THE LIFE OF

LORD CURZON

Being the Authorized Biography of

GEORGE NATHANIEL

MARQUESS CURZON OF KEDLESTON, K.G.

by

THE RT. HON. THE

EARL OF RONALDSHAY

———— ✕∽o∾✕ ————

BONI AND LIVERIGHT

Publishers   *New York*

LONDON: ERNEST BENN LTD.

Bouverie House, Fleet Street

PRINTED IN GREAT BRITAIN

PLATE I.   UNDER SECRETARY FOR INDIA

The Hon. G. N. Curzon, M.P., 1891

Reproduced from " Vanity Fair "

PREFACE

LORD CURZON'S life falls quite naturally into three well defined periods—the first forty years from his birth in 1859 to his appointment as Viceroy of India in 1898 ; the seven years of his Viceroyalty from 1898 to his return to England in December 1905 ; and the last twenty years of his life from 1905 to March 1925. It is with the first of these three periods that the present volume deals.

The first forty years of George Curzon's life were unusually full, for into them were packed the meteoric performances of his early manhood at Eton and Oxford ; the great series of journeys upon which he was engaged almost continuously between 1883 and 1895, including two voyages round the world and expeditions into Central Asia, Persia, the Pamirs and Afghanistan ; and the whole of his comparatively brief but unquestionably brilliant career in the House of Commons. And apart altogether from achievements in these various fields which a man of far maturer years might well have contemplated with something more than mere satisfaction, he found time during these crowded days to write three books of outstanding merit on the peoples and politics of Central Asia, the Far East and Persia, the last of which, at least, demanded an immense amount of patient and sustained research, and to carve for himself a special niche in a social circle which gave to the world a number of distinguished figures in literature, politics and art.

From the first he displayed symptoms of a very complex personality, and it is during these early years that can best be studied those conflicting elements in his temperament and character that often made him so difficult to understand. To the public he appeared as a pompous and even arrogant figure—cold, haughty and aloof; to his intimate companions as an emotional and sensitive being, warm-hearted and impulsive, within whose frame there lurked eternally the spirit of incorrigible youth. To the former he appeared to have been born old; to the latter it sometimes seemed that he had never quite grown up. " Most men," he once observed in a letter to the first Lady Curzon, "are not understood of their own generation, for human nature is really very complex, and yet ignoring our own complexity we expect everyone else to be simple." Of no one could this have been said with greater truth than of George Curzon himself. How could the public who saw him only from the far side of the footlights—who were used to seeing him depicted, always as " a most superior person," in countless caricatures, cartoons and paragraphs published broadcast in the popular press—know that behind the scenes of the theatre he bubbled over with animal spirits, danced, joked, did all those things that high-spirited youth in love with life and with a consuming passion for laughter insists on doing the wide world over ? Or that he possessed a spirit of hospitality that made of him the most charming of hosts and a sense of humour that rendered him inimitable as a raconteur ?

In the first of the three Volumes, therefore, in which the story of his life is told, space has been found for some analysis of his personality which, it is hoped, may prove of assistance to the reader who follows him through the succeeding volumes as he threads his way across the crowded stage on which the drama of his public life was played.

* * * * * *

It would be difficult, even if it were possible, to mention by name all those to whom I have been indebted for assistance. George

PREFACE

Curzon never, when he could avoid doing so, made use of clerical assistance. And since his curious aversion to the employment of such aid necessitated his writing all his letters in his own hand, it follows that except in very special cases, no copies of what he wrote were made. I have, consequently, to thank all those who have placed at my disposal such letters written by him as they may have received and preserved. For material for the chapters on George Curzon's undergraduate days I am indebted more particularly to Lord Midleton, Lord Sumner of Ibstone and Professor J. W. Mackail ; and indeed my debt to Lord Midleton extends over a period far in excess of George Curzon's Oxford days.

Finally to Lord Curzon's Literary Executors, Dr. F. W. Pember, Warden of All Souls College and Vice-Chancellor of Oxford University, and Sir Ian Malcolm, K.C.M.G., and to Lady Curzon, I desire to express my gratitude, for the courteous consideration which they have at all times shown me in the discharge of a task which, if a pleasure, has nevertheless not been wholly free from difficulty. Indeed it is not too much to say that without the constant readiness which Sir Ian Malcolm has shown to respond to the many demands which I have made upon him, this Biography could scarcely have been written.

RONALDSHAY.

Dec. 1st, 1927.

CONTENTS

CHAPTER I

EARLY DAYS—KEDLESTON, WIXENFORD AND ETON—
1859–1878

Love of Kedleston—discipline under Miss Paraman—and under Archibald James Campbell Dunbar—symptoms of precocity—from Wixenford to Eton—school successes—a rebellious and insubordinate pupil—death of Lady Scarsdale—sense of humour—a bundle of contradictions—wild escapades—Pop and the Literary Society—a Lecture on India—invitation to Mr. Gladstone to visit Eton—speech by Mr. Gladstone at the Literary Society—President of the Literary Society—literary activities—editor of the *Etonian*—publication of " Out of School at Eton "—success as a speaker—a memorable Fourth of June—interest in cricket and other games—farewell to Eton . . . . pp. 17-36

CHAPTER II

LIFE AT BALLIOL—1878–1882

Arrival at Balliol—Balliol under Jowett—a grave physical weakness —first appearance at the Union—an acknowledged leader—his striking appearance and qualifications as a speaker—mannerisms— " a most superior person "—origin of the rhyme—undergraduates and politics—the danger of prolixity—advice from Jowett—President of the Union—Secretary of the Canning Club—a successful function—his political creed expounded—female suffrage—maturity of his views . . . . pp. 37-50

7

CONTENTS

CHAPTER III

OXFORD AND AFTER—1878–1882

The beginnings of a great friendship—a critical examination—disappointment—winner of the Lothian Prize—elected a Fellow of All Souls—winner of the Arnold Prize—farewell to Oxford—great ambitions—early maturity of mind—words over a cracked teapot—a complex personality—sense of humour—a good story and an epigram—wielder of an ironic pen—capacity for friendship—an artistic temperament—love of beauty—its influence upon his life—an emotional and highly strung personality—little-suspected humility—physical suffering—his sterling courage—tribute from Sir W. Harcourt—love of travel—a conspectus of his journeys from 1877 to 1895 . . . . pp. 51-71

CHAPTER IV

EARLY JOURNEYS—1882 AND 1883
ITALY, GREECE, EGYPT, PALESTINE AND CENTRAL EUROPE

Advantage derived from foreign travel—attention to detail—Italy—ancient Rome—the *via sacra*—the Colosseum—St. Peter's—the approach to Athens—the Acropolis—the paramount influence of Greece upon Western Civilization—characteristics of modern Greece—the beauty of Greek art—plea for the restoration to Athens of the Caryatides and the missing panels of the frieze of the temple of the Wingless Victory—criticism of Greek Parliamentary life—the charm of travel in Greece—its humours—Mr. Gladstone's popularity—the bombardment of Alexandria and the battlefield of Telel Kebir—Cairo—characteristics of Arab architecture—the Egyptian countryside—Sakkhara—Karnak—critical appreciation of ancient Egyptian monuments—reconstructing the past—the chain of culture—the vocal Memnon—Cairo society—Palestine—the delight of fitting Biblical scenes into their geographical and historical setting—Mount Carmel—the sea of Galilee—influence of his tour of the Holy Land upon his mind—eastern and central Europe—the Lothian History Prize . . . . pp. 72-89

8

CONTENTS

CHAPTER V

FIRST ATTEMPT TO ENTER PARLIAMENT
SUMMER OF 1883—JANUARY, 1886

A Fellow of All Souls—the Arnold History Prize—a platform campaign—a budding orator—his political creed—his attack upon Mr. Gladstone's Administration—indignation at the death of Gordon—a remarkable historical parallel—miscellaneous writings— assistant private secretary to Lord Salisbury—the General Election of 1885—defeat—estimates of men, Lord Randolph Churchill, Sir Michael Hicks Beach, Lord Salisbury, Lord Cowper, Lord Lytton, Mr. Jesse Collings . . . . . pp. 90-104

CHAPTER VI

ENTRY INTO THE HOUSE OF COMMONS—1886–1887

Financial stringency—candidate for Southport—defeat of Mr. Gladstone's Government—Lord Salisbury back in office—Curzon's victory at Southport—his success at Bradford—Lord Randolph Churchill's resignation—Democratic Toryism—Curzon's enthusiasm for—but no need to follow its chief author into the wilderness —a brilliant maiden speech—success on the platform—a wide range of interests . . . . pp. 105-117

CHAPTER VII

FIRST JOURNEY ROUND THE WORLD—1887–1888

Canada—Chicago—the Grand Canyon—the Yosemite Valley— Japan—the exhilaration of novel scenes—temples and mausolea— exquisite scenery—Kioto—a hurried glance at China—Great Britain in Asia—remarkable demonstrations of loyalty at Hong-Kong— Canton, its temples and its examination halls—Monasticism in China, an intriguing subject for literary treatment—Singapore and Penang—Ceylon—the shadow of Adam's Peak—buried cities— an architectural riddle—Dravidian art—the miracles of Mme. Blavatsky—Calcutta—renewal of acquaintance with Lord Dufferin —the panorama from Darjeeling—the Taj Mahal at Agra—admira-

CONTENTS

tion for Moghul buildings—from Delhi to the North West Frontier —Baluchistan—the Ultima Thule of the Indian Empire—Amritsar, Jeypore, Amber and the Caves of Elephanta—" middle-class method "—provisional conclusions—the civilising mission of Great Britain—an eventful and a fateful enterprise   .   . pp. 118-133

CHAPTER VIII

HIGH POLITICS AT HOME AND ABROAD—1888-1890

Fresh laurels in the House of Commons—reform of the House of Lords—the hereditary principle not a sacrosanct element in the composition of the House of Lords—elements in the national life that ought to be represented—a constructive scheme put forward—reform must come from within—the campaign not based on a spirit of iconoclasm—reception accorded to the scheme—writings on the Indian Frontier—a journey to Central Asia—publication of " Russia in Central Asia in 1889 "—purpose of the book—an illustration of early maturity of mind—high praise .   . pp. 134-145

CHAPTER IX

PERSIA AND THE PERSIAN QUESTION—1889-1892

The defence of India—a military question—Persia—articles for *The Times*—Turkish red tape—the trials of a traveller—an exhausting journey—politics and literature—ill health—a sojourn at St. Moritz—progress with his book on Persia—appointed Under Secretary for India—an awkward question—the publication of " Persia "—the reception accorded to the book—a letter from Thomas Hardy   .   .   .   . pp. 146-157

CHAPTER X

SOCIAL INTERESTS

The Crabbet Club—its vicissitudes—its activities—the Souls—the Bachelor's club dinner party—" doggrel appalling "—a second dinner party—rumours about " the Souls "—intellectual games—Curzon's power of assimilation—his industry with his pen—his

CONTENTS

private correspondence—qualities little suspected by the public—
wide range of his interests—a visit to Lord Tennyson—friendship
with Ouida and Amelie Rives . . . pp. 158-172

CHAPTER XI

THE WRITTEN AND THE SPOKEN WORD

Love of language—the secret of his success—imagination—the
tyranny of mere words—the fascination of the pen—his distrust of
clerical assistance—a high standard of composition demanded of his
subordinates—an amazing letter—his appreciation of sound and
rhythm—a style that appealed—description of a sunset—modern
Parliamentary eloquence—the oratory of Mr. Balfour—of Lord
Rosebery—of Lord Hugh Cecil—a remarkable echo—an unattractive speaker—Curzon's speeches translated into Greek—his
love of poetry—its appeal to his feelings—Clough and Longfellow
criticised—admiration for Tennyson—and for D. G. Rossetti—
the " Blessed Damozel "—the quality of his speeches . pp. 173-186

CHAPTER XII

UNDER SECRETARY FOR INDIA AND SECOND JOURNEY
ROUND THE WORLD—1891-1893

Under Secretary for India—comments on the appointment—first
speech as a Minister—the Indian Councils Bill—the General
Election of 1892—out of office—departure for New York—Asia
once more—the great Khmer Empire—back in England—great
ambitions—the new Imperialism—India, the strength and greatness
of England—diverse interests—opposition to women as Fellows of
the Royal Geographical Society—France and Siam—the Protocol of
July 31st, 1893—criticism of . . . pp. 187-198

CHAPTER XIII

THE PAMIRS AND AFGHANISTAN—1894-95

Publication of " Problems of the Far East "—fortunate in the time
of its appearance—the war in the Far East—conflicting opinions

CONTENTS

about the book—verdict of the public—determination to visit the
Pamirs and Afghanistan—uncertainties of the political situation in
1894—a letter to the Amir—opposition in official quarters—refusal
to accept failure—opposition withdrawn—extent of the journey—
award of the gold medal of the Royal Geographical Society—
Monograph on the Pamirs—the essentials of successful travel—
the journey to Kabul—interviews with the Amir—desire of the
Amir to visit England—the Amir's estimate of George Curzon—
return to England . . . . . pp. 199-214

CHAPTER XIV

COURTSHIP AND MARRIAGE—1890-1895

An early disappointment—Miss Leiter—life in Washington—Persia
a bond between them—England through American glasses—the
call of the Pamirs—French animosity—return from the Pamirs and
Afghanistan—his engagement announced—a romantic story.

pp. 215-227

CHAPTER XV

WHEN IS A PEER NOT A PEER ?—1895

Death of Lord Selborne—a Bill to enable a peer to sit in the House
of Commons—a test case—death of Lord Pembroke—ingenious
arguments—the case of the Hon. Bernard Coleridge, M.P.—Sir
William Harcourt's dilemma—a Committee appointed—Lord
Selborne's move—attitude of the Speaker—a Select Committee
appointed—the eldest sons lose—Lord Salisbury's gibe—fall of the
Government—George Curzon offered the Under Secretaryship for
Foreign Affairs—his acceptance—becomes a Member of the
Privy Council . . . . pp. 228-235

CHAPTER XVI

UNDER SECRETARY FOR FOREIGN AFFAIRS—1895-1898

An altered outlook—growing popularity of Imperialism—George
Curzon's advocacy of it—the Uganda railway—difficulties with
France—George Curzon and Lord Salisbury—differences between

CONTENTS

them—attention to detail—in search of information—national animosities—the burden thrown upon the Foreign Office and the Under Secretary in particular—a visit to Berlin—holidays in Scotland—a visit to Mr. Gladstone—death of Mr. Gladstone.

pp. 236-250

CHAPTER XVII

THE TRIALS OF AN UNDER SECRETARY—1895-1898

George Curzon's impatience of Lord Salisbury's caution—question of an appointment—French encroachments in West Africa—George Curzon's loyalty to his Chief—the Siamese question—throwing bones to dogs—George Curzon's published views on British policy in the Far East—his sensitiveness—the Uganda railway again—a bout with Sir William Harcourt—physical infirmity—a warning unheeded .   .   .   . pp. 251-261

CHAPTER XVIII

THE CONCERT OF EUROPE—1895-1898

The Concert of Europe—a brilliant speech—a contrast—attacks in the House of Commons—hostilities in Egypt—the Cretan question—Greek *v.* Turk—a great performance—defence of the Concert of the Powers—speaking to a brief—the break-up of the Concert—question hour in the House of Commons—an enhanced reputation

pp. 262-274

CHAPTER XIX

CLOUDS IN THE FAR EAST—1898

George Curzon's published views on policy in the Far East—his difficulties in Parliament in consequence—résumé of recent events in the Far East—letter to Lord Salisbury of December 29th, 1897—official optimism—lease of Port Arthur and Talienwan to Russia—anxiety of the public—an embarrassing position—reasons for not resigning—Memorandum of March 13th, 1898—attendance at

13

CONTENTS

Cabinet meetings—urges the acquisition of Wei-hai-wei—his success—railways in China—the Pigtail Committee—George Curzon's triumph in the House of Commons—his fight against ill health —last speech in the House of Commons .   .   . pp. 275-290

CHAPTER XX

APPOINTED VICEROY OF INDIA—1898

Close of Lord Elgin's Viceroyalty—the state of India—importance of Lord Salisbury's choice—candidates for the post—Mr. Curzon appointed—reception of the announcement—Russian fears—shared to some extent in England—a forward policy?—Mr. Curzon's views on Anglo-Russian rivalry—his speech in the House of Commons on February 15th, 1898—view of *The Times* on his appointment—letters of congratulation .   .   . pp. 291-306

CHAPTER XXI

PREPARATIONS FOR DEPARTURE—JULY–DECEMBER 1898

India the goal of George Curzon's ambition—his comprehensive programme of works on Asiatic countries—books contemplated but never completed—his passionate desire to serve as Viceroy—a letter to Lord Salisbury—search for a private secretary—Walter Lawrence—visit to Queen Victoria at Balmoral—life's little comedies—question of a title—acquisition of No. 1. Carlton House Terrace—Old Etonian dinner—Royal Societies' club dinner— oratory—a " Souls " dinner—presentation at Kedleston—Lord Curzon and Lord Kitchener—a nation's farewell . pp. 307-318

ILLUSTRATIONS

PLATE

I   *Under Secretary for India,* 1891 .   .   . *Frontispiece*

Facing Page

II   *A Memorable Fourth of June,* 1878 .   .   .   33

III   *Committee of the Oxford Union,* 1880 .   .   .   39

IV   *The Canning Club in* 1881   47

V   *Friends at Oxford*   63

VI   *Gilgit,* 1894, *en route for the Pamirs* .   .   .   203

VII   *The Hon. Mrs. G. N. Curzon*   221

VIII   *A Holiday in Scotland*   243

IX   *Discussing the Future of China*   271

X   *Kedleston Hall, Derbyshire*   309

THE LIFE OF LORD CURZON

CHAPTER I

EARLY DAYS
KEDLESTON, WIXENFORD AND ETON

1859—1878

GEORGE NATHANIEL CURZON, eldeſt son of the Reverend Alfred Nathaniel Holden Curzon, fourth Baron Scarsdale, and of Blanche, daughter of Joseph Pocklington Senhouse, of Netherhall, was born at Kedleston, in Derbyshire, on January the 11th, 1859. Here within the walls of the ſtately Adam mansion built on the site on which for nigh on eight centuries had ſtood the home of an unbroken line of Curzons, he spent his boyhood, ſtrangely sensitive to the appeal of his surroundings and acquiring half consciously, perhaps, a deep affeƈtion and admiration for the building itself, which, as years rolled by, grew into something akin to reverence. This early attachment to Kedleſton Hall exercised a laſting influence upon his attitude towards architeƈture, leading him not merely to admire great and hiſtoric buildings as Works of Art, but to inveſt them with a definite personality of their own. As will afterwards appear, it was the mainspring of a special aspeƈt of his aƈtivities in an un-usually full and varied life.

His early years were not a time of unmixed happiness. They were dominated by a ſtrange and forceful influence in the person of the lady who for ten years had charge of the upbringing of George Curzon and the four members of the family next to him in age. Of Miss Paraman, who appeared upon the scene when George Curzon was seven years old, he has himself said that she taught all subjeƈts well, and in addition inculcated in her charges habits of economy and neatness, and a dislike of anything vulgar or fast ; that in her saner moments she was devotedly attached to her pupils ; but that there were frequent occasions on which she acted with all the savagery of a brutal and vindictive tyrant. [1] The many ingenious forms of punishment which she devised were such that, in after years, he declared that he doubted if any children well born and well placed cried so much or so justly. [2] There can be little doubt that this ferocious discipline to which she subjected her unfortunate charges did much to foster that rebellious spirit of the existence of which, sometimes latent, at other times disastrously active, George Curzon was himself aware throughout his life. It is but fair to add that these paroxysms of ferocity cloaked a real if wayward affection for those who were their victims. To others she spoke of the young Curzons as model children. She bequeathed what little money she possessed to the eldest of the girls whom she had taught and terrorised, and when in 1892 she passed away, conspicuous among the figures seen standing by her grave was that of George Curzon, then a member of Her Majesty's Government.

From the hands of Miss Paraman he passed into those of another masterly personality in the shape of Mr. Dunbar, the second master at the Reverend R. Cowley Powles's school at Wixenford—the latter " a perfect gentleman, an amiable character and a graceful scholar," [3] who had established his seminary for young gentlemen at Wixenford in order to be near his friend Charles Kingsley, at that time Rector of the adjoining parish of Eversley. But the reverend gentleman had neither the power nor, perhaps, the inclination to assert himself so long as he commanded the services of so forceful and competent a lieutenant as Mr. Archibald James Campbell Dunbar. This remarkable man left on young Curzon's mind the same uneffaceable mark as Miss Paraman had done—and for much the same reason. Indeed, he seems to have been of the same violent and unstable disposition as she was, and one cannot but be struck by this strange coincidence. Like Miss Paraman, he was an admirable teacher ; like her, he was often savage and cruel to the boys. Like her again, " though he never spared us one jot or tittle of his displeasure or punishment if we had provoked either, he could

[1] Pencil notes by G. N. Curzon.   [2] *Ibid.*   [3] *Ibid.*

18

be extremely nice to us when he was in a gracious mood, and was as genuinely fond of us as we were—at a distance—attached to him." [1] As in the case of the lady, " his vigour and resourcefulness were overpowering," [2] and it is difficult to refrain from speculating upon the possible consequences had either chanced to have been drawn by Fate into the orbit of the other. He had other inconvenient characteristics, for if he was of a passionate and imperious nature, he was also extremely sensitive and was constantly imagining that people were deliberately bent on outraging his feelings. The result was that sooner or later he exasperated and alienated most of the friends that he made. For more than twenty years George Curzon kept up a firm friendship with him, when, in one of his unaccountable moods, the latter suddenly broke off all communication with his former pupil and their relations came to an abrupt end. [3] He died in 1923, but not apparently before he had destroyed the voluminous correspondence which George Curzon had maintained with him for twenty years.

Young Curzon's three years at Wixenford brought out something of the quality of his mind. Before leaving he became head of the school and during his last term created a record by carrying off five prizes, though one—as with becoming modesty he has been careful to point out—was for " the best collection of moths and butterflies, of which we were passionate pursuers." [4]

They also made it clear that his was no ordinary turn of mind. A boy who, at the age of ten, could observe in a letter to his Father— " What a congress of people you talk about in your letters " ; who, when still a junior boy at a private school, could mention casually that he supposed that Parliament would soon be opening, [5] and who, on returning to school after the holidays, at the age of eleven, could write that in crossing London he drove to Eaton Square, passing on his way " Hyde Park, St. James's Park, Green Park, Stafford House, Apsley House, Buckingham Palace, etc.," [6] was, to say the least of it, original.

---

[1]Pencil notes by G. N. Curzon.   [2]*Ibid.*   [3]*Ibid.*   [4]*Ibid.*
[5]Letter to Lord Scarsdale dated February 11th, 1870.
[6]Letter to Lady Scarsdale on his return to school in 1870.

Even when treating of the things with which the average school-boy of his age was wont to interest himself, he exhibited a certain originality of style :

" Now for my requests. First, as it is the half term, a hamper is undoubtedly requisite under the present circumstances, as we hadn't one last term. This hamper must contain : one fine fat brawn, as usual, several pots of superior jam, including, *mark me*, apricot, etc., whilst pots of potted meat are indispensable. Oh ! but above all things, one of those very jolly cakes which are so nice and big and which Mrs. Halliday fully knows how to fabricate." [1]

He also acquired thus early the habit of concise and methodical exposition which made of him in after years so lucid and successful a debater :

" Johnston is going to London sometime this term and there are three things that he wants me to ask you.

" 1st—which I know you won't grant—he wants me to go an exeat with him to London, to his Grandmother's.

" 2nd—which perhaps you may grant—will you let me go up to London with him for one day—go in the morning and come back in the afternoon ?

" 3rd—if you won't let me do this, may he get me a football jersey and a football cap and a belt ?

" If you agree to 1st or 2nd requests, will you mention the day, or if to the 3rd, say yes or no." [2]

The excellent grounding which he had received at the hands of the two remarkable characters on whom had devolved his early training became apparent when, at the age of thirteen, he proceeded to Eton and distinguished himself by taking ' remove,' the highest form open to a newcomer, and by heading the list of competitors in mathematics—a branch of study for which he was wont to say he had a natural distaste.

[1] Letter to Lady Scarsdale dated November 5th, 1871.
[2] Letter to Lady Scarsdale dated November 5th, 1870.

Among the vast and varied collection of documents extant in George Curzon's own handwriting is a fragment in which he speaks of the next six years as a happy and glorious time—" perhaps the happiest and most glorious that it will ever be given to me to enjoy."[1] They gained something, doubtless, by contrast with the tumultuous emotions of his more tender years, spent in constant apprehension of the violent vagaries first of Miss Paraman and then of Mr. Dunbar. Though he never reached quite the foremost rank in scholarship, his six years at Eton were marked, nevertheless, by brilliant and almost uninterrupted success. He progressed rapidly up the school until, in 1877, he reached the highest place open to a non-colleger, that of captain of the " oppidans," so-called, it may be observed for the benefit of those who were not themselves brought up at Eton, because they live outside the college in the town. He was usually at the top of his form, either in school work or in examinations, and never far from it.   He won no less than seventeen first prizes and was " sent up for good " on twenty-three occasions, a record shared only by one boy, some few years senior to himself, Mr. J. E. C. Welldon, destined to accompany him twenty years later to India as Metropolitan and Bishop of Calcutta, and now a distinguished figure of the church in England. Nor was this all, for to this remarkable record of achievement must be added his success during his last year at school in getting into " the select " for the Newcastle Scholarship—the greatest distinction open to an Eton boy in the way of scholarships—the scholar and medallist on this occasion being two King's scholars, W. O. Burrows, afterwards Archdeacon of Birmingham, and W. R. Inge, afterwards Dean Inge.

During his time at Eton he cultivated a taste for literature which stood him in good stead in after life as a writer and public speaker. He took prizes in French and Italian and in Shakespeare, and in 1877 was awarded the prize for declamation, i.e., for the best Latin oration on a set subject in the style of the oratory of ancient Rome, both in the Lent and Michaelmas terms.   On one occasion the Headmaster, Dr. Hornby, whose quiet sense of humour appealed strongly to George Curzon, turned the tables neatly on the preco-

[1]From a note-book kept at Eton.

cious boy. When giving out the result of the competition, he said :
" The best declamation has been written by Foley, the second best
by Mr. Curzon." This announcement was received by the expectant
listener with dismay. But Dr. Hornby had not finished. " Unfortunately in the greater part of what he has written Foley has been
anticipated by Cicero. The prize therefore goes to Mr. Curzon."
The studious turn of his mind was hall-marked by the award of no
less than four holiday task prizes during his last two years at the
school, and at the end of his last term he took away with him prizes
for history, for English verse, and for the best essay in Latin.

A model boy, surely, and the joy of any master's heart ! Yet
truth demands the admission that this was not so. His relations
with the majority of Eton masters were, as a matter of fact, the
reverse of harmonious, as he himself freely admitted. The spirit
of rebellion, of which mention has been made, was easily kindled by
contact with authority, resulting in acts of insubordination and an
impertinent demeanour, which made him anything but *persona grata*
with the teaching staff. Very early in their acquaintance his tutor,
the Reverend Wolley Dod, complained of a tendency on his pupil's
part " to say silly things and to make silly answers about the lesson ";
and, he added, " Being young for his place in the school and a
popular boy, he is in some danger of being spoilt by associating
too much with boys older than himself."[1] He, in his turn, was
piqued by the inability of his masters to discount these ebullitions
and to perceive beneath the surface the earnestness of the man. He
took an unholy delight, consequently, in demonstrating to them in
signal fashion their mistake. The capture of the French and Italian
prizes was the outcome of an impish determination to score off the
French and Italian masters with whom he had fallen out. He left
the classes of both, read with fiery energy week after week far into
the night, and won, first, the Prince Consort's prize for French
by a larger percentage of marks and at an earlier age than had ever
been done before, and subsequently, to the surprise and annoyance
of the Italian master, the Italian prize, his sardonic sense of satisfaction at this triumph being enhanced by the fact that among the
vanquished was the favourite pupil of the latter, a lad partly of

[1]Letter from the Rev. Wolley Dod to Lord Scarsdale dated December 10th, 1872.

Italian extraction who had been brought up at Florence. A history prize fell to him in similar circumstances. Stung to the quick by a disparaging remark from Mr. Cornish, the lecturer on the subject, he withdrew from his class. In due course, to the astonishment of most people, he presented himself at the examination—and carried off the prize. To the credit of both, be it said, there sprang up in after years between Mr. Cornish and his intractable pupil relations of mutual good-will and esteem.

That this state of tension between teacher and taught was due in large measure to the boy's temperament seems to follow from the fact that it was the almost invariable rule. With few exceptions, of which his happy intimacy with Mr. Oscar Browning provides the most notable example, his intercourse with his teachers was marred by friction. On one occasion he wrote home describing a scene with his tutor which ended in the latter " in an awful foam " dashing himself down on to a chair and saluting the culprit " with the pleasant appellation of ' impertinent brat.' "[1] At another time he complained bitterly of his tutor's attitude towards him. " It is a well-known thing through the house that he especially spites me. I use the word *spite* because it is true . . . . I have been so loaded with his punishments during the last week that I haven't had a moment to myself."[2] This was almost the last letter that he wrote to his Mother, for in April 1875, she died. The sorrow which he felt at this tragic bereavement, mingled with his feelings of attachment to Kedleston, found expression in verse, which he committed to paper at the age of sixteen with the title, " Kedleston " :

> Monarch of the grassy parkland,
>   Sheltered by ancestral trees,
> For a century thy pillars
>   Have grown hoary in the breeze.
>
> For a century around thee
>   Bud hath blossomed, flower hath blown,
> Many a wooded glade thou ownest,
>   Many an acre is thine own.

[1] Letter to Lady Scarsdale dated March 17th, 1873.
[2] Letter to Lady Scarsdale dated March 16th, 1875.

CURZON, 1872–1878

Still as ever, proud thou ſtandeſt,
   Green thy meadows as of yore,
But a chill of desolation
   Mid the sunbeams clouds thee o'er.

Merry voices that but lately
   Laughing echoed through thy halls
Sound no longer there, and silence
   Reigns inſtead within thy walls.

Heedless of thy frowning presence
   Lichen creep along the ſtone
And the weeds grow long and dreary
   Where thou ſtandeſt all alone.

Towards the end of his time at Eton he was transferred from the tutorial care of his own house-maſter, Wolley Dod, to that of Mr. E. D. Stone. It cannot be said that the change made any difference either to the relations between himself and his tutor, or to his own academic success. He was convinced that Stone looked upon him as " a nimble-witted farceur,"[1] and he smarted under his continual upbraidings on the score of what the former insiſted on regarding as his shallowness and lack of serious purpose. Once again the want of discernment on the part of the teacher was demonſtrated when the liſt of the Firſt Hundred examination was published with the name of Curzon ſtanding at the head of the school.

But if his attitude towards life was in the main a serious one, he possessed also a lively sense of the ludicrous. On his return to Eton on one occasion he was apparently requeſted to look after the younger members of the family, who were being sent to Brighton. The journey from Derbyshire was not altogether free from mishaps, and in due course he submitted the following ſtatement of his out-of-pocket expenses to his Father :

[1]Pencil notes by G. N. Curzon.

EARLY DAYS : KEDLESTON

" Lord Scarsdale Dr. to Hon. G. Curzon.

	£	s.	d.
To attendance on nurses, children and servants....		10	6
Getting Miss Paraman out of pawn		15	6
Rent in seat of trousers from extreme tension running up and down platform		8	3
Re-soleing boots from wear and tear of do.........		4	9
Samuel's fare from Victoria to Brighton		7	9
Fare for person engaged to take care of Samuel.....		7	9
Telegram to Brighton to say Samuel had missed the train and lost all the luggage		1	0
Do. to say Samuel and luggage was found and would proceed to his destination at 5 p.m.		1	0
Wear and tear of mind consequent upon the frightful consequences involved in the aforestated trouble.	1	0	0
Synopsis of foregoing account	3	16	6

" Being much pressed at present time to meet several large demands, shall esteem it a great favour to have His Lordship's cheque for the above small and moderate charges.

" G. N. Curzon."

He could forgive much in others provided they enjoyed a similar sense of humour. He used to recall with obvious relish a joke to the credit of a master of the name of Day with a " very squeaky voice," but " a keen sense of humour." [1] A boy charged with a message from some other master threw open the door of Mr. Day's class room on one occasion when work was in progress and waited the latter's permission to speak. " Your name ? " enquired Day. " Cole," replied the boy. After a silence of some minutes Day looked up from his work and exclaimed, " Well then, Cole— scuttle ! " The boy in question was A. C. Cole, who afterwards became Governor of the Bank of England. A mordaunt piece of humour on the part of another master, of the name of Austen Leigh,

[1] Pencil notes by G. N. Curzon.

tickled his sense of the ludicrous and lingered in his memory. In incisive terms Austen Leigh made known to one of his class, Sclater Booth—afterwards Lord Basing—his opinion of him. " Sclater Booth, in the whole course of my experience I have only known one boy worse than Sclater Booth this term," was the name of this prodigy of misconduct Curzon perchance ? But no—" and that was," continued his judge, in measured terms, " Sclater Booth last term."

To many the George Curzon of those days must have seemed a curious bundle of contradictions. He was, indeed, in some sense the sport of certain strongly marked and conflicting features in his character. There was the spirit of rebellion fostered, as I have before observed, by the tyranny of Miss Paraman. But equally powerful was a constant urge deep down in his nature to excel in competition with his fellow men. If the former drove him into open warfare with those in authority over him, the latter impelled him, if not to sit at their feet, at least to serious study. Hence, he was at once rampantly undisciplined and extraordinarily studious. To add further to the confusion aroused by these two antithetical characteristics was a tendency, not uncommon with the boyhood of our public schools, to conceal his virtues and represent himself as worse than he was. He shrank from being regarded wholly as a " sap." Hence, wild exploits of insubordination. He made it a point of honour to proceed every year to Ascot races—not because he cared for racing, but because it was forbidden. For a similar reason he kept a stock of claret and champagne in the drawer of the bureau in his room—not because he cared for drinking, but because he enjoyed the supreme effrontery of giving wine parties under the nose of his housemaster. But perhaps the most audacious of his escapades—at which, as he himself confessed in after years, he still stood aghast[1] was a sudden determination to play a game of tennis in Upper School—the long panelled room adorned with busts and decorated with carved names innumerable, hallowed, if ever a room was, by a long tradition of decorous behaviour and bathed in a gentle atmosphere of learning. This wild idea was duly given effect to and for an hour the hovering silence was broken by the

[1]Pencil notes by G. N. Curzon.

boisterous laughter of four irreverent schoolboys, while tennis balls cannoned off the heads of Chatham and Canning and other giants of former days. The hour was well chosen and the desecration escaped detection. And the heir to Kedleston and his accomplices flattered themselves—no doubt with justice—that they were the only persons who had ever played tennis in Upper School.

But in spite of these and similar aberrations, learning was by far the most serious of his pursuits at Eton. Neither were his literary activities confined to school hours nor within narrow limits. In 1876 and 1877 he was elected successively to the Secretaryship and Presidentship of the Eton Literary Society, and to membership and later to the post of auditor of Pop, the famous Eton Society—the most select club, perhaps, in all the world—which he described in a farewell speech as being " not so much a debating society as a friendly and social confederation whose members are all friends in one common friendship."[1] Election to this exclusive circle bears unimpeachable testimony to his standing among his school mates. Athletic or intellectual distinction of themselves availed a man nothing. Unless to these attributes was added " that indefinable quality, good fellowship, which is born, not made,"[2] the suppliant knocked at its doors in vain. Nor did those within show the smallest hesitation in making known their disapprobation of the aspirant who was, and who they considered should remain, without the pale. One such in Curzon's day received no fewer than twenty-four black balls at a meeting at which eighteen members only were present.

How came it that so aristocratic a company sailed under so plebeian a name ? Mr. Gilbert Coleridge offers an explanation. The name Pop, he tells us, was derived from " popina," a " cook-shop," because the original habitation of the society when first formed in 1811 was a room over a well-known " sock-shop " of the day.[3]

The Literary Society, of which George Curzon became President in 1877, had been founded by Oscar Browning in 1871 and throughout the seventies was almost as exclusive a body as Pop. A small

[1]Speech delivered on August the 1st, 1878.
[2]The Hon. Gilbert Coleridge in " Eton in the Seventies."   [3]Ibid.

coterie of thirty, it was managed entirely by the boys themselves. A heavy responsibility rested on the President, for besides presiding at the ordinary meetings at which papers were read by members of the Society, he was expected to arrange for periodic lectures to the school by men eminent in their own line of life in the larger world beyond its walls. Masters, other than those who had been admitted to honorary membership, desiring to attend such lectures could only do so by obtaining tickets from the boys. Within the charmed circle of membership itself matters were taken very seriously in Curzon's day, absence from an ordinary meeting being punished with a fine. With the departure of the giants of those days—Cecil Spring-Rice, afterwards to make his mark in diplomacy; J. K. Stephen, son of Sir James Fitzjames Stephen and author of " Lapsus Calami "; W. O. Burrows, afterwards Archdeacon of Birmingham, and now Bishop of Chichester; C. Lowry, afterwards Head Master of Tonbridge—the society fell upon evil days, discipline lapsed and interest languished. But under the Presidentship of George Curzon and his immediate predecessors it flourished exceedingly, and under its auspices lectures were delivered to the school by a number of distinguished persons including Sir John Lubbock, Sir James Stephen, Dr. Carpenter, Matthew Arnold, John Ruskin and William Gladstone. It was at one of these lectures that Curzon's thoughts were first directed towards India, with consequences destined to influence profoundly his whole future life. So deep an impression did the theme and the manner of its unfolding make upon him, that nigh upon forty years afterwards he could still conjure up a vivid picture of " the vast head, the heavy pendulous jaw, the long and curling locks of Sir James Fitzjames Stephen as he stood at the desk "[1] and spoke to a spellbound audience of Eton boys about India.

In accordance with the practice of the Society, Curzon had to choose and secure the attendance of suitable lecturers, and casting about in his mind for a man of mark, he conceived the bold idea of enlisting the services of Mr. Gladstone. The letter in which he conveyed his invitation is of interest as being, in all probability, the first official letter to a public man which he ever wrote.

[1] " Eton in the Seventies."

"Dear Sir,

I trust you will excuse the great liberty I am taking in writing to you, my only excuse is the nature of my request. I am captain of the Oppidans and President of the Literary Society at Eton, and I write to ask you if you will some time this summer do us the great honour to come down there and lecture to us . . . I need not say how enthusiastically every one at Eton would greet the news that you are coming and how hearty a reception you would meet with ; but I have heard it observed that an Eton audience beats any other in the expression of its pleasure and gratitude. Should you do us the honour to come, might I suggest some such subject as the Homeric question as one in which Eton is specially interested and which no one is so fitted as yourself to expound. . . . I hope you will excuse my adding that as I leave Eton for Oxford at Midsummer I should consider it a special distinction if the last few months of my presidency were marked by the favour of a visit from you."

A sympathetic reply encouraged him to follow up his letter with a personal call upon Mr. Gladstone at his town house, and the following account of the visit has been preserved among the written fragments relating to his life at Eton.

" On Ascension Day, May 30th, 1878, being in London for the day, called on the Rt. Hon. W. E. Gladstone with reference to the possibility of his coming to lecture at Eton on Homer. Sent in my card. He was at breakfast with a large party of ladies and gentlemen, but came out at once, shook hands most kindly, and took me into small side room, where he said he looked upon the visit as a bargain which was certainly to be kept. Said he considered himself bound to do anything for Eton."

A later entry mentions a second visit :

" Called again on June 20th : introduced me to Mrs. G., Young G., Albert Grey and others. Everything arranged."

The undertaking thus given was faithfully fulfilled. On July the 6th, Mr. and Mrs. Gladstone arrived at Eton to spend the week-end with the Headmaster, Dr. Hornby, and in the evening he delivered his lecture on Homer. It had required some courage on the part of George Curzon to sponsor him, for he had sometime before spoken critically of Eton in a speech delivered at another school, a proceeding which had caused no little resentment at Eton. His courage was amply rewarded, for the impression which the speaker made upon his audience was immediate and profound. We have it on the authority of one who was present that " his prestige, his pale face, his blazing eyes, his sweeping gestures and the timbre of that marvellous voice, which had an almost physical effect upon the nerves, kept the audience spell-bound."[1] While a contributor to the press declared that after the charming references to his old school with which he prefaced his main theme, " the recollection of a certain speech at Marlborough could no longer have rankled in any breast and the reconciliation was perfect."[2]

On Sunday, Curzon escorted the distinguished visitors into Pop, where they routed out the old records in which were chronicled Mr. Gladstone's own past activities. " He laughed much over his own remarks as reported therein, and still more over the votes he had given." Thus George Curzon in the desultory diary which he kept of his doings at Eton. Small wonder that he laughed, for what he found in " the musty volumes of the Pop book " were " his Tory opinions fossilised in faded ink," along with " other youthful extravagances of many great ones of the earth."[3] Curzon adds to his account of this visit to Pop that Mr. Gladstone was much pleased at the painted photograph of himself hanging upon the wall. But he makes no mention of what might have proved an awkward contretemps had it not been for the presence of mind of Mr. C. M. Smith, who, as President, was one of the party. On account, presumably, of the criticisms of Eton to which reference has been made, the portrait had been turned face to the wall. It was not until he was actually on the stairs that a recollection of this

[1]Mr. A. C. Benson in " Eton in the Seventies."
[2]Land and Water of July 13th, 1878.
[3]Mr. Gilbert Coleridge in " Eton in the Seventies."

indignity flashed across Smith's mind. "It hung juſt inside the door, on the left hand side, and I had juſt time to run up and turn it the right way round before he entered the room ; and I don't think that he noticed that it was ſtill swinging."[1]

From Pop they proceeded to Curzon's own quarters, where Mr. Gladſtone, " noticing the general prettiness and refinement of my room, ſtocked as it was with pictures, china, prizes, armchairs and flowers, went on to make some remarks about the luxury of Eton."[2] Such an atmosphere, he thought, muſt exercise an enervating influence upon the boys. This view was warmly contested by Curzon, who argued that cultivation, even in such external details must tend to elevate. " Thus talking we reached the Head Master's door, where he said good-bye and asked me to go and stay with him at Hawarden, where, he said, we would resume the discussion."[3]

George Curzon's Presidentship of the Literary Society fostered his taste for literary work of all kinds. It provided him with an excuse for putting into practice a natural facility for letter writing, which made of him in after life so prolific a correspondent. In addition to the two visits which he had paid Mr. Gladstone in London, he wrote him four long letters in connection with his visit to Eton. And among other letters which he wrote to public men at the time, was one addressed to Mr. Ruskin, then Slade Professor at Oxford, congratulating him upon his recovery from a serious illness. " I need not say that during your long illness we have watched with anxiety the news of its slow and painful progress, and that we now welcome with pleasure no less intense the announcement which I have lately seen in the papers of its final defeat."[4] To how many schoolboys would it have occurred to write a similar letter ?

In 1876 he became the editor of *The Etonian,* a fortnightly school paper which had been ſtarted the year before by H. St. Clair Feilden, and in the absence of other contributions, he sometimes wrote an entire number himself. The labour proved too exacting, and on his giving up the editorship the paper perished. His occupation

[1]Mr. C. M. Smith in " Eton in the Seventies."
[2]Fragments relating to Curzon's life at Eton.　　　　[3]*Ibid.*
[4]Letter written in April 1878.

of the editorial chair, however, had fired him with a new ambition, no less a one than that of publishing a book. The volume, a short anthology of prose and verse, appeared anonymously under the title " Out of school at Eton," and was described in the preface as a collection of miscellaneous writings " with the composition of which we Eton boys have from time to time occupied our leisure hours." Though published anonymously, it is now known that among the contributors besides George Curzon himself were C., afterwards Sir Cecil Spring-Rice, M. T. Tatham, J. K. Stephen and St. Clair Feilden. The selection and arrangement of the contents were undertaken by Curzon on his own responsibility alone with the object, naively admitted, of proving that literary talent or, at any rate, the literary spirit was not extinct at Eton. Indeed the public were asked to accept the book as " an attempt, the first which has been made for many years, to vindicate the literary prestige of Eton." Not all the critics were persuaded that the object aimed at had been attained. If the *Eton College Journal* thought it " a very amusing little volume deserving all the pleasant things which friends of the contributors would say of it,"[1] the *Eton College Chronicle* was of opinion that there was " no adequate cause for the book being produced at all," and that it was one of those " which the world—both the larger world without and the smaller world of Eton—would willingly let die."[2] And if the *Spectator* commended it as " a bright, harum-scarum, open-air book,"[3] the *Athenaeum*, with a pontifical severity which scarcely seemed called for, dismissed it with the churlish complaint—familiar enough from the pen of the *laudator temporis acti*—that, " a straining after the facetious which is not comic and an occasional grandiloquence which is anything but impressive " had taken the place of " the scholarship and culture, good-taste and fine wit " of former days.[4] The most caustic among the critics agreed that the collection contained one contribution of real merit, a description in verse of " Our House Debating Society." Of this particular piece, however, George Curzon was not the author. In academic circles

[1] The *Windsor Gazette and Eton College Journal* of July 28th, 1877.
[2] The *Eton College Chronicle* of October 11th, 1877.
[3] The *Spectator* of August 11th, 1877.
[4] The *Athenaeum* of September 15th, 1877.

PLATE II.   A MEMORABLE FOURTH OF JUNE

The Hon. G. N. Curzon in 1878

at Cambridge the prevailing opinion was that the prose was boyish but tolerably promising, the poetry never below a fair level and now and then very high in merit. [1]

But if the reception accorded to this first attempt at authorship was not wholly encouraging, George Curzon had no reason to complain of any lack of readiness on the part of the critics to acknowledge his ability as a speaker. While still in his teens he developed a love of sonorous language and highly polished periods which made him in later years so impressive a speaker. Writing many years afterwards, Mr. A. C. Benson recalled the awe with which, when a small boy, he listened to an animated discussion on some political topic between George Curzon and a boy of the name of Wallop, in the school library. " I was amazed and even stupified at their eloquence and the maturity of their diction." [2] Critics of maturer years were equally impressed. His performances at the speeches on the Fourth of June, 1877, were described as " decidedly above the level of school recitation," [3] and as standing out in dramatic intensity. So much so, that " the immortal Scapin of Moliere, the familiar Don Abbondio of Manzoni's *I Promessi Sposi*, and George Eliot's *Spanish Gipsy*, seemed to live in the intelligent and vivid rendering of Mr. Curzon without the adventitious aid of Costume." [4]

His ability was so marked at the speeches of the following year, that those who heard him already began to speculate upon his future. [5] The happy recipient of so much praise was justifiably elated by his success and at the end of the day took unconcealed pleasure in jotting down his impressions of it. " June 4, 1878— the proudest day, I *expect*, of my life. Speeches in the morning. As soon as they were over, gents whom I had never previously seen seized me by the hand : ' Well done, you were the best of them all !' An elderly French lady tremendously voluble with her, ' Je vous felicite monsieur.' In the evening tent dinner at Surly . . . Ponsonby, my great friend, got up and proposed health of Captain of Oppidans. Drunk with musical honours in tent and all down

[1] Letter from the Hon. E. Lyttelton dated August 20th, 1877.
[2] " Eton in the Seventies."
[3] *Daily Telegraph*, June 5th, 1877.
[4] *Ibid.*   [5] *London*, June 8th, 1878.

boat tables. Had never been done before. Later on my health proposed here by Dod. Such fun!"[1] Perusal of these jottings when the first intoxication of success had worn off, seems to have excited qualms, for there is appended something of the nature of a postscript : " All the above is pure and unadulterated conceit, but as the truthful memento of a successful day may suffice in after years to recall the pleasurable emotions which it at the time excited."[2]

Immersed in these pursuits, it is unlikely that George Curzon would ever have found the time for games which anyone ambitious of athletic triumphs must devote to them—even if he had not been handicapped by physical disabilities. Throughout his school life he was particularly liable to juvenile ailments, and was already a victim to the weakness in his back which was the source of so much suffering throughout his life. And in 1875 he had the misfortune to break his arm on the football field. But it would be a mistake to suppose that he was in any way contemptuous of games or that his own record was a mean one. Cricketers, oarsmen and footballers who had won their school colours constituted " the Presiding spirit of Eton society, which could not flourish without them," and he acknowledged the undisputed, though not exclusive, right of such persons to the title of " swagger."[3] At the age of fourteen he himself started a junior cricket club in South Derbyshire and enjoyed some success as a bowler. In the archives of the *Derbyshire Advertiser* reposes an account of a match between a team captained by himself and one captained by a Mr. Devas. The opposing side was dismissed for eighty-six runs, thanks, in large measure, to the accuracy of Curzon's bowling, which was responsible for five of the enemy's wickets. The batting of his team did not, unfortunately, reach the same high standard as the bowling, and the whole eleven were dismissed once for fifty-one and a second time for twenty-eight, the match thus going to Mr. Devas' side by an innings and seven runs. Good cricket it always gave him pleasure to look on at, and for many years he was a frequent visitor at Lords. " I think at present that my chief regrets at being in India," he told

[1]From a note-book kept at Eton. [2]*Ibid.*
[3]In an article entitled " Swaggers " in " Out of School at Eton."

Alfred Lyttelton in 1901, " are that I cannot see Jessop slog, or shoot a grouse myself." At football he met with some success. " I play football a good deal—about four times a week—and I like it very much,"[1] and he eventually got his house colours, playing for the team for two years. In 1877 he was paid the compliment of having his name included in the list of Oppidan wall choices, though if he took any part in the time-honoured match between Collegers and Oppidans—the great event of the football term at Eton—it was as an onlooker only. During his last summer term he became senior keeper of Middle club at cricket, and as a compliment was given his " lazaroni " colours by the Captain of the school eleven. Was it a reference to this, perhaps, that J. K. Stephen introduced into his parody on Homer which appeared in the *Eton College Chronicle?*

> " Λοδδαιῶν ἦρχον μετα δαιδαλέοισι κολῶριτι
> Λουγλασίοιο βίη και Κυρσονέης Ωρὰτωρ"

" From Dod's with curiously wrought colours,
Douglas the Strong and Curzon the Orator led the way."[2]

When, in July, 1878, the time came for him to bid farewell to the school which he had grown to love so well, he was assailed by those poignant regrets which all sensitive natures experience when faced with the inexorable necessity of closing a chapter in their lives for the last time. In a farewell speech to the members of the Literary Society, he recalled the sad complaint of Sir Bevidere at the breaking up of the Round Table. They should not, however, give way to despair. They should call to mind the nature of the reply given by King Arthur " in words that are true both yesterday, to-day and for ever—' the old order changeth yielding place to new.' We who are going are the old order. Those who take our place are the new. We must not grieve too much . . . but must remember that we have had our time to make the most of, short-lived though it seems to have been."[3] A farewell speech in Pop was marked by

---

[1]Letter to Lady Scarsdale dated October 20th, 1872.
[2]I am told that it is more likely that the reference was to Wolley Dod's house colours, a curious mixture of purple, yellow and red.
[3]Speech on July 30th, 1878.

passages of real pathos : " Many of us now here may not be together in the same room again for years—some never. . . . We have
been a very friendly body, some of us will, I trust, remain friends
for life ; none, I am sure, can forget their last year of Pop at Eton.
The time has come for us to say good-bye, not only to institutions
like this, but to the great school itself among whose followers we
are proud to be enrolled.   I will not say anything about the sorrow
of leaving *that*, but I think we all of us feel on occasions like this,
when we are breaking up old times and dissolving old associations,
the truth of the words that

> ' Nothing in life shall sever
>   The chain that is round us now,'

and that we shall all go forth into the world with a happy and a
living recollection of our last year at Eton." [1]

---

[1] Speech on August 1st, 1878.

CHAPTER II

LIFE AT BALLIOL

1878-1882

GEORGE CURZON went up to Oxford in the autumn of 1878 with great expectations blunted little, if at all, by his failure to win the Balliol scholarship, for which he sat during his last year at Eton. The four years which he spent at the University were years of deliberate preparation for a clearly pre-ordained career. " I do not know that I build many castles in the air for Oxford specially," he told a friend. " My castles come later on in life and perhaps have dim chances of realisation ; but I recognise, at any rate, that they cannot have any unless this Oxford time is spent in laying the foundations and preparing for the superstructure." [1] Even before he reached Oxford his friends were speaking of " the brief interval which must intervene between Eton and the Cabinet." [2] No one among them ever doubted his ambition. " You are very ambitious, I know, and right ambition is very noble and wholesome, but it must be directed to some altruistic not egoistic end." [3] Their fear was rather that ambition so definite, formed at so young an age, might atrophy the finer feelings of the heart. " This doctrine of altruism is the sum, the upshot, the cream of all philosophy. . . . Prizes, distinction, tinsel are poor substitutes for the reverence of an humble gratitude of even one human heart " ; [4] and on his leaving Eton : " You know that you have been accused—as I believe, so wrongly—of a general superficiality of heart and mind.

[1] Letter to the Hon. R. B. Brett, afterwards Lord Esher, September 20th, 1878.
[2] Letter from the Hon. St. John Brodrick, afterwards Lord Midleton, May 29th, 1878.
[3] Letter from the Hon. R. B. Brett, afterwards Lord Esher, March 5th, 1878.
[4] Ibid.

37

. . . Superficiality means plenty of intellect and not enough heart. Dear George, let your feelings have full play, and you will get round everybody as you have got round me." [1]

These early judgments are interesting, because they show that even at this youthful age the veil which all through his life hid the real man from the public gaze and gave rise to such false estimates of him was not easily penetrated, even by his friends.

It was to Balliol college that he proceeded in October, 1878, and Balliol college was the obvious and fitting setting for his period of probation. For Balliol, under Jowett, had become by the late seventies a famous nursery of Public men. With a wide catholicity of taste, it welcomed men of varying types and from different strata in society. Within its walls scholars from democratic Glasgow rubbed shoulders with the fine flower of the aristocracy of England. And Balliol was justified by her children. In his " Social and Diplomatic Memories," Sir Rennell Rodd mentions the names of a whole galaxy of men of his generation who went forth from her portals to make their mark in public life—Lansdowne, Loreburn, Oxford and Milner, of a rather earlier date, Curzon and Midleton, of his own time, and a little later Grey of Fallodon. In the ranks of diplomacy Cecil Spring-Rice, Arthur Hardinge and Louis Mallet, all of his own year; in the world of scholarship J. W. Mackail and W. P. Ker; among athletes, W. H. Grenfell, afterwards Lord Desborough, and Savile Crossley, afterwards Lord Somerleyton; and in the front rank of journalism St. Loe Strachey and Sidney Low. Nor was this list by any means exhaustive; and at a dinner held at Balliol rather more than a decade later to those of its old pupils who were in either House of Parliament, it was found that there were forty-one in the then House of Commons alone.

Between his departure from Eton at the beginning of August and his arrival at Oxford in October, George Curzon had experienced a severe attack of the trouble with his back, which accentuated the disability for games, from which he had always suffered. He returned in September from a brief visit to France, with what was already recognised as an incurable curvature of the spine. " Since

[1] Letter from the Hon. R. B. Brett, afterwards Lord Esher, August 23rd, 1878.

PLATE III. COMMITTEE OF THE OXFORD UNION, 1880

E. I. Horsburgh   C. Arnold-White   B. R. Wise
Librarian   *Treasurer*   *Ex-President*

H. C. Macleod   R. Dawson   Hon. G. N. Curzon   E. T. Cook   R. A. Germaine

I came back from France," he told Mr. Brett, "I have felt out-shooting pains in my side, in the region of the hip, and noticed an unusual prominence of that member. I went up to London about it and saw the best men. They said it was weakness of the spine resulting from natural weakness and overwork, and that I must give up Oxford for the present and lie down on my back. Paget, to whom it was settled I should go as a final opinion, saw no harm in my going to Oxford if I obey strict injunctions—wear an appliance, lie down a good deal and take no violent or, indeed, very active exercise." This in itself made very little difference to his career at Oxford, for his ambition lay in other directions, and inability or disinclination to play games was of far less account at the University than at a Public School.

Both the nature of his ambitions, and his qualifications for achieving them, were made clear at his very first appearance at the Union. The motion before the House was a vote of confidence in the Government in respect of their Afghan policy, and a contributor to *Land and Water*, in a brief description of the proceedings, remarked that "the first half dozen speeches were very good, the Hon. G. N. Curzon making a very successful beginning as a speaker at the Union."[1] The Government were accorded the confidence of the House by sixty-two votes to thirty-nine ; but not content with this, Curzon followed it up the next term by carrying the war into the enemy's camp with a motion denouncing the attitude of the Opposition in Parliament towards the war then in progress beyond the Indian Frontier. Of his speech on this occasion, a writer in *Land and Water*, singling him out as "quite a new member," said : "He spoke at some length with much fluency and classical quotation."[2] The *Undergraduate Journal* viewing the proceedings, possibly, from a slightly different angle, said much the same thing in somewhat different language : "Balliol scholarship was painfully conspicuous in the opener's speech."[3] It may have been, for he had acquired at Eton a love of sonorous language and an aptitude for classical quotation ; but whatever the defects of his

[1]*Land and Water* of November 16th, 1878.
[2]*Land and Water* of February 8th, 1879.
[3]The *Undergraduate Journal,* February 6th, 1879.

style, he quickly became the acknowledged leader of the Young Conservatives at Oxford.

There are men alive to-day who can paint from memory graphic pictures of him as he appeared when first he flashed, comet-like across the horizon of undergraduate political life. A striking figure, tall, straight and rigid, bearing himself with a loftiness uncommon among men of his age, he made an immediate impression upon all with whom he came in contact. Among his friends his bearing was a subject of admiring comment. " I am miserable to have missed a sight of your shapely form " ; " My bonny boy " ; " I should very much enjoy a sight of your shapely figure " ; " My shapely boy " are all phrases taken at random from letters written to him at Oxford. To these physical advantages of form and stature was added a complexion so unusually brilliant as always to catch the eye. Many years after he had left the University his pink cheeks continued to be the subject of good-natured banter. " The complexion of a milkmaid, the stature of an Apollo and the activity of an Under-Secretary," was the description of him given in one newspaper, when, in 1893, he was busy organising a memorial to his old master, Jowett, of Balliol.

In manner and conversation he struck those who were not within the circle of his own particular friends as self-confident and rather boisterous, and as being impatient of opposition. The greater maturity of mind and the superior knowledge of public men and affairs which were apparent from his earliest days at Oxford gave him special prestige among his contemporaries. And added to this initial advantage, were accomplishments as a speaker which, whether regarded as assets—as they were by those in sympathy with him ; or as defects—as they might easily have been by those opposed to him—were, in any case, extremely effective in debate. Self-possession too easily to be mistaken for self-esteem ; a powerful voice employed with equal effect to appeal to the emotions of those in sympathy with his views and to castigate those hostile to him ; admirable and carefully studied elocution and a style elaborate and ornate which, while impressive to his friends, was apt to suggest artificiality to his critics ; a particularly orderly and well-stocked mind, which led him to cover his ground with a thorough-

ness and detail that too easily lent itself to charges of prolixity;
a command of language which envy was apt to dub verbosity;
an alertness of mind enabling him to barb his shafts with a sarcasm
and repartee which, while delighting his supporters, were regarded
as heavy-handed rather than light-winged by those who were their
targets; an aggressiveness which could be regarded as powerful
advocacy or over-bearing declamation, according to the disposition
and predilections of the listener—these were the attributes of a
personality which in controversy both attracted and repelled, but
which in the one case as in the other, most emphatically refused to
be ignored.

It was not unnatural, perhaps, that undergraduate democracy
should be a little inclined to turn up its nose at airs and graces
which seemed to it, in the case of so young a man, to verge on the
ridiculous. And this feeling found expression in the rhymes
which, in one form or another, stuck to him for life. The original
version of the lines appeared in the *Balliol Masque*, a collection of
rhymes mainly by J. W. Mackail, now Professor of Ancient Literature to the Royal Academy, and H. C. Beeching, afterwards Dean
of Norwich, on dons and prominent undergraduates of the day.
They may be seen in the original issue of the publication presented
by Mackail to the college library, and are as follows:

> " I am a most superior person, Mary,
> My name is George N-th-n--l C-rz-n, Mary,
> I'll make a speech on any political question of the day,
> Mary,
> Provided you'll not say me nay, Mary."

These lines, in their turn, were a parody on a song written by
George Curzon himself for *Waifs and Strays*, a terminal magazine
of Oxford poetry, started by Rennell Rodd and a friend in 1879.
The first two stanzas of this composition, which excited some deri-
sion on its first appearance, read as follows:

> " When I was a little lad, Mary,
> And thou wert a little lass,
> Ere ever we knew what we had, Mary,
> To make us together life pass,

CURZON, 1878

I used in those days to say, Mary,
That the girl I should claim as my own,
Provided she'd not say me nay, Mary,
Would be one that I had not then known."

The better known version of the rhyme usually, though I believe
incorrectly, attributed to Cecil Spring-Rice runs thus :—

" My name is George Nathaniel Curzon,
I am a most superior person,
My cheek is pink, my hair is sleek,
I dine at Blenheim once a week."

But if his manner was irritating to many, and if it seemed to some
that his triumphs in debate were of a quasi-physical rather than of
a purely intellectual nature, there were few who would have denied
that his style and argument were admirably suited to their purpose.
And with all his zeal and aggressiveness in political warfare, he
earned the respect, and often the regard, of those who differed
from him.   One who at Oxford met him more often in debate
than in intimate social intercourse has paid him a fine tribute when
declaring that though he recalls his kindness in those distant days,
he can remember no ill-will throughout. [1]

Perhaps one of the most interesting pen portraits of George
Curzon as an undergraduate that has been handed down to us, is
that contained in the letter of a young American, whose obvious
detachment gives his opinion a special value.   The writer, Mr. L. R
Johnson of Bollinger County, Missouri, wrote a year or two after
leaving Oxford, where he had spent some time as an undergraduate,
to ask of Curzon the favour of a photograph.   In explanation of
so unusual a request by one who was " an entire stranger," he said
that the portrait, if given, would represent not so much an individual as a proud and powerful political party.

" As an undergraduate at Oxford I attended the Union
debates and noted the best speakers.   As an unprejudiced
observer I was interested more in studying the types of men

[1] Lord Sumner of Ibstone.

42

than in weighing their political arguments. You were the only man I found who perfectly filled my ideal of what a young representative of the Conservative, and especially the aristocratic, party should be. It was the intense aristocratic turn of your disposition which forcibly struck me; for which, indeed, I had been abundantly prepared by works of fiction, but which I had never seen exemplified. . . . You were to me a type."

And he concluded by saying that having seen the ease with which he took and held the lead of his party at the Union, he felt little doubt that he would with equal ease at some future time, become the leader of the Conservative Party in the country.[1]

Politics certainly occupied a large share of George Curzon's time at Oxford and became a serious rival to his academic studies, thus justifying to some extent, perhaps, the dictum of Professor Ruskin that young men had no business at all with such matters. Against this view, needless to say, Curzon protested vigorously. "My dear Sir," demanded the Professor, "what in the Devil's name have you to do either with Mr. Disraeli or Mr. Gladstone. You are students at the University and have no more business with politics than you have with rat-catching."[2] To which Curzon replied that since politics was merely a synonym for contemporary history, education itself demanded of a man that he should take an intelligent interest in it. Moreover, in 1880, politics thrust themselves upon the young men at Oxford; for following upon the General Election had come the renewed fight for Sir William Harcourt's seat at that city on his appointment as Home Secretary, and following upon his defeat, the trial of the election petition to which it gave rise. Realising how grave were the temptations to which the undergraduate world was subjected by these events, the University authorities had decreed a penalty of £5 against any undergraduate found taking part in a political meeting. This action on their part may, or may not, have proved effective in reducing temporarily the effervescence which the undergraduate element im-

[1] Letter dated September 6th, 1884.
[2] "Arrows of the Chase," Vol. II.

ported into the political gatherings of more sober citizens, but it can hardly have proved other than an advertisement for politics in general. In any case young Oxford was in no mood to fall in with the fatherly advice of Professor Ruskin. With an extraordinary zest it flung itself into the political arena, thought about politics, discussed politics, formed opinions on politics—refused any longer to accept a political creed ready made and at second-hand. "To assume that young men under the conditions of modern education are Conservative or Liberal merely because their fathers were before them, is to demand that the shadow shall return upon the dial, and to shut our eyes to the point which the mental development of the race has attained."[1] And wherever the ardent political spirits of the University were gathered together —whether at the Union, or the Dervorguilla Society of Balliol, or the Canning Club—there was George Curzon to be seen prominent in their midst.

Paradoxical though it may seem, his enthusiasm and earnestness fostered the very defect which most seriously threatened his reputation as a speaker ; and by the end of his first year at the University, when his position in the Union was established, his prolixity was exciting universal comment. "Lengthy and somewhat discursive though eloquent " were terms applied to his speaking by a writer in *Land and Water*[2] ; while a contributor to the same paper observed on another occasion that though at times good, he certainly exhibited " a lamentable tendency to become prolix. As it was, he spoke for about fifty minutes and would have gone on for fifty more had not the President interposed."[3] Friends who were fully persuaded of the fine quality of his mind warned him constantly of the insidious nature of this besetting sin, and none with greater solicitude than Jowett. "As you know, success in politics depends upon good sense, the power of work and the power of speech "[4] ; but this latter power must not be allowed to run riot. "I think you have many advantages and one disadvantage—too much to say in a

[1] "The Conservatism of Young Oxford," George Curzon in the *National Review*, June, 1884.
[2] *Land and Water*, October 25th, 1879.
[3] *Land and Water* of May 24th, 1879.
[4] Letter dated July 15th, 1882.

speech or in conversation. It is a good fault if corrected—but a most serious one if left uncorrected, because it destroys the impression of weight and of thought and gives the impression, probably very undeserved, of conceit and self-sufficiency."[1] So conscious was he of the danger which this failing threatened to the career of one of the outstanding figures that had gone forth from his beloved Balliol, that he continued to press his views upon him long after he had passed from his immediate ken. " May I tell you something—only a hint, which may, perhaps, be rather impertinent now that you have ceased to be ' in statu pupillari ' ? It would be better if you were shorter in speaking, writing, conversation. I think it is worth your while to consider how you can correct this defect—probably the only bar which stands in the way of your rising to eminence."[2] That this excellent and well-meant advice was accepted in the spirit in which it was tendered was amply apparent when, in due course, George Curzon threw himself heart and soul into the project for raising a memorial to the late Master of Balliol and, indeed, bore on his own shoulders the whole brunt of the undertaking.

Early in 1880 interest in politics was stimulated by the General Election which, after a long period of exile, had brought the Liberal party back to power with Mr. Gladstone at its head, and with a considerable infusion of the strong wine of radicalism—that very advanced brand of liberalism which only stopped short of socialism —represented in the new Government by Sir Charles Dilke and Mr. Joseph Chamberlain. These events roused the conservative instincts deeply rooted in George Curzon's nature, and at the earliest opportunity he moved in the Union " that this House views with sincere regret the results of the General Election." He spoke " in his best style and was listened to with profound attention for three-quarters of an hour. Both as regards manner and matter it was by far the best speech I have heard at the Union for a long time past."[3] The debate excited widespread interest. Twice it had to be adjourned, and on April the 29th, when the final stage was reached, the new

[1] Letter dated December 31st, 1884.
[2] Letter dated September 13th, 1889.
[3] *John Bull* of April 13th, 1880.

hall was crammed to suffocation, it being estimated that more than a thousand people were present.[1] " The debate ended with a House tumultuously impatient to hear Mr. Curzon's reply, which, indeed, was well worth hearing. He carried his audience completely with him, and his motion by a considerable majority."[2] The actual numbers were : for the motion 228, against 113 ; majority 115.

The following month George Curzon was elected President of the Union by 308 votes to 193, a majority of 115 over Mr. Sargeaunt, the representative of the Liberal section of the House, who had the advantage of being the nominee of the out-going President, Mr. B. R. Wise. The honour was no empty one, for the Union at that time was justly regarded as a nursery of statesmen. Asquith in 1874, Milner in 1876, had each occupied the Presidential chair— and each had found it a stepping stone to a distinguished Public career. The same year he added to his responsibilities by accepting the secretaryship of the Canning Club—an exclusive organisation, representing the flower of Young Oxford Conservatism, which had been founded in 1860, but which had fallen somewhat into neglect. This in spite of the fact that a protracted enquiry into principles which had marked the transactions of the club in the late seventies had placed opinion in the Canning " years ahead of the party at large."[3]

With a vigour and a success that earned for him the title of second founder of the club, he set to work to make of the Canning Club a real centre of Conservatism in the University. During the first year of his tenure of office the maximum number of undergraduate members permitted by the rules, namely, twenty-five, was reached for the first time for a number of years, and the total living membership brought up to two hundred and twelve, including five members of each of the two Houses of Parliament. During the same period the club met regularly once a week throughout the academic year, a record never previously reached, and at every one of the twenty-four meetings George Curzon was in attendance. He frequently took part in the debates and always drafted in masterly style minutes

---

[1]*Cambridge Review* of May 5th, 1880. [2]*Ibid.*
[3]An account of the Canning Club compiled by Mr. H. Steinhart and printed privately for circulation amongst its members.

PLATE IV.   THE CANNING CLUB IN 1881

Viscount Curzon.   E. C. Owen.   C. L. Selater Booth.   J. G. Pemberton.   J. A. R. Marriot.   Viscount Cranborne.   J. C. Bower.   E. G. Mowbray.
                              W. Bromley-Davenport.   W. P. Burn
G. L. Talbot.   A. T. Thring.   W. W. How

of the proceedings, which provided summaries of the debates so admirable, that at the close of his two years of office the club determined to have them printed and bound as a permanent record of its proceedings. He always regarded debate as the primary purpose of the club's existence, and it is clear from the method which he adopted of reporting the discussions that he assumed that the papers which gave rise to them would be preserved separately. They certainly were during his time, for at its close he handed them to his successor ; but while his summaries of the debates have been preserved, the papers themselves have disappeared. In the sympathetic atmosphere of the club he spoke with marked effect. " He was master, even in those early days, of a style . . . . always vigorous and effective and at times rising to a stately eloquence."[1]

Apart from the debates, the chief feature of the club's activities was an annual dinner held in conjunction with a kindred body, the Chatham club, to which prominent public men were always invited. The newly-appointed secretary was determined to prove that this function could be made, not only an effective political demonstration, but a financial success. With a faith that deserved and won success, he hired the city buildings, gave the contract for the dinner to the cook of Balliol college, reduced the price of tickets from twenty-five shillings to a guinea, and awaited with confidence the result. On June the 18th, 1881, a record number—one hundred and thirty— sat down to dinner, among the guests being two prominent members of the Opposition, Sir Richard Cross, M.P., and Mr. E. Gibson, M.P., who responded to the toasts of Her Majesty's Opposition and the Houses of Parliament, proposed by Mr. Curzon and Lord Cranborne respectively.

It was with legitimate satisfaction that he penned his subsequent report on the proceedings. Instead of resulting in a deficit, as had almost invariably been the case, " the dinner left in the coffers of the club a handsome and unprecedented surplus." The success of the banquet as a political and social function was equally decisive. " It only remains to say that the dinner appeared to give very general satisfaction, and that so late were the festivity and speech making protracted, that it was a quarter past twelve before the town hall

[1] Mr. W. W. How, Fellow of Merton College, a member of the club at the time.

was vacated, and the members of the two clubs returned home after the most successful dinner ever chronicled in the annals of the Canning and Chatham."

It must have been a source of no little gratification to him that many years later Mr. Steinhart, in an historical survey of the activities of the club during a period of fifty years from its foundation in 1860, should have declared of his term of office, " during which Toryism was slowly recovering from the smashing blow of the General Election of 1880," that it was " the golden age of the Canning club."

Reference has been made to the early maturity of his mind. His political beliefs were formed at a very early age and changed singularly little throughout his life. The politics of Eton, so far as there could be said to be any, were doubtless conservative by tradition. " Very nearly all Eton fellows are Conservatives," he informed his Mother at the time of the election of 1874, " and we all wore dark blue ribbon in our buttonholes."[1] But his political views were much more definite than those of the average schoolboy, and being " the protagonist of conservative ideas, he soon found himself the uncrowned leader of a Government perpetually in power."[2]

Before he left Oxford his conception of Conservatism was comprehensive and clear cut. It was in the main the creed expounded by Disraeli in his political novels, " Coningsby," " Sybil," and " Tancred." In this creed of a young England party he saw " a great deal that was visionary, much that was doomed to disappointment, and a little that was absurd " ; but from it Conservatism had derived one great principle which was, and must continue to be, the sheet anchor of its domestic programme, namely, " the amelioration of the condition of the lower orders of society." This principle he desired to see raised " from the dream of the philanthropist to the duty of the statesman." But this was not to be effected by what a British administrator at a later date and in a different connection aptly described as " catastrophic change."[3] The Monarchy, the Estates of the realm, the Established Church—institutions which

[1] Letter to Lady Scarsdale, February 5th, 1874.
[2] " Eton in the Seventies."
[3] Lord Chelmsford when Viceroy of India.

48

had "raised England from a collection of petty principalities to a great Power whose fame overshadowed the world "—must be sedulously guarded and preserved. Social revolution involving a war of classes, "of the landed and monied interests, of aristocracy and democracy, of the rich and the poor, of the landlord and the tenant," was fraught only with disaster.

His outlook upon foreign affairs was emphatically and frankly Imperialistic. Nor could he understand how anyone brought up at Oxford could hold a different creed. "At a place and amid institutions whose roots are buried in the past, and whose history is intertwined with that of the nation, whose sons have carried its name to the corners of the World and stamped their own on the fabric of imperial grandeur, it would, indeed, be strange were there found any acquiescence in the sordid doctrines of self-effacement, in a policy of national or territorial disintegration, in the new-found obligation to shirk admitted duties, or in the application of the system of a parochial vestry to the polity of a colossal empire." [1]

A striking example of the fixity of his views on political and social questions is provided by his attitude towards the enfranchisement of women. He was convinced that any encroachment by one sex on the rightful sphere of the other must lead to social disintegration, and he opposed on principle all movements in this direction. During his second year at Oxford a proposal was put forward by the library Committee to permit lady students to make use of the Union library. The proposal was one which occasioned considerable excitement, though "when the librarian announced that the ladies would not themselves appear in the Union, there was a groan of disappointment." [2] Nevertheless the proposal supported by the President, Mr. E. T. Cook, and opposed by Mr. Curzon, was carried by a narrow majority, 254 voting for, and 238 against the motion. It was one of the few—possibly the only—occasion on which Curzon suffered defeat in any debate of first-class importance at the Union. With him the matter was one of principle, and fifteen years later he

---

[1] This and the previous quotations are from an article entitled "The Conservatism of Young Oxford," by G. N. Curzon, which appeared in the *National Review* of June 1884.
[2] *Land and Water* of November 22nd, 1879.

was opposing with equal zeal—and for the time being with success—
the admission of ladies to Fellowship of the Royal Geographical
Society. Later still he stood out as one of the most convinced and
powerful opponents of woman suffrage.

His opinions of persons, expressed with the unabashed candour
which gave to his conversation so piquant an interest, were marked
by the same maturity as his views about things. Writing from Blenheim, where " the conversation was largely political," he told his
friend Farrer that he thought Sir Michael Hicks Beach " the
most incompetent Cabinet Minister " he had ever set eyes on. With
Randolph Churchill he was more favourably impressed as " a smart
fellow possessing all the audacity which his performances give him
credit for." [1] This impression remained and was, indeed, heightened
by the latter's brilliant leadership of the famous Fourth Party, for
two years later he wrote of him in a still more admiring strain—
" Randolph Churchill has made most remarkable strides in estimation both inside and outside the House. He may not always have
been judicious, but he has shown extreme capacity and is walking
away from all his contemporaries." [2]

---

[1] Letter to R. R. Farrer, October 17th, 1880.
[2] Letter to R. R. Farrer December 2nd, 1882.

CHAPTER III

OXFORD AND AFTER

1878-1882

GEORGE CURZON's abilities were such as might have won for him a brilliant academic career. They did win for him brilliant academic successes, though they failed to give him the former. No man ever worked harder than he did, but his absorbing interest in political and social life claimed too much of his time and energy to permit him to concentrate steadily on the studies comprised within the University curriculum. His successes, brilliant—even startling—as they sometimes proved to be, were flashes of genius rather than indications of steadily pursued study. As at Eton, so at Oxford, his academic spoils were taken by storm rather than by patient and carefully prepared siege. It was his phenomenal power of rapid assimilation that made him so formidable a candidate in the competitions for which he entered. His friends were wont to expostulate with him on this score: ". . . . You might do anything you liked if you borrowed some of the steadiness of mediocrity. You will be grumbling at this old story by this time; but an acquaintance of yours up here (Cambridge) was saying the same thing lately and stirred me up anew."[1] And a year later—" So you have won another prize. I hope you are not tired of them yet. Remember O(scar) B(rowning)'s dictum that success is no criterion of a good education; . . . . its merits are not quite clear to you now, I dare say."[2]

His chances of a Balliol scholarship were prejudiced, if not altogether spoilt, by his insisting upon sitting up nightly until three a.m. or 4 a.m., discussing with his new found friend, St. John

[1] Letter from the Hon. E. Lyttelton, December 5th, 1876.
[2] Letter from the Hon. E. Lyttelton, November 11th, 1877.

Brodrick, every aspect of life—social, political and religious. He had jumped breathlessly into a railway carriage and the latter's friendship one day when proceeding on long leave from Eton. The present Lord Midleton tells how, just as the train was moving off, a " tall, pink-faced and breathless individual " was pushed unceremoniously into the carriage occupied by himself and Alfred Lyttelton, the great hero of the school at the time, and how, having seen him announced as the winner of the Prince Consort prize for French that morning, he recognised him and proceeded to put him at his ease. Such was the beginning of a friendship which lasted for thirty years before great events cast their shadow over it and embittered the relations which had brought into the lives of each so much real pleasure. For these intimate talks far into the night, in 1877, though they may have lost Curzon a Balliol scholarship, laid the foundations of a remarkable friendship. " If I were to tell you what a pleasure it is to exchange thoughts and feelings with one who is to run the same course as oneself, with the same aims and many mutual friends and associations, you would believe that I was only flattering you ; but I know that you will agree with me that it is something beyond a mere community of interests which has enabled us to talk so unreservedly on so short a friendship on subjects which most people, if they enter on them at all, touch upon only when they have proved their confidence in each other."[1]

This habit of sitting up late was already attracting the unfavourable notice of his friends. " Now I want to harangue you about going to bed in rather better time. Ever since my brother Arthur, who was one of the strongest brained men I ever saw, broke down, I vowed that I would not see anyone running the risk of making himself, by sitting up, incompetent for the rest of his life to make any sudden spurt in work—for that is what it comes to."[2] All such warnings fell on deaf ears ; yet neither social nor political distractions succeeded in robbing him of success in the first great test of the use to which he had put his time at the University, for he took a first-class in Honour Moderations in classics in 1880. And the following year Jowett wrote enthusiastically to Lord Scarsdale—

[1]Letter from the Hon. St. John Brodrick, December 2nd, 1877.
[2]Letter from the Hon. Alfred Lyttelton, Christmas 1879.

" Your son is doing extremely well at Balliol. He works very steadily and successfully." [1]

Nevertheless his friends were fearful lest he should fail to do himself justice and continued to proffer good advice. This solicitude on his behalf he acknowledged gratefully.

> " I know how true what you say is, and that Oxford life and work are not to be treated in a chance and casual manner. I hope that this coming term, several former distractions being absent, I shall be able to buckle down in greater earnestness. Anyhow, I recognise that there is something more to be done than indulge in delightful but not, perhaps, very profitable intercourse with charming friends." [2]

But the attractions of social and political life militated against these good resolutions, and as the date of the final examination approached we find him depressed and full of forebodings. " I am thoroughly sick of work, have long realised that I did not begin putting my back into Greats till a year too late, and shall be quite content still further to dignify class two by the insertion of my name." [3] For six months he had been working at high pressure to make up for lost time, and when at last the ordeal was over, he fell a prey to anxiety as to the result. " As to the exam, I am harassed by conflicting doubts and emotions." He tried to estimate his chances. His history papers he was satisfied with, his translations he thought were on the whole quite good, but the papers on logic and philosophy he marred " by totally misunderstanding, and therefore writing bosh on one important question in each." His proses he reckoned to have been moderate.

> " Now you see my extremely critical position. My history is pulling me up, backed by my translations. My logic and philosophy are remorselessly pulling me down. Which will win ? Honestly, I think either. I tell you the truth. I do

[1] Letter dated October 21st, 1881.
[2] Letter to R. R. Farrer, January 14th, 1880.
[3] Letter to R. R. Farrer, March 4th, 1882.

not think I am absolutely out of the chance of a first; but, upon my word, I am far from in it . . . bearing in mind the superior importance attached to philosophy . . . I am inclined to believe that the betting is on a second." [1]

Six weeks were to elapse before these anxieties could be laid to rest, and he turned to political and social engagements for distraction—a long promised motion at the Union, the Canning Club dinner, and two balls, the Vincent and the 'Varsity, which he helped to organise. It was not until the blow fell that he realised how much he had set his heart upon a first and how greatly he had expected success. "Disappointed I freely confess I was and am. And I was also rather disgusted, for in spite of occasional doubts . . . . I felt tolerably confident, on the whole, of getting a first, and still think I did about well enough to do so." [2] And it was characteristic of the man that he should have exclaimed on learning his fate—so at least runs the story—"Now I shall devote the rest of my life to showing the examiners that they have made a mistake." What he cared for most was the effect which his failure might have on his future career. "In the public eye I am, of course, stamped with the brand of respectable mediocrity." [3]

His friends and admirers hastened to reassure him. "I think that it should be regarded as an accident," wrote Jowett, "for the first-class was certainly deserved both by ability and industry; and I trust that you will not abate one jot of hope or heart in entering upon the political career which is your natural sphere." [4] Among the first to write and discount the effect of failure was Alfred Lyttelton, the Eton hero into whose railway compartment he had been unceremoniously ushered eight years before. "Of course, you could have got the first-class for certain if you had denied yourself the Union, the Canning, and those other literary, political and social enterprises which have earned you the name of the most famous Oxonian that in my knowledge of Oxford I can remember." [5] Jowett's estimate of the result as an accident was a sound one. The

[1] Letter to R. R. Farrer, May 28th, 1882.
[2] Letter to R. R. Farrer, July 23rd, 1882.   [3] Ibid.
[4] Letter from Jowett, July 15th, 1882.
[5] Letter dated July 4th, 1882.

decision had hung in the balance, and it was only at the last moment and by a feather's weight that the scale had fallen against him. His performance, when all the circumstances are taken into consideration, was one of which he had little reason to be ashamed.

Some little time before he had been placed " proxime accessit " for the Chancellor's Latin verse prize, and in the summer of 1881 had suffered the same fate in an attempt to capture the Lothian history prize. His Essay on John Sobieski, King of Poland, covering one hundred and eight large quarto pages of neat manuscript, was described by one of the judges as " a decidedly good narrative Essay with a considerable amount of careful reading," the author's treatment of " the political causes which led Sobieski to change from a French to an Austrian policy " being regarded as particularly good. But it was marred by " a certain pretentiousness of style and character,"[1] and was judged inferior to the essay of Mr. E. H. R. Tatham of Brasenose College, who was proclaimed the winner. Thus, with his second-class in the final school of Literæ Humaniores, his undergraduate life at Oxford came to a somewhat disappointing end.

It was not, however, his last tilt at fortune in this particular arena. A year later he atoned for his previous defeat by winning the Lothian Prize for the best historical Essay on Justinian, in circumstances recalling his most brilliant and dramatic onslaughts on the prize fund at Eton. The story of this achievement will be told presently. The same year he was elected a Fellow of All Souls, an ambition which he had cherished, but which he had hesitated to put to the test, twelve months before. " Do you recommend me to stand for All Souls this year ? " he had asked his friend Farrer, in July, 1882. " I am very doubtful," he added. " I don't know much history and am not inclined to read all August, September and October . . . . It seems to me only a hundred to one chance, particularly after I have only got a second."[2] And, finally, by winning the Arnold Prize for the best Essay on Sir Thomas More, in 1884, he created a new record, no one man having previously won the two most important University prizes in history.

[1] Letter from Dean Kitchin to R. W. Raper, May 11th, 1881.
[2] Letter dated July 23rd, 1882.

This last triumph was the outcome of a sudden whim on a par with the impulse which had led him to withdraw from the Italian class at Eton, only to reappear at the examination and under the Italian master's nose, to snatch the prize from the latter's favourite pupil. Strolling one day into the Bodleian Library, he noticed Mr. A. Hawkins—afterwards to win fame under the nom-de-plume of Anthony Hope—whose Essay in competition for the Lothian Prize had been singled out for " honourable mention," at work with a view, as he thought, to wiping out his defeat in the former competition by capturing the Arnold Prize.[1] The effect was like that of the smell of the field of battle in the nostrils of Bucephalus. His spirit of emulation rose within him, and from that moment he made up his mind to enter the lists. He spent many days at the British Museum reading, with an imperious determination to succeed and an apostolic faith in his ability to do so. And in due course he had the satisfaction of being acclaimed the victor. Thus the mishaps which had befallen him as an undergraduate fell into the background before the glittering rewards which crowned his student days.

These final academic victories were won after his undergraduate days were over ; and two years earlier we see him emerging from the University and stepping expectantly across the threshold of the greater world awaiting exploration and, unless he was much mistaken, conquest. Earlier still, at the festivities with which his coming of age at Kedleston had been celebrated in January, 1880, he had made plain the standpoint from which he looked forward to the future. " I am fully conscious of the fact that should I ever do anything worthy of the humblest mention, it must be looked for not in the boyhood which has now closed behind me, but in the manhood which from to-day opens before me."[2]

This side of his character is plain enough. George Curzon was, and always had been, a man of great ambitions. One who knew him from his Eton days once said of him that he seemed to realise the ideal of Aristotle's $\mu\epsilon\gamma\alpha\lambda\acute{o}\psi\nu\chi\circ\varsigma$, a man who regards himself as worthy of greatness and who is worthy.[3] It is a coincidence that is

[1] He was quite wrong in the conclusion to which he jumped, for Sir A. H. Hawkins tells me that he never entered for the Arnold.
[2] Speech to the tenantry at Kedleston, on January 11th, 1880.
[3] Rev. J. E. C. Welldon.

not without significance, surely, that at a much later period of his life a very different person should have been struck with the same idea. One day in March, 1902, Lady Curzon sat in the verandah of a house in Darjeeling, gazing out at the snow-white peak of Kanchenjunga, and fitfully turning over the pages of Macaulay's " Life of Pitt." As she glanced casually at the letterpress, her attention was suddenly arrested by a description of that statesman, which she at once applied to the man who always filled her thoughts and who was, at that moment, toiling in the service of his country in the steaming plains below. Pitt's self-esteem, she read, " was not that of an upstart who was drunk with good luck and with applause . . . . it was that of the magnanimous man so finely described by Aristotle in the ' Ethics '—of the man who thinks himself worthy of the great things, being in truth worthy."

If, then, George Curzon had long dreamed dreams of coming greatness, it was natural enough that now, when the vista of life was opening out before his gaze, these ambitions should have risen to the surface and should have tended to obscure the many other characteristics lying behind the mask which was too often mistaken for the man. For these we must glance back at the early formation of character during his eventful school-days and the rapid crystallisation of habits and opinions at Eton and Oxford which, far more than in the case of most men, make it important to study George Curzon as a boy and undergraduate.

His precocity was amusingly apparent in his correspondence— already considerable even before he reached Oxford. Returning from Dinard at the age of nineteen, he undertook to escort to England a small boy of eight who was being sent to school for the first time. " I had no notion that children at that age could be so interesting or could say such extraordinary things," he wrote in a letter to R. B. Brett on September the 20th, 1878. " He quite enlivened our fourteen hours' passage, and we trudged about Southampton two hours together before our train left for London, where his father met him and smothered him with kisses and me with thanks. I never saw a father and a little boy so glad to see each other and it was quite refreshing to watch them." He commented freely on the books he read. " I have been reading by way of light, but withal advantageous material *Gil Blas*. It is an amusing jumble of love stories and pedantic narration of a bygone, amorous and extravagant age, destitute of morals and keenly appreciative of the present. Life couldn't by any possibility be called dull in those days ; the only question is if they ever existed."[1]

To his contemporaries at Oxford it seemed that he had never passed through a stage of immaturity at all. Nettleship and Strachan-Davidson, his tutors, took him as they found him and left him so. It has been said of him with much truth that before he ceased to be an undergraduate he had touched upon as much political and social life as most men of thirty. " What think you of Oxford socially ? " asked St. John Brodrick before the end of Curzon's first year at the University. " You are a great experiment there, you know. So few fellows of public school fame come up with so many impressions of the outside world and settle down to Oxford. You began there where most fellows leave off, so the result is especially interesting."[2] And a year later, when congratulating him on his coming of age— " If the day is not a crisis in your life, it is because you can look back on many experiences which usually succeed it."[3] Before leaving college he had already paid several visits to the continent. And in the course of his incursions into society he had become engaged to be married—a project which withered and died as a result of the chilly reception which his engagement at so young an age met with from his father.

Reference has been made in the account which has been given of his life at Eton to a certain fastidiousness of taste—exhibited by the furnishing of his room—which had attracted the attention of Mr. Gladstone and caused him to comment on the increasing luxury of life at our public schools. The same thought was suggested to others by the appearance of his rooms on the ground floor of the small block, familiarly known as " the cottage," beyond the new Hall at Balliol. " They were furnished rather more elaborately than was usual ; they were always kept spick and span, and gave a sort of impression of opulence and of that ' superiority ' which became

[1]Letter to the Hon. R. B. Brett, August 21st, 1878.
[2]Letter dated March 10th, 1879.
[3]Letter dated January 10th, 1880.

crystallised in a famous phrase."[1] His determination to have everything kept not merely tidily, but in its appointed place, was a source of no little perturbation to the " scout " of number twelve staircase,[2] who found it difficult to keep his master's rooms quite as he wished them. Words over a cracked teapot led to the highly-tried servant being had up before the redoubtable Jowett—the solitary occasion during forty years of meritorious service on which such a thing happened to him. It was not that George Curzon was intentionally hard upon those who served him or deliberately inconsiderate, it was simply that he expected others to exhibit the same efficiency in the discharge of their duties as he displayed himself. It was a characteristic which grew rather than diminished with advancing years, and marred with increasing frequency his relations with his subordinates. Let it be added that when it occurred to him that they were required, no one knew better how to speak the kindly word and perform the gracious act that turn away wrath. In the case of his old scout the occasion presented itself many years later, at a dinner given at Balliol in his honour, on his return from India. He was quick to take it. That one act of courtesy was never forgotten, and among the great throng that flocked to Westminster to attend Lord Curzon's funeral was the old scout of number twelve staircase, there to pay his last tribute of respect to his former master.

It is not, in reality, strange that the impressions which he made upon men of his own age in these days of early manhood should be conflicting, for, Janus-like, he looked with two faces upon the world around him. To the generality of mankind he was ambitious, self-confident, amazingly industrious, haughty, coldly aloof. Fifty years before he had made his mark at the Oxford Union, representatives of the undergraduate life of Oxford and Cambridge had crossed swords in a famous debate on the respective merits of Byron and Shelley. Monckton Milnes, afterwards Lord Houghton, had said of a Christ Church undergraduate on that occasion that he was " a very superior person." Gladstone, like Curzon, did undoubtedly stand out as something different from his undergraduate contem-

[1] Professor J. W. Mackail.
[2] Now number 22.

poraries. Beyond this it would hardly be justifiable to press the analogy; but just as both differed from the men of their own times, so both possessed characteristics which were far from attractive to the majority of their fellows. Macaulay had written of Gladstone in 1839 that " it would not be at all strange if he were one of the most unpopular men in England." Similarly, one who was an undergraduate with George Curzon at Oxford has said of him—" He was not popular in college; nor did he wish to be. His scale of values was his own."[1] None suffered fools less gladly than he did, and he made enemies, if not deliberately, at least with an indifference which those who were interested in his future viewed with feelings not far short of dismay. " A politician," urged Jowett, " should make friends wherever he goes; the social part of his life is quite as important as the political, and in early years perhaps more so."[2] But he was temperamentally incapable of mitigating the crude force of an iron hand by the use of a velvet glove.

There was much behind the mask, however, that the generality of mankind never saw. The man himself—the ego behind these outward expressions of a virile and sometimes irritating personality, was something almost unimaginably different. Throughout his life the man outwardly so complacently self-confident was curiously dependent upon spiritual aid. He once confided to one of his closest friends that he never embarked upon any undertaking, however trivial, without uttering a prayer for help. Yet through the fundamental seriousness of his nature there ran an astonishing streak of boyishness and naivety, which was constantly displaying itself to the infinite edification of his intimate friends. When in company that he found congenial, he could be the most entertaining of mortals and at once became the centre of attraction. " George Curzon was, as usual, the most brilliant; he never flags for an instant either in speech or in repartee. After him George Wyndham, Mark Napier and Webber."[3] His humour welled up endlessly and bubbled over from sheer exuberance. No one enjoyed either the hearing or the telling of a good story more than he did.

[1] Professor J. W. Mackail.
[2] Letter dated December 1884.
[3] From the Diary of Wilfred Scawen Blunt, July 1st, 1893.

"The Duke of Marlborough had an Emu given him. It was sent to Blenheim, and great interest was taken in the chances of its capacity for procreation. Eventually it laid an egg. The Duke and Duchess were absent from home. A telegram was sent to the latter by the agent to apprise her of the event. 'Emu has laid an egg. In the absence of Your Grace, have put goose to sit on it.' "[1]

And so delighted was he with an epigram believed to have been composed by A. W. Verrall on his old friend Oscar Browning, that he wrote it down and preserved it carefully among his private papers.

> O be obedient, O.B.,
> To nature's stern decrees,
> Else singular as now you are
> You'll soon be ⎰too obese.
> ⎱two O.B.'s.

His own wit was not always devoid of sting, for he passed easily from humour to irony, as anyone who invited a rebuff was not unlikely to discover. Finding himself on one occasion the recipient of a presentation copy of a book in which he thought that he detected sundry borrowings from publications of his own, he penned the following acknowledgement:

"Many thanks for the copy of your most interesting and valuable book. It contains a mass of information and brings our knowledge with wonderful accuracy and minuteness up to date. In glancing through it, I observe that you have made a clean sweep of all my most cherished quotations. I give you the following instances. I dare say there are many more .. Either our reading must run on curiously parallel lines, or you must have absorbed what I wrote with a completeness which is, in any case, a compliment. Hoping that you are in good health and spirits and ready either to conquer new worlds or to resume your triumph over old ones. I am, etc. . . ."

[1] Letter from George Curzon to Cecil Spring-Rice, July 11th, 1880.

Sarcasm, even when its edge is dulled by humour, is apt to wound. Yet those who succeeded in penetrating the hard outer shell of apparent callousness and hauteur, found beneath it a being eminently lovable. " What are you reading and thinking about ?" asked R. B. Brett in a letter in which he added " I am full of affection for you."[1] And Dick Farrer's devotion to him was so great, that all through his long and wasting illness, which culminated in his early death in July, 1883, he wrote constantly to him, even when the mere effort of putting pen to paper was distasteful and the exertion of doing so a severe tax upon his strength. The bond between them was one of very real affection ; and in a letter opened after his death, he stated that George Curzon's " affectionate thoughtfulness so conspicuous during my long illness," had been a great help to him in his sore trial.

As time went on his love of social life tended to widen the circle of his friends. While still at Oxford he had flung himself with zest into the pleasures of society. With the removal of the restrictions which college discipline necessarily imposed upon his freedom, he plunged into a whirl of social engagements. His spinal trouble made it impossible for him to enjoy riding ; but dinner parties and dances in London, and good company and shooting in the country, filled a large part of his leisure. " I have had just over four weeks' season, which I have enjoyed enormously," he told Farrer after leaving Oxford. " During that time I have only dined at home once and have been to a dance (excluding Saturdays and Sundays) every night but one."[2] Later in the year, when entertaining was less in evidence, he turned his attention to the theatres. "'Much Ado About Nothing' draws crowds to the Lyceum to admire the sumptuous scenery and appurtenances and (strange fact !) the really first-class acting of Irving as Benedick. Gilbert and Sullivan have produced a new comic opera called ' Iolanthe.' It is a satire upon the House of Lords and as such elicits yells of delight from the mob."[3] Singing and acting appealed to his artistic sense. Some years later he went to see the Italian actress, Eleanora Duse, when she first came over to

[1]Letter dated August 19th, 1878.
[2]Letter to R. R. Farrer, July 23rd, 1882.
[3]Letter to R. R. Farrer, December 2nd, 1882.

PLATE V. FRIENDS AT OXFORD

G. N. Curzon.

Hon. W. W. Palmer,
(afterwards Earl of Selborne)

E. K. Douglas.

electrify a London audience, and was fascinated by the perfection of her art. Though she was " a woman not too young, not pretty, not shapely, not painted, not adorned," yet she drew immense and enthusiastic audiences, for " she acted on the stage as though she were doing the very actual and real thing in life, and as though one wall of the room where she was so doing it had accidentally been torn down, so that an outside audience could intrude upon her privacy." [1]

His correspondence with his many friends certainly showed no trace of the " superior person " and would have been read with astonishment by those who were unwilling to credit him with the quality of companionableness. From Farrer he received an amusing account of his experiences at a house-party in Scotland.

> " Most of the shooting was over except black game and blue hares. . . . Four real guns got nearly three hundred one day. I say *real*, because the Celtic keepers and gardeners, the York-shire flunkeys and Belgian cook are all allowed to carry guns and pot away freely at grice, hares, beaters or each other, according to their own sweet will. It is fancied that if asked to beat, they would be stiff and proud, but they enjoy the dig-nity of *La Chasse*. The cook in particular is eyed with aver-sion. I saw him rake the line and all but massacre the tutor and two small lads." [2]

And Curzon wrote in the same strain of boyish exuberance. " . . . I went to the Wharncliffes for a party. We jugged some conies. I developed unexpected and unwonted accuracy in my attempts upon that animal's existence this autumn—a deadliness not extended in similar proportion to the fowls of the air. However, a little at a time." [3]

He had a great love of the beautiful wherever it was to be found— in the human form both male and female, in natural scenery, in

[1]Letter to Miss Leiter, June 4th, 1893.
[2]Letter from R. R. Farrer, October 3rd, 1880.
[3]Letter to R. R. Farrer, December 2nd, 1882.

poetry, in buildings, in pictures and, indeed, in every kind of art. "The Taj is incomparable," he told St. John Brodrick when describing his feelings on seeing it for the first time, "designed like a palace and finished like a jewel—a snow-white emanation starting from a bed of cypresses and backed by a turquoise sky, pure, perfect and unutterably lovely. One feels the same sensation as in gazing at a beautiful woman, one who has that mixture of loveliness and sadness which is essential to the highest beauty."[1] This sensitiveness to beauty exercised a great influence upon him, for it was a powerful factor in extending the range of his interests and in adding to the intensity of the joys and the depth of the sorrows of life. From Dresden, where he found himself for a few days the year after he came down from Oxford, he wrote with evident delight:

> "Here I naturally spend my time in looking at pictures or listening to music. The gallery is all that one could hope for, and the world-famed pictures are all one had imagined. Perhaps more than anything else I am struck by the cleverness of Holbein. I did not know before that he was a painter of such surprising talent. The Madonna of Raphael seems to me to deserve its recognised pre-eminence over his other works. It is softer and more ethereal."[2]

And the satisfaction which he derived from the contemplation of a striking landscape was as vivid and as intense as the joy which he found in a beautiful work of art. He could scarcely find words to describe his sensations when the mist melted away and he saw—not for the first time—the towering pinnacles of Kanchenjunga outlined against a turquoise sky. "Suddenly there outshone, hung up, as it were, by chains in the sky, that most incomparable of all visions in the entire universe, Kanchenjunga and his satellites, free from cloud, bright as silver, royal as a king. Oh! my God, it was sublime, worth everything else in the world rolled together."[3]

It is important to realise the strength of this element in George

[1] Letter dated, January 1st, 1888.
[2] Letter to R. R. Farrer, May 27th, 1883.
[3] Letter to Mr., afterwards Sir Ian, Malcolm, February 24th, 1902.

Curzon's nature, because it explains much that is otherwise difficult to understand. An artistic temperament adds to the fullness and richness of life, but it carries with it certain defects. Those who possess it are almost invariably emotional and highly strung. They are seldom content to plod along the well-trodden and uneventful groove that suffices for the average man. They are apt to find the punctilio of a sober and conventional formality irksome. George Curzon was emotional and highly strung. He was easily moved to tears, both of sorrow and of joy. He once went to the Albert Hall to hear Adeline Patti, and was profoundly affected by her singing. " Though fifty-three years old she is still a miracle, and the tears came like water springs to my eyes."[1] In the same way, when playing the part of Dr. Primrose in some *tableaux vivants* at a country house, to the Olivia of a friend of his, he was so carried away by the feelings of the character he was impersonating, that he could not help trembling with mingled compassion and affection.[2] It was inevitable that he should be profoundly affected by the sorrows of life. There are those alive who cannot to this day recall without emotion a pathetic incident many years later than the time of which I am now writing, of which he was the central figure. At a dinner at Bombay given by the then Governor, Lord Lamington, to welcome him on his return to take up for a second time the toils and res-ponsibilities of the Viceroyalty, he rose to respond to the toast of his health, and that of Lady Curzon, too unwell, unhappily, to accompany him from England. Overcome by a sudden wave of emotion induced by the proposer's kindly reference to this mis-fortune, he stood for some moments choking with sobs unable to utter audibly the opening sentences of his reply.

Paradoxical though it may seem, this emotional sensitiveness goes far to explain both his hauteur and aloofness towards the generality of mankind and an epicene and almost Bohemian sociability where his personal friends were concerned. In the presence of strangers he was instinctively on his guard. His attitude towards them was determined by the same instinct of self-preservation which causes

[1] Letter to Miss Leiter, June 4th, 1893.
[2] The house was Stanway the seat of Lord Elcho ; and the part of Olivia was taken by Miss Balfour, now the Hon. Mrs. Alfred Lyttelton, D.B.E.

the hedgehog to withdraw to the shelter of its spinous coat when confronted with the unknown. In congenial company, on the other hand, his emotional vivacity caused him to rebel against the drab tyranny of a conventional purism, just as when a boy it had made him restive under the restrictions imposed upon his freedom by school discipline.

It is possible that to this same source must be traced another characteristic wholly unsuspected by the majority of those who knew him. Persons of emotional temperament are proverbially prone to extremes of feeling. If they have their moments of exaltation they have also their periods of profound depression. There were times when George Curzon seemed able to view himself with curious detatchment and to subject himself to dispassionate analysis. On one such occasion he astonished an intimate friend by exclaiming at the end of a long dissertation on the career that he was planning for himself, that he made no pretence to being a first-class man.[1] This was far from being an isolated example of a certain innate humility. Replying to a letter from a friend who had written to congratulate him on his appointment as Under Secretary for India in 1891, he spoke of the burden of his political work. " I have a lot of meetings, and shall retail rubbish with a solemnity that will make the people think it all very grand and fine. One of the greatest delusions is that I can speak. I know one person who knows very well the reverse, and that is, Yours etc."[2] Three or four years later, when he was at Simla, on his way to the Pamirs and Afghanistan, he noted down in his diary his surprise at the " palatial proportions " of Viceregal Lodge, and added : " as I entered I could not help wondering if I should ever do so as its master ?" This proved a fascinating topic on which to speculate, yet he concluded that while he would like to succeed Lord Elgin in five years' time, Harris might prove a " formidable and worthier rival." There were, indeed, occasions on which he took an almost absurdly diffident view of his own powers. Early in 1904, when his period of office in India was drawing towards a close, he received an invitation to write the official Life of Lord Beaconsfield. He

[1]This statement was made to Miss Balfour, now the Hon. Mrs. A. Lyttelton, D.B.E.
[2]Letter to Miss Leiter, dated November 29th, 1891.

understood and appreciated the compliment, but he declined. " Personally, I do not think for a moment that I should have been equal to the task," he told Lady Curzon in a letter written on March 3rd, 1904. " I have not the perception, or the analytical powers or the requisite literary style." These modest estimates of himself were not the erratic affectations of moments of theatrical self-depreciation ; they were considered judgments formed, it may be, during periods of depression, but steadfastly adhered to, nevertheless, as being substantially correct. Years after he had left India he sat down in one of these strange moods of detachment and committed to writing estimates of himself which reproduce almost verbatim these statements made within a decade of his leaving Oxford.

> " I have, and always have had, opinion of my abilities and accomplishments—such as they are. I am never in the society of able men without recognising their intellectual superiority. I have no opinion at all of what are sometimes alleged to be my powers of speech. When I ' carry away ' a big meeting, no one is more astonished than myself. . . . To say that I have a high estimate of myself, makes me, who know the reality, smile." [1]

In these days of research into the sub-conscious working of the human mind such admissions as these would provide the psycho-analyst with a key to the hauteur and aloofness of his bearing in public. They would be attributed to what, in the jargon of the new learning, would be termed an " inferiority complex."

Of course it is easy enough to set against these displays of humility innumerable examples of bombast. There is the well-known story of his offer to bet the late Mr Henry Wardle, M.P., who defeated him for South Derbyshire on his first attempt to enter Parliament, in 1885, that he would be the first to make his maiden speech in the House of Commons—a confidence on his part which was justified by the event. And on another occasion when an appointment which he had expected to be offered was given to someone else, he wrote

---

[1]These musings were jotted down characteristically on a half sheet of note paper in 1910 and put away in a drawer at Hackwood where they were found after his death.

in anything but a spirit of humility—" If I do not some day leave— (the successful rival) standing as still as a church steeple, I am not your obedient servant writing this letter."[1] The answer to the obvious comment that no man can have seriously entertained estimates of himself so glaringly discrepant, is that a man's judgment of himself is affected by his moods, and that in the case of persons of emotional temperament their moods swing after the manner of a pendulum from extravagant optimism to excessive pessimism.

There was one other quality which George Curzon possessed in high degree, which often played a decisive part in determining his actions. He was a man of very unusual courage. Many of his exploits as a boy, even when not in themselves meritorious, had demanded no little courage for their successful accomplishment. In later years he frequently took a course which called for the exercise of great moral courage. On the question of the Indian cotton excise duty, he voted against the material interests and the vigorously voiced wishes of his Lancashire constituents, because he believed that to do otherwise would be to act unjustly towards the inarticulate masses of the Indian peasantry ; and again, in later years in India itself, he displayed the same inflexible courage when as Viceroy he took up so uncompromising a stand in the case of collisions between British soldiers and the natives of the country. And throughout his life he faced, with a fortitude and courage of which few had any conception, the unceasing struggle with physical suffering, seldom in his later years far off and often excruciatingly severe.

"Who knows," he asked in one of his moments of self-examination, " what an effort and often a pain to me is public appearance of any kind ? I am supposed to seek the footlights. Little do they know what a business it is to get me on to the stage ! How many of them, I wonder, have any idea of the long hours spent in bed, of the aching back, of the incessant nerve pain in the leg, of the fearful steel cage in which I have to be incased when I undergo any strain in which standing up is involved ? They think me strong and arrogant and self-

[1] Letter to Miss Leiter, October 10th, 1891.

sufficient. Little do they reck that it is an invalid addressing them, who has only been driven to the duty because it is a duty, who has to be mechanically supported in order to stand upright for an hour, and who probably goes back to his bed to writhe in agony as an expiation for his foolishness." [1]

In the attempt which I have made to draw aside the veil behind which the real man lay hidden from the public gaze, I have travelled here and there over ground which still lies in front of me. An endeavour at this early stage to draw a detailed portrait of the man is justified in the case of George Curzon by the early maturity on which emphasis has been laid. In his case neither character nor plan of life was built up slowly from year to year ; both were ready-made from an unusually early date and remained singularly little affected by the external incidents of his subsequent history. And without an adequate knowledge of the man, no attempt to read aright the story of his life would be likely to prove successful. With his portrait before us we may return to the autumn of 1882 and follow him with a better chance of understanding him along the road on which he had now set foot.

He took part in public functions as occasion offered—in an important Conservative demonstration at Derby, in October, and in the festivities held to celebrate the opening of a new Art Gallery in the same city, in November. On this latter occasion he drew a graceful tribute from Sir William Harcourt for the manner in which " with all the grace and the wit of an accomplished orator," he had managed " delicately to propose the House of Commons coupled with the name of one who belongs to a different political party from himself." But in the autumn of 1882 there was little prospect of an election ; and keenly though he enjoyed the distractions of social life in England, there was one thing in which, with his enquiring mind and enterprising spirit, he delighted even more, and that was travel in foreign lands.

While still at Eton he had accompanied Oscar Browning during the Christmas holidays in 1877 to France and Italy. This man was one of the few Eton masters who really understood him as a boy—

[1] Notes found on a sheet of note paper in a drawer at Hackwood.

he writes in one of his letters to his Mother of being taken by him to see the churchyard where Gray wrote his elegy and the room in which Milton wrote "Paradise Lost"[1]—and in the summer of 1880 the two joined forces once more and proceeded, during the Oxford long Vacation, to Oberammergau to see the Passion Play, and on to Switzerland. On leaving Oxford in 1882, he embarked on a longer and more ambitious journey, travelling to Rome and to Greece with three boon companions—Edward Lyttelton, Welldon, and Cornish—and thence alone to Egypt and Palestine, and home *via* Constantinople, Vienna, Dresden, Prague and Berlin. This journey was followed after an interval of less than a year by a visit to Spain and Tangier; and the spring of 1885 saw him first at the Italian lakes and then in Sicily, Tunis, Carthage and Kairwhan. After his return from this journey in the summer of 1885, he was kept in England for some time by the General Election of that year and by his subsequent entry into the House of Commons in 1886 as member for Southport. But in August, 1887, he left England once more, this time for Canada and the United States and on *via* Japan and China to India. It was during the concluding stages of this journey that he first visited and began to write about the Indian Frontier. He returned to England in 1888, but he was too much bitten by the fascination of travel to remain long at home, and during the autumn of the same year he made the journey to Central Asia which resulted in his first important book on the problems and politics of the East, which was published the following year with the title :—" Russia in Central Asia in 1889." Some part of the spring and summer of that year was spent on the continent and the whole of the autumn and ensuing winter in Persia, where he was engaged in collecting material for his second big book on Asia :—" Persia and the Persian Question"—which came out in two large volumes in 1892.

During 1890 and 1891 George Curzon's health was giving cause for some anxiety, and he spent a good deal of time on the continent— at St. Moritz, and in France, Italy, Greece and Turkey. He was sufficiently restored in health to embark in August, 1892, on his second journey round the world ; the main object of this expedition being the collection of material for his book on Japan, Korea and

[1]Letter dated July 23rd, 1873.

China, which was published in 1894 and, under the title of "Problems of the Far East," met with immediate and gratifying success. It had scarcely passed through the press when the opportunity, which he had long sought, of visiting the Pamirs and Afghanistan, presented itself, and by August, 1894, he was once more on his way to the East. The spell of the countries beyond the confines of eastern Europe—vast in extent, stretching far back into the dim and shadowy twilight which preceeded the dawn of history, at once alluring and illusive, was strong upon him. "Asia," he wrote to a friend, as he steamed down the Red Sea, "looms before me, vast, magnificent, inspiring." It was for his work in determining the source of the Oxus river on this journey that he subsequently received the Gold Medal of the Royal Geographical Society. With his return to England in February, 1895, his series of journeys to the East came to an end, for new duties and responsibilities claimed his presence at home.

For more than twelve years he had been travelling almost continuously, for, from December, 1882, until February, 1895, no year had passed, with the solitary exception of 1886, some part of which had not been spent in foreign countries. So extensive a programme of travel had necessarily taken him away at frequent intervals from his Parliamentary duties, with the result that in the Whip's room there was some not unnatural opposition to his inclusion in the Government in 1891. Lord Salisbury, however, appreciated the objects with which his journeys had been undertaken and offered him the post of Under Secretary for India, as will appear hereafter. Further reference to his Asiatic journeys will be made in due course ; in the mean time some description of his tour in 1883 will give an idea of the spirit in which he embarked upon, and the profit which he derived from foreign travel.

CHAPTER IV

GEORGE CURZON was fitted both by natural aptitude and by training to derive the maximum advantage from foreign travel. He brought an alert and critical mind to bear upon other peoples, and the delight which he obtained from the ruins of ancient cities and the scenes of vanished greatness, was enhanced by the facility with which a well-stored mind enabled him to reconstruct the past and to infuse into the *disjecta membra* of history the life and colour which had once been theirs. Of this he was himself fully conscious. " Greece," he once said, " to anyone not acquainted with and fond of the classics, must be like a page of Egyptian hieroglyphics to one who cannot decipher them—curious, interesting, even beautiful, but ceaselessly unintelligible." [1]

His deep love of the beautiful in nature and in art served to keep a fine edge on his powers of observation. " The plain of Marathon was alive with flitting magpies guiltless of the timidity of their English cousins. Elsewhere in Greece we were perpetually charmed by the noble flight of the large hawk, now poised motionless in the still air, now flashing like a meteor round the brow of a hill." His animal spirits and sense of humour enabled him—in retrospect, at any rate—to make light of the minor discomforts and contretemps of travel. " A fog enabled our boat to lose its way in crossing the channel, hence two hours' soundings off the French coast" ; and the passion for thoroughness, which was one of his characteristics, caused him to enter with enthusiasm into the minutest details

---

[1] From a note book kept by G. N. Curzon during journeys in Italy, Greece and Egypt. All quotations in this chapter are from the same source unless otherwise specified.

of the arrangements for his journeys. "For three people travelling together a *fauteuil lit* is strongly to be recommended. Complete isolation and reasonable comfort at night at half the price of *wagon-lit.*" Perhaps in this last observation are to be traced subconscious memories of the stern injunctions on the subject of economy administered in the school-room by the imperious Miss Paraman.

The notes and comments, which he never failed to compile when travelling, make instructive and exhilarating reading. Italy delighted him. "Every fresh sweep discloses to the foreigner, however fastidious, some spot where it would be no penalty to dwell. This can scarcely be said of any other country." And then came Rome. The obtrusiveness of the modern city troubled him ; the Rome which he had come to see he had to search for, so much so, that " a stranger might be in the town for hours without being aware that he was in the centre of the greatest historic memories in the life of the world." But when, approaching by way of the forum of Trajan and Augustus, he turned the corner and suddenly found the forum at his feet, " the full tide of memories " burst upon him, and he forgot the present and was with Cato and Cicero and Pompey and Julius Cæsar. Of all the relics of this ancient civilisation the one that moved him most was " the distinct and sinuous track of the *via sacra,*" for here he was gazing upon " the unmistakable paving stones in their original beds which echoed to the chariot wheels of Scipio, Sulla, Cæsar Germanicus, Titus and Trajan." And it was this famous way that summed up the history of Republican Rome without a break from its rise to its fall, and of Imperial Rome from Julius to Constantine. For Rome was a military power, and the Sacred Way was especially consecrated to her military triumphs, and " speaks, therefore, more of the majesty of Rome than any other ruin."

The most disappointing feature in Rome was the Capitoline Hill, for the reason that it was so overrun with modern buildings, that it was impossible to picture it as it appeared in its ancient setting. " Where exactly was the summit ? How long—how broad ? Where can we locate the templum and the arx ? Where was the Tarpeian rock ?" From the summit of a church tower outside the city he tried to distinguish the different hills whose separate existence had given to Rome the name of the City of the Seven Hills. But while from this point of vantage the Capitoline, Palatine and Aventine hills were clear, the rest had become merged into the modern town and their individuality lost.

The Colosseum he thought "perhaps the most impressive thing in the world." He tried to picture it at its prime—"those endless tiers crowded with a sea of faces, a vast awning stretched over that gigantic and open roof, the floor even turned into a miniature lake on which rode galleys and ships of war, or given up to the combats of men and beasts"; but even the mind's eye could barely compass its possibilities at its prime. Of St. Peter's he noted "the great stretches of gleaming marble and the golden altar beyond," forming a splendid vista. "You have to pace the floor to credit the distances, ostentatiously, but usefully inscribed upon it, to mark its superiority over all extant edifices." And then his sense of humour, never very far hidden below the surface, asserts itself and a whimsical thought occurs to him—What in St. Peter's would be the remark of the British sportsman who, after slowly pacing down the nave of York minster, was heard to observe, "a long shot for a partridge."

The cone of Stromboli, "the most imposing feature between Naples and Athens," is the subject of a passing reference, and then Athens claims his whole attention. The eye is caught first by a lofty peak commanding the town on the north-east side, "certainly by far the most prominent feature in the landscape"—Mount Lycabettus—and he notes down in his diary that the unwary may well mistake this for the Acropolis itself. But when once the latter has been identified, Lycabettus, for all its imposing appearance, may be dismissed from the mind. The Acropolis, "that majestic rock bearing on its summit the noblest ruins in the world and still fortified by the massive walls of Themistocles and Cimon, appealing by its temples to the memories of a splendid religion, and by its shattered defences to those of an even more splendid history," stirred his emotions to their depths. Rome might possess greater majesty, but here "there is far more beauty and an infinitely greater pathos." The people "whose genius stares from every stone" of these hallowed ruins were only a small nation, struggling precariously, even during the golden epoch of their history, for supremacy with

74

another small power. " They did not mould history to anything like
the extent that Rome did ; but they moulded minds much more."
The influence of Greek civilisation upon the world—this is the
thought which fills his mind as he passes through the pillars of the
Propylæa, and stands amid the collection of " vast uninjured drums,
abaci and architraves lying in criminal confusion " on the Acropolis,
faced by " the superbly graceful proportions " of the Parthenon.
Criticism of the people of ancient Greece was easy enough ; they
were " excitable, passionate, frivolous, talkative, disputatious, not
always honest." But their vices weighed lightly in the balance
against their virtues. " Where would the world have been," he
muses, " without the philosophy of Socrates, Plato and Aristotle ;
the history of Thucydides ; the poetry of Æschylus and Sophocles ;
the eloquence of Demosthenes ; the sculpture of Phidias ; the
example of Aristides and Pericles." The question was one which
seemed to him to be well worth pondering, for " each of these had
confessedly been the model upon which a whole art or science or
category has since been constructed, and without the copy, what
becomes of the copyist ?"

He found some of the less meritorious traits which he assigned to
the ancient Greeks reproduced with tolerable accuracy in their
nineteenth century descendants. The central street of the modern
city " is filled with a clamouring crowd from morn to night. At
no moment of the day is there any respite in the clatter of aimless
conversation." The people " argue and declaim and gesticulate "
with extreme violence ; but they are unstable even in their
animosities, " and those who have been shaking their hands in one
another's faces at one moment are exchanging cigarettes the
next."

Unlike Rome, where " the core of the old town is embedded in
the centre of the new," the modern city in the case of Athens lies
apart from the old. This is a great advantage and permits a clear
view of the setting of the ancient city which, with even greater
reason than in the case of Rome, might have been called " a city of
Hills."

The architectural beauty of the buildings on the Acropolis appealed strongly to him. Amongst the virtues with which he endowed

the ancient Greeks was "a taſte for the beautiful and chaſte which has never been approached in any other age or by any other people"; and he approached Greek art in a spirit of reverent admiration and alert to discover keys to the secrets of its diſtinctive beauty. He found one to the particular beauty of the Propylæa, in the employ-ment of Doric pillars in the outer corridor, and Ionic in the inner Veſtibule of the building—"a combination of the simple grandeur of the Phidian age with the exquisite delicacy and taſte beginning to make itself felt with a softening and refining, though also an even-tually demoralising, influence." He was ſtruck, again, by the oblique lines in the orientation of the different buildings on the Acropolis—"a sacrifice such as we moderns do not underſtand, of actual to ideal symmetry." Similarly, his attention was arreſted by the out-ward slope from the centre in the floor and ſteps of the Parthenon. "What was it for?" he asks. The obvious explanation that it was to drain off rain water was rejected as inadequate ; more probably, he thought, it was "in obedience to some now unknown law of symmetry."

The rich, creamy colour "merging at times into a russet brown or a tawny gold which all ancient Greek ſtatues possess and no modern ones can attain," while due in part to accident—the supe-riority of the marble available and the softening effect of climate—was not wholly so ; it was assiſted by a preparation of oil and wax rubbed over the surface by the sculptor.

His reverence for ancient buildings—which caused him when he was in a position to do so, in India, to undertake an extensive pro-gramme of reſtoration—led him to view with regret the removal from their natural surroundings of the Greek marbles by Lord Elgin. His only juſtification for doing so was the inexplicable disregard shown by the Greeks themselves for their hiſtoric monuments ; and he would gladly have seen these things reſtored to their proper setting whenever the Greek people showed that they were prepared to treat them with due respect. Some years later he came to a definite conclusion as to what our attitude in this matter ought to be. He realised that wholesale reſtitution was neither practicable nor desirable. The Parthenon marbles could never be set up again as integral parts of the building to which they originally belonged.

They were destined, wherever located, to "an everlasting museum,"[1] and he thought it preferable, therefore, that they should remain in the British Museum, where they would be seen by an infinitely larger number of people than they would be, if housed in a museum in Athens. The case of such relics as could be placed once more amid their original surroundings, "*in situ ipso antiquo* on the sacred rock,"[2] was, however, in his opinion an entirely different one. There were two notable examples of such relics in the Greek collection at the British Museum. All who were familiar with the appearance of the Erectheium would agree that the most graceful and best preserved portion of the building was the projecting portico, "whose coffered marble ceiling is upheld by six female figures, chiselled at the culminating period of Athenian art . . . sometimes called the Attic virgins, more commonly the Caryatides."[3] While five of these still stood amid their natural setting on the building, one was to be seen in sorrowful isolation in the British Museum "where, like Niobe, she seems to weep her desolation in stone."[4] Similarly on the right of the Propylæa, the beautiful temple of the Wingless Victory, long since skilfully restored, "presents much the same appearance in the nineteenth century after as it did in the fifth century before Christ." But the walls of the temple once bore a frieze, some panels of which are to be seen *in situ*. "The rest, four in number, were carried off by Lord Elgin, to London, and now adorn the walls of the British Museum."[5] It was for the restoration of these relics that George Curzon pleaded, first by appealing to Mr. Gladstone as the friend of Greece, and afterwards, when, on the advice of Sir F. Leighten, his appeal was rejected, by propaganda in the press. While he admitted that the creation of an embarrassing precedent would be open to objection, he denied that the act of restitution which he himself urged could be regarded in this light, "for the reason that the broadest distinction in principle exists between a restoration not merely to ancient locality, but also to ancient site, and a restoration to the former only."[6]

With Parliamentary life in modern Greece he was not favourably impressed. He found everywhere "an equality almost incon-

[1]From a letter written by George Curzon to the *Fortnightly Review*, April 4th, 1891.
[2]*Ibid.*   [3]*Ibid.*   [4]*Ibid.*   [5]*Ibid.*   [6]*Ibid.*

ceivable to an Englishman." Much of the failure which he detected in the system of government was due, he thought, to the grant of far too large a measure of representative government too precipitately. " A people just awakening from the night of four hundred years of Turkish oppression is hardly fit to receive the mead of full enlightenment." On the other hand, he found the Greek spirit essentially democratic and anti-monarchical; with the result that while his subjects were supremely indifferent to him, the Monarch soon ceased to take any interest in them.

The visit to Greece concluded with a tour through the north-east Peloponnese and Bœotia which, owing to it having become known that Edward Lyttelton was a nephew of Mr. Gladstone, became at times an embarrassingly triumphal procession. " At Nauplia began a series of extraordinary and enthusiastic receptions of our party, which gradually increased in publicity and zeal until they culminated at Delphi, and then gradually waned till the last flicker went out in the appropriate surroundings of boorish Bœotia."

These days of travel were happy times for George Curzon. Everything pleased. Each new place visited possessed some fresh interest. Where the outward features were meagre, scholarship stepped in and endowed them with an interest which was not apparent on the surface. He quickly discovered that the man who was familiar with his Herodotus enjoyed sensations which no one else could possibly share. Scenery and weather were superb. The country in the neighbourhood of Delphi excited the highest admiration of the travellers, and overhead as they neared the end of their day's march " was displayed the pomp of a gorgeous sunset, like a golden and crimson banner flung across the sky." Even the attentions of municipal and other bodies—the outcome of Mr. Gladstone's phenomenal popularity in Greece—irksome though they tended to become when too frequently repeated, were remembered chiefly for their humorous side. On the way to Delphi the party was accorded an elaborate welcome at the villages through which they passed. Coffee and oranges were handed round, formal introductions were gone through, and at one place there were presented to them a veteran who had fought in the War of Independence and

EARLY JOURNEYS : ITALY, ETC.

"an old fellow of eighty-five years, who had been guide to Mr. Gladstone when he had ascended Parnassus in 1856. He took a special interest in Edward Lyttelton, to whom he gallantly offered the loan of his horse. The rest of us were more humbly accommodated with mules, and mounted thus we shortly left for Delphi." It was episodes such as these that he had in mind, no doubt, when he wrote " though I could neither claim nor receive any portion of the credit attached to our party as representatives of the Grand Old Man, I was not averse to being treated with respect as an Englishman."[1]

At the conclusion of this tour the party broke up, George Curzon proceeding alone from Corfu to Alexandria, which he reached towards the end of January, 1883. The bombardment by the British fleet had taken place during the previous summer, and he found more to interest him in the effect of the naval fire on the Egyptian forts than in the few antiquities of indifferent interest of which the town could boast. For the rest he found Alexandria worth little time, and " with a sigh for that burned library with its million of priceless volumes," which was one of the prices paid by the world for the triumph of Cæsar, he proceeded to Telel Kebir on his way to Cairo. Here the remnants of the battle of the previous September lay scattered in profusion over the ground, and with characteristic thoroughness he rode twice over the whole field of battle, reconstructing as he did so the scene which it must have presented on the morning of September the 13th. He left with one outstanding impression on his mind, namely, the amazing luck which had enabled the English troops to miss, and to remain themselves unnoticed by, the Egyptian detachment in the advanced redoubt erected five hundred yards in front of the enemy's main line of defence. Reflection on this most fortunate accident gave rise to other thoughts, for example, that Sir G. Wolseley had many of the characteristics of Sulla—first and foremost that " he was emphatically Felix."

The glamour of the East had long excited his curiosity and struck a responsive chord in his innermost being. And it is easy to picture the feelings of keen anticipation with which he pulled aside the

[1] Letter to Mr. P. A. Barnett, dated March 26th, 1883.

curtain and took his first glimpse at the mysteries that lay behind. Cairo with its four hundred mosques, " each with one or more than one minaret, always a graceful object and sometimes grand," provided an appropriate introduction. Nothing, it seemed to him, could be more interesting than " to stroll about the streets, dropping into one mosque after another, noting the devout Arabs at prayer, remarking their scrupulous obedience to the Moslem ritual and hearing, maybe, a muttered curse at the dog of a christian." With practised eye he quickly picked up the main features of Arabian architecture and stored them up in his mind for future reference— the pointed horse-shoe arches and elliptical domes, the general avoidance of columns and the preference for open courts, the stress laid upon superficial as distinct from structural ornamentation, the delicate mosaics of coloured marble, the stalactite corbellings or clusters of cellular woodwork to round off the corners and blend the vertical with the horizontal lines, and the broad friezes running everywhere round the interior of the buildings, with sentences from the Koran inscribed in bold and beautiful characters upon them.

As was his invariable custom, he brought a mind richly endowed by previous study to bear on all that he saw. But previous acquaintance with the views of others served to stimulate rather than to dull his critical faculties. He dissented altogether from current notions of the Gama Sultan Hassan as " the finest existing monument of Arab architecture "[1] and as " perhaps the most beautiful mosque in the world."[2] He felt quite certain that it was not the latter, and he thought that it was in far too dilapidated a condition to be the former.

When he passed beyond Cairo into the land of ancient Egypt he fell, as was only to be expected, under the spell of her length of days. On all sides he saw the massive monuments of a vanished epoch in the history of mankind. And the sense that he had opened a long closed chapter in the story of the human race was not confined to the buildings themselves ; it became associated with the scenery and the people. The strongest impression which his journey up the

[1] Bædeker.
[2] Miss Edwards.

Nile left upon him was a sense of the unchanged and, as it seemed, unchangeable life and character of the people.

" These rude felaheen . . . . who are liable to be pressed into compulsory labour by the State . . . are identical in a thousand respects with the peasants from whom Pharaohs and priests wrung the fruits of their toil, and whose lives they poured out like water in the construction of monuments as senseless as they are grand. Here are the same men of the same build and stature, with the same dress or undress and the same implements, plying the same business as did their ancestors of five thousand years ago, so wonderfully depicted on the bas reliefs of royal and private tombs . . . civilisation is foiled by a country which refuses to be civilised, which cannot be civilised, which will remain uncivilised to the end."

At Sakkhara he gazed fascinated at what, upon all the available evidence, he believed to be the oldest building in the world. This was the great step pyramid. True, the experts differed on the question of actual date ; but " when you are drawing a cheque upon the actual bank of Time " such differences are of little real moment ; the imagination recoils, in any case, before " an antiquity which makes the visit of Abraham to Egypt a thing of yesterday." In many cases the artistic beauty of these buildings was as great a cause of wonder as their age. The sculptures executed in low relief on the walls of the sepulchral chamber of the Queen of Ti, four thousand years, certainly, and possibly six thousand years old, appealed to him as " among the most marvellous and beautiful things in the World." Yet his attitude towards the buildings of ancient Egypt was one of critical appreciation rather than of undiscriminating praise. At Philæ, which he visited from Assouan, he was at once struck by the exaggerated *asummetria* of all the buildings on the island. " Not one is either parallel or at right angles to another. There are oblique lines and obtuse angles everywhere," the irregularity extending even to the interior of the temple of Isis. He sped back in imagination to the Acropolis at Athens which he had so recently visited, and came to the conclusion that the Greeks, " who produced their effect by a deviation from the symmetrical so slight as to be scarcely noticeable at first sight," displayed a superior artistic genius.

Similarly, at Karnak he differed strongly from the ordinarily accepted view of the superlative architectural merits of the building known as the great hall. He duly made note of Miss Edwards's eulogy—" How often has it been written and how often must it be repeated that the great hall at Karnak is the noblest architectural work ever designed and executed by human hands ? " But he did so only to dissent from it. He thought its breadth much too great for its length and the large number of subordinate pillars much too short for their enormous bulk, besides being inelegant and clumsy in shape. Moreover, they appeared to him to be crowded together so closely that the effect of distance which their great number, if skilfully disposed, should have enhanced, was sacrificed. As a monument of architectural grandeur this Hypostyle Hall of Sethi I might be without rival ; " but judged from the effect it produced upon myself, it can only be pronounced disappointing in the extreme."

On the other hand he was lavish in his praise of buildings which satisfied his own æsthetic standards, and he was astonished at the magnificence of some of the less well-known temples. " While Karnak is known from China to Peru," comparatively few people seemed to have heard of the temple of Edfou, which he had no hesitation in regarding as the finest thing in Egypt, " with all the glories of Denderah with many more added." This was high praise indeed, for he had been profoundly impressed by Denderah, " the effect of whose long-pillared aisles, the light fading as you advance first into shade, then into gloom, finally into impenetrable darkness, is so solemn that judged by its influence upon the senses alone, it must rank almost first among Egyptian temples."

As in Italy and Greece, so in Egypt, he was constantly bringing his knowledge of history to his aid in the fascinating task of reconstructing episodes of which the ruins that he visited had been the actual, though mute, witnesses. And he had frequent cause to call down blessing on " the garrulity of Herodotus—greatest of chroniclers if not greatest of historians "—for the flood of light which it let in upon the dark passages of time. Had he not committed to paper amongst much gossip about Cambysses and his doings a story of the wanton impiety with which he had stabbed in the thigh Apis, the sacred bull of Egypt ? And here at the Serapeum, or tombs of the Apis, at Sakkhara, had been found, in 1850 of the Christian era, an Apis mummy, and within the wrappings the actual animal of which Herodotus had written, as the condition of its thigh bone showed. In one respect only Herodotus had erred, for he had spoken of the bull dying of the wound, whereas a tablet found in the Serapeum made it clear that the animal had recovered and had survived for some years. Before this dramatic episode in the story of archæological exploration the spirit of Romance itself might well stand dumb.

Often he came upon sights linking the history of Egypt with that of Greece and Rome. In the rock tombs of Beni Hassan he detected the exact prototype of the Doric shaft, the abacus and the architrave of Greece—evidence as conclusive as could be demanded that the Doric style, the earliest in Greece, was not indigenous but an importation from Egypt. At Denderah still survived bas reliefs of Cleopatra—" an evil looking, voluptuous countenance retaining, even in the conventionality of decorative sculpture at that epoch, something of the matchless beauty that made Cæsar a fool and Anthony a knave."

But perhaps the relic that intrigued him most was the colossal seated figure known as the vocal Memnon. As he gazed up into its contemptuous, unseeing face, and thought of the men who had stood there too—Germanicus, Strabo and Hadrian among them— all equally baffled by the secret which it had retained inviolate for 3,500 years, he determined to probe the mystery. " That great speechless image with its marvellous and romantic history is one of the most fascinating objects I have ever seen. I must get to the bottom of it." The result of this decision formed and recorded on the dusty banks of the Nile, appeared many years afterwards in the volume of " Tales of Travel " which he published not long before his death. Therein he set forth in thirty-five large octavo pages of print his researches and conclusions in the matter, in the hope that they might be regarded as " a positive contribution to historical and archæological research." [1]

¹From the Preface to " Tales of Travel," published in 1923.

83

From this visit to the land of Egypt he certainly derived a very full measure of satisfaction, and on his return to Cairo he summed up in a sentence the dominant impression which it had left upon his mind. " Temples, colossi, tombs are splendid, of proportions so stupendous that the ordinary senses find themselves bewildered and rich with the blazoned history, every letter of which is now intelligible, of four thousand years ago." [1]

Most people who devoted to the monuments of Egypt the amount of time and study that George Curzon did, would have found little leisure and still less energy, perhaps, with which to enjoy the amenities of society. Not so this indefatigable traveller. At Luxor he was a guest at an Arab dinner of thirteen courses—an experience into which he entered " with zest," but which, he noted at the time, " should not be too frequently repeated." And in Cairo he made the acquaintance of many persons of note—Lord Dufferin, " the temporary king of Cairo, residing in a palace and surrounded by a court . . . . as evidently a first-rate diplomatist as he is an attractive man "; Colonel Synge, " a man to be looked at, considering he cost the British Government £10,000, [2] a sum which, with commendable astuteness, they are now deducting from the Turkish revenues of Cyprus "; Dr. W. H. Russell, " the *doyen* of foreign correspondents . . . . full of anecdotes and information, charmed to accept a dinner at your hands and to repay you by amusing talk "; the Bishop of Limerick, " a most amiable and courtly divine . . . . with interesting experiences to relate of Wordsworth and Hartley Coleridge "; Baron de Malortie, the author of an admirable book in English on Egypt, who, though " one of those numerous men who can write but not talk, was far from being a dull companion, and in addition to (or fortunately often instead of) his own society, gave me that of his beautiful and charming wife," and many more.

Social engagements did end, indeed, by making inroads upon the time which he had intended to devote to more serious pursuits. " All this made life in Cairo seductive, but it also made it rather unprofitable, for here one was living the London life over again

[1]Letter to R. R. Farrer, February 9th, 1883.
[2]He had been captured by brigands and held to ransome.

without the London justification ";[1] and though he got to know the principal features of the city and its environments fairly well, " social engagements were so pressing that many I did not see as often as I should have done, and a few I did not see at all."[2]

His proximity to the " Holy Land " determined him to visit it before returning to England, and on Easter Day, March the 25th, his steamer from Port Said brought him to land at the little port of Jaffa. To follow him in any detail on this journey would require an amount of space which it is impracticable to give to it. His notes and comments, covering page after page of a stout notebook, with line upon line of minute, closely written, but marvellously well-formed handwriting, provide ample material for a whole volume. The task of fitting scenes familiar to him from his earliest years into their historical and geographical frame delighted him. As he travelled north from Jerusalem to the sea of Galilee he found the boards of a comparatively narrow stage crowded with events from the Old and New Testaments.

Entering the plain of Esdraelon, the floodgates of memory were opened, and chapter after chapter of Old Testament history passed in rapid succession before him. Here it was that " Barak went down and ten thousand men after him " to roll back the armed forces of Sisera towards the west ; here, too, that Gideon brought down the people from Mount Gilboa and smote the Midianites, the Amalekites and the children of the East camped on the plain " as grasshoppers for multitude." Nor was this all, for " if Esdraelon was famous for the glories of two of Israel's greatest judges, it was also famous for the tragic death of two of her kings." Further, it had produced " the two finest bursts of poetry in the Hebrew, perhaps in any tongue : the noblest pæan of conquest[3] and the most pathetic dirge of despair."[4]

From the summit of Mount Carmel he gazed over the rich expanse of the plain as it stretched away up to the walls of Jezreel, ten miles or more to the east, and in imagination he saw speeding across it the agile form of the prophet as he ran before Ahab to the

[1]Letter to R. R. Farrer, March 24th, 1883.
[2]Letter to P. A. Barnett, March 26th, 1883.
[3]Song of Deborah and Barak, Judges v. 2.
[4]The lament of David over Saul and Jonathan, II Samuel, i.

entrance of the city. Then turning his gaze westward, he pictured the gradual forming on the horizon of the little cloud no bigger than a man's hand, as it first appeared to the straining eyes of Elijah's servant, standing on the self-same spot on which he now stood. And as he looked from the summit of Carmel to the muddy track of the river Kishon, " creeping along in sinuous coils over the fertile plain below," he pictured the scene on that memorable day before the breaking of the drought, when the dramatic trial of strength between Elijah and the four hundred prophets of Baal ended in the humiliation and slaughter of the latter and the triumph of Jehovah. With his imagination stimulated by his surroundings, he saw the sea of upturned faces of all Israel fixed upon them as they " called upon the name of Baal from morning even until noon, saying, O Baal, hear us " ;[1] and later, under the taunts of Elijah, " cut themselves after their manner with knives and lancets till the blood gushed out upon them."[2] And then towards " the time of the offering of the evening sacrifice,"[3] the suppliant figure of the prophet of the Lord silhouetted against the western sky, and the vast concourse of people falling on their faces when the fire of the Lord fell upon the altar which he had made, and crying out in their fear, " the Lord He is the God ; the Lord He is the God,"[4] and, finally, the horrible dénouement when the sluggish waters of the river Kishon were further sullied with the blood of the four hundred and fifty prophets of Baal, who had been given over to the fanatical wrath of a duped and now disillusioned people.

When, on the Sunday morning on which they visited the heights of Mount Carmel, a clergyman of the party read the morning service and he himself, in place of the lesson of the day, " that glorious chapter I Kings xviii," standing with his companions as nearly as possible on the site of " the most dramatic scene in Jewish history," he felt that the breath of life had indeed been breathed into the dry bones of the dead past.

Of the many places forming the background of the gospel story, he was as much moved by his first vision of the sea of Galilee as by any other. After a long pull up the slope of the last elevation—

[1] I Kings xviii, v.26.　　　[2] I Kings xviii, v.28.
[3] I Kings xviii, v.36.　　　[4] I Kings xviii, v.30.

EARLY JOURNEYS : ITALY, ETC.

" We reach its summit and suddenly at one step are presented with an entirely new and wonderful prospect. Deep down below us lies the sea of Galilee. The most hardened sensibilities must confess to a thrill of genuine emotion. We are looking upon the most sacred sheet of water in the world, upon the now glassy but erstwhile stormy surface whereon the Saviour walked, upon the shores which He trod, upon the scenes of His most active and most successful ministrations."

Every minute of the four weeks which he spent in the Holy Land had been full of interest ; and looking back, as was his custom at the close of his frequent journeys, to sum up the impressions left upon his mind he asked himself—" What is my judgment ? " And he replies—not with complete conviction, it seems, to one who reads his summing up with care—that he has not been disappointed. He had not expected monumental remains such as those of Egypt, nor particularly attractive scenery, such as he had come across in some parts of Greece. The interest of the country lay, as he well knew before starting, in its associations, " which come up in long procession whenever the mind chooses to summon them." The associations themselves made an irresistible appeal, but it had been irritating to find in connection with them so great an amount of imposture and superstition. " In the whole country there are not above a dozen sites of absolutely unquestionable authenticity, though there is not an event described in the Old or New Testament that is not localised by the inventive capacity of clerics and accepted by the credulity of pilgrims."

Moreover, in spite of his denial he was undoubtedly disappointed in the actual sights of Palestine. The mud hovels of the villages, the dirty Arab population, the constant presence of his own dingy cavalcade, fitted ill with the pictures of his mind. To appreciate properly a tour of the Holy Land solitude and quiet thought are essential. " Afterwards as we ponder over it alone the deformities of modern surroundings disappear and the original features stand out in all their solemnity and fascination." The sting of his disappointment—disillusionment almost—is apparent from the nature of the cross-examination to which he subjects himself. He had expected that a visit to the actual places made memorable by the birth, the life and the death of Christ, would give rise to " a spiritual re-awakening, a stirring of torpid pulses, a kindling of dormant fires." Yet he was unable to detect in himself any moral influence resulting from his tour. " I feel a kind of interest I never did before in the circumstances of the gospel narrative. But they do not appeal to me with a different force. They breathe a thousand memories ; but they teach no lesson. I do not find it any easier after visiting the country and dwelling place of Christ to live more like Christ." But if he experienced no tangible spiritual benefit from his visit, he repudiated the suggestion that a man's religious belief might be impaired by his experiences in Palestine. He had himself seen enough in the site of the temple of Solomon to produce great satisfaction and in the Holy Sepulchre to create a corresponding irritation ;[1] " but to go into a fictitious Holy Sepulchre, to walk along a modern *via dolorosa,* to see an imaginary Holy House at Nazareth does not— cannot—make me sceptical as to the truth of the narrative which they only secondarily illustrate."

The beginning of May saw him at Constantinople ; and from there he travelled in leisurely fashion across Europe, steaming up the Danube through the Iron Gates and the far finer Defile of Kasau, and pausing at Bucharest, a city " notoriously immoral," Buda Pesth, Vienna, " with the finest modern buildings, with the possible exception of Paris, of any continental capital," Prague, " the prettiest place seen since leaving England," Dresden, where he spent his time " looking at pictures or listening to music," and Berlin. [2] It was in a cafe at Buda Pesth that he learned that what must, I think, be regarded as the most remarkable performance of the whole of this notable journey, had been crowned with success. In a copy of *The Times*[3] a day or two old, he read the following notice under the heading *University Intelligence* :

> " Oxford, Lothian Prize. The judges have awarded this prize to the Hon. G. N. Curzon, Balliol. They also consider

[1]Letter to P. A. Barnett, March 26th, 1883.
[2]Letter to R. R. Farrer, May 27th, 1883.
[3]Of May 14th, 1883.

the essay by A. Hawkins, Balliol, deserves honourable mention."

The story of this amazing achievement is told in a letter to his great friend, R. R. Farrer. Writing to him from Dresden, he explained the reasons for the secrecy which he had maintained. His chance of success seemed to him so slight that to make known his intention of competing, even to his closest friends, appeared likely to end only in publishing to the world another rebuff. The memory of his failure to obtain a first in the Final School at Oxford was still a bitter one and the thought of a further possible humiliation was more than he could bear. How, indeed, in the circumstances of the present case could he hope to elude defeat? " I had to get through all my reading in London in less than a fortnight to take notes of what I had read and from them, a Gibbon and a French edition of Procopius, to do the composition in trains, on steamers in the intervals of sea-sickness, or sight-seeing in Greece, Cairo and on the Nile. No composition was ever put together at such a jumble of times or in such a jumble of places." [1]

That success should have been won under conditions so little favourable, must have gone far to compensate him for previous disappointments. In face of determination so dogged and courage so high, may we not fittingly exclaim—" Palmam qui meruit, ferat."

[1] Letter to R. R. Farrer, May 27th, 1883.

CHAPTER V

DURING George Curzon's absence abroad, St. John Brodrick had written on New Year's eve his good wishes for the coming twelve months. The year just over—with its university disappointment—might not stand out in his life as some already did and as others yet to come most certainly would ; but it had been, nevertheless, "wondrous satisfactory, and not least in the continued agglomeration of devoted friends around you." It is a tribute to the force of his personality that his absence from their midst was genuinely and very keenly felt. " I look forward to May when we shall see you back fresh, buoyant, baby-cheeked, and bursting with new words and astounding epithets " ;[1] and shortly before his return : " You will just be back for Ascot, and how glad we shall all be to see you again."[2] And George Curzon himself looked forward impatiently to the society of his friends once more, for he wrote from Constantinople that he would rush home from Berlin " very homesick. For already I long for a sight of distant faces, and a sound of distant voices, and a pressure of distant hands."[3]

The time was near, however, when weightier matters were to claim his attention. He was anxious to embark upon the political career which he had marked out for himself ; but he still hankered after academic distinction, and on his return to England he began reading for the All Souls Fellowship which he coveted. " I am not

[1]Letter from the Hon. St. J. Brodrick, March 17th, 1883.
[2]Letter from the Hon. St. J. Brodrick, May 15th, 1883.
[3]Letter to the Hon. St. J. Brodrick, May 5th, 1883.

doing any political work," he wrote St. John Brodrick, in August, " but am trying to glean a superficial acquaintance with modern history." At the same time he apologised for the grandiloquent phrasing of his letter, which he thought must be " the result of reading Gibbon, three volumes of which I have been attempting to despatch in less than twice the number of days, with the result of confusing my brain and prostituting my style."[1]

It is evident that he was undergoing one of those periods of fierce and concentrated work which had been a peculiar but familiar feature of his school and college days ; for he added that since returning to Kedleston he had only been away for a weekend, and had refused invitations for Doncaster races and for a coming of age party at Longleat. He remained at Kedleston till October " doing nothing but see the days succeed each other with regular monotony," getting through an immense amount of reading and coming to the conclusion at the end of it all that however jaded he might be, no one could be the worse for having got through Gibbon and Hallam. On October the 14th he wrote to St. John Brodrick from London :

> " Next week I may perhaps go up to Oxford ; but it really seems hardly worth while. The effort to get even a superficial grasp of the entire range of history in less than three months, I have found to be excessive, if not absurd. And it seems preposterous to go and compete with men who have studied history for years and to challenge their profundity with one's own shallowness . . . Still I shall probably enter by way of satisfying myself that my scruples against entering are well founded[2]

How baseless such scruples were was proved by the result, for he obtained his Fellowship, and that, too, in a year in which there were among the candidates " a large number of able scholars, especially of good men in the history schools."[3] The way now seemed clear

[1] Letter to the Hon. St. J. Brodrick, August 15th, 1883.
[2] Letter dated October 14th, 1883.
[3] The *Derby Mercury*, November 14th, 1883.

for him to devote himself to politics. Yet he was still dazzled by the lure of academic success, and the course of political speaking on which he had determined had once more to be postponed, while he split yet another lance in the arena of the university. The circumstances in which he suddenly decided to enter for the Arnold Prize have been related in chapter three. For fifteen weeks he lived the life of a recluse in London, spending long hours at the British Museum and working daily from 11 o'clock one morning until 4 o'clock the next. He is himself responsible for the following laconic description of the manner in which the resulting Essay was completed and handed in. " I took down the unfinished Essay to Oxford on the day on which it had to be handed in at midnight and continued writing until then. I took it over to the old schools, rang up the janitor (who was in bed) as the clock struck twelve. I apologised for waking him, on the ground that it was the winning Essay. It was." [1]

Twice during this period of concentrated study—the second within nine months—he made a fleeting appearance on a political platform in South Derbyshire, where his presence by the side of Sir H. Wilmot, the sitting member for the Division, gave rise to interested speculation. " That a gentleman so liberally endowed with the qualities which most adorn political life should long remain aloof from the race for Westminster " [2] was inconceivable to political friend and political foe alike. The significance of these appearances became apparent within a few days of the announcement of his success in winning the Arnold Prize. In March, Sir H. Wilmot made known his intention of retiring at the end of the existing Parliament, and Mr. Curzon and Mr. Fitzherbert Wright were formally selected as the future Conservative candidates.

From now until the dissolution and General Election in the autumn of 1885, with the exception of a few weeks during the spring of 1885, when he visited Spain, and a similar break in the early summer of 1885, when he travelled in Italy and north Africa, the newly selected candidate was kept busy addressing meetings throughout the constituency. His energy was such as to excite the sarcastic

[1]See an article by Sir Ian Malcolm K.C.M.G., in the *Quarterly Review* for July, 1925.
[2]The *Derby and Chesterfield Reporter.*

comment of the local Liberal press :—"Sir Robert Peel," snapped one Liberal paper in the constituency, " summed up his advice to the Conservative party of the day in the memorable and eminently practical words, ' Register, Register, Register.' The Conservatives of South Derbyshire seem to think that a better programme still is that of ' Talk, Talk, Talk.' "[1]

Nor were his meetings confined to his own constituency, for he had already gained a considerable reputation as a speaker. While still at Oxford he had come under the favourable notice of Lord Randolph Churchill. " I must write you a line to thank you very much for your speech at Woodstock last week. I hear from two or three reliable sources that your audience was interested and delighted with the way in which you treated the topics of importance at the present moment " ;[2] and Lord Lytton, after attending the Canning club dinner in 1882, had written of his " remarkable ability as a speaker."[3] In the House of Commons a phrase from a speech of his had been quoted by one of Her Majesty's Ministers who, in acknowledging his indebtedness, had said of him that if ever he entered the House, he would be " an ornament to the other side."[4] The opinion expressed in a leading article by the chief Conservative organ in the county, that his speeches were " admirable alike in their assertion of Conservative principle and their criticism of Radical performance " and that they were distinguished by " a marked cleverness of style and phrase,"[5] was something more than the conventional puff of a party paper ; it was a view which was shared by persons who were wholly free from party bias.

" I heard something very nice about you the other day," wrote one of his friends, " which I must tell you, even at the risk of adding to your self-esteem. I was helping to entertain old—— at his political trotting out in Glasgow the other day, and amongst other terrible civic entertainments we had to go to, was a luncheon at the Lord Provost's, where I was

[1] The *Derbyshire Advertiser*, May 23rd, 1884.
[2] Letter dated March 3rd, 1881.
[3] Letter dated June 7th, 1882.
[4] Sir Henry James, the Attorney General, on November 10th, 1882.
[5] The *Derby Mercury* of January 23rd, 1884.

taken in by a portly gentleman whom I had never set eyes on
before. . . . In beating about the bush for a subject for conversation, I chanced to fall upon speechifying, when he launched
forth into a panegyric on the unusual excellencies of a speech
he heard the other day at a dinner in Derby. . . . Of course I
was dying to hear who this young orator was. Imagine my
pride and joy when I was told it was you and could say it was a
friend of mine ! Even amidst the desolation of pink jellies
and gold crackers I had found an interest. I am afraid I shall
make you horribly conceited by telling you all he said. Your
speech was most eloquent, interesting, incisive, with a splendid peroration, and was admired with equal enthusiasm by
both parties. You were considered a most promising orator
by them both, and, in fact, you took them all by storm." [1]

At the outset of his campaign he gave a clear definition of his
conception of the principles on which Conservatism was based.
These consisted in :

" An affectionate regard for our existing constitution, both
in church and state ; a passionate loyalty to the English name,
with the thousand sacred associations which the name involves;
an unselfish recognition of our Imperial position and the responsibilities it entails, and a desire by prudent legislation and
by consistent efforts at home to educate the unlearned, to
support the feeble, to raise the humble, to ameliorate the condition of the oppressed, to teach the English people the lessons of a steady and graduated progress so that, first of all
under the guidance of others, and lastly on their own accord,
they may learn to be happy and God-fearing and free, so to
train them above all that they and their children may learn to
become fit inheritors of a noble patrimony and worthy citizens of this unequalled Empire." [2]

The honour of England's name ; the splendour of the Imperial
heritage that was ours—these were the things that extorted from

[1] Letter from Lady Ribblesdale dated December 28th, 1882.
[2] Speech at Stapenhill in February, 1884.

him the homage of a willing worshipper, the passionate admiration of a true devotee. And it was on the ground of their failure to maintain untarnished the English name with the thousand sacred associations which the name involved, that he based his most scathing denunciation of the Government of the day.

It must be admitted that circumstances had conspired to provide him with an ample quiver from which to draw shafts for his attack, for from the moment that Mr. Gladstone had become Prime Minister misfortune had seemed to dog his footsteps. He had been obliged at the very outset of his term of office to make public apology to the Emperor of Austria for language used in the course of his Midlothian campaign, and by so doing had placed the Prime Minister of Great Britain in a position of humiliation which had not unnaturally excited feelings of resentment. This inauspicious beginning had been followed by a series of events all mortifying to the Englishman's *amour propre*. In Afghanistan a grave defeat had been inflicted on British arms, and the remnants of her stricken forces had been besieged in Kandahar, whence they had only been extricated by Sir Frederick Roberts' famous march from Kabul. In South Africa British prestige had been subjected to even greater humiliation. The recently annexed territory of the Transvaal had been wrenched back by force of arms, and the British commander, Sir G. Colley, had lost his life at Majuba Hill—a mere reference to which ill-fated name was sufficient in the heated atmosphere of the hustings, to excite feelings of violent indignation. And now, at the very moment when George Curzon was called upon to play the congenial part of a Missionary of Empire on the political platforms of the constituency which he aspired to represent in Parliament, it seemed to many—Liberals as well as Conservatives—that the Government by their inexplicable indecision were paving the way to further humiliation. His recent study of the Egyptian situation on the spot had quickened his appreciation of its dangers. He was quick to point out the lamentable results which had already attended the fatal lack of purpose which the Government had displayed. As was only to be expected, the half-hearted attitude which had been adopted had resulted in all the assurances which had been given being brought to nought. The despatch of ships to Alexandria, that were to effect their purpose without firing a shot, had resulted in the bombardment of the town ; the promise given, that not a man would be landed, had ended in the invasion of the country ; the party, which had protested its abhorrence of war, had been responsible for the battle of Tel-el-Kebir. " We have heard a great deal about the false prophet in Egypt ; it seems to me that we have got a dozen false prophets at home." [1]

Worse was yet to come. Gordon had been sent to the Sudan to extricate the garrisons beleaguered by the insurgent hordes enrolled under the banner of the Madhi. And Gordon was himself a prisoner in Khartum ; and still the Government hesitated to act. Gordon himself, in a despatch which had " touched a chord of commiseration in the heart of every man or woman who had read it," sounded a note of despair. The Government had stated their intention of not sending a relief expedition. Well, he would hold on where he was as long as he could, and if he could suppress the rebellion he would do so. If this proved beyond his power, he would retire to the equator and leave to the Government the indelible disgrace of abandoning the garrisons. In a recent division on the Government's Egyptian policy, their proud majority of one hundred and thirty had fallen to twenty-eight. " I should like to know," asked the speaker, " where the hundred are. No doubt Sir William Harcourt and his friends tried to spur them to action and cheered them on with the words of the greatest of our poets :

' Yours not to make reply
Yours not to reason why,
Yours but to vote a lie,
    Noble one hundred.'

But, gentlemen, the one hundred did not see it." [2]

In the end the Government acted ; but not until it was too late, and before Khartum could be relieved Gordon was dead.

There is no doubt that George Curzon felt very bitterly on the subject. Apart from the loss of prestige, which was deeply morti-

[1]Speech at Swadlincote, January 18th, 1884.
[2]Speech at Hilton in May 1884.

fying to one who held so lofty a view of the civilising mission of the British Empire, he, like many others, had come under the spell of the man whom he had described in the speech above referred to as, " an unique and heroic figure." Sometime before, he had met him unexpectedly when walking with a friend in Pall Mall. At the moment he had not realised who the figure " rather shabbily dressed in a seedy black frock coat, trousers that did not come down to the boots, and a very dilapidated black silk topper with a particularly narrow brim and silk mostly brushed the wrong way,"[1] was. But the meeting left a profound impression on him, all the same. And when, during his visit to the Holy Land, he heard that Gordon was living on the Joppa road some miles out of Jerusalem, bent on identifying the site of the Crucifixion and Holy Sepulchre with a bare hill—said to resemble a skull in outline—that stands outside the Damascus gate, he expressed a strong desire to ride out and find him ; but was dissuaded by his fellow travellers, who were unwilling to spare the time. His chance of an intimate talk with the man who had so impressed him thus passed, never to recur.

But he could not dismiss Gordon from his mind ; nor could he forgive the Government which had sent him to his doom. And brooding on his strange and eventful life and the manner of its ending, he was profoundly struck with the parallel which it presented to that of another historic figure " whose character, career and fate offer points of such extraordinary similarity to those of Gordon, as to excite our astonishment and to justify a passing examination." In Germanicus, the nephew of the Roman Emperor, Tiberius, " whose brilliant life and premature death elicited from his unimpressionable countrymen an outburst of feeling that illumined a degenerate era," he saw an exact historical prototype of General Gordon. With a scholarly pen he traced in the pages of the *Oxford Review* the remarkable parallelism, not only between the characters and careers of the two men, but, more striking still, between their respective fates and the feelings which in each case they aroused in the public. In the case of Gordon, some had been satisfied with lamentations over the loss of a hero ; others had deplored the vacillation that had led to his sacrifice ; a third party had not con-

[1] Note of a meeting with General Gordon, by G.N.C.

cealed their indignation with those in high places whom they held
to have been primarily responsible for the calamity of his death.
His name had been mentioned in public worship ; we might be
sure it had been breathed in many a private prayer. " The resemblance, I would rather say the identity, between these circumstances
and those that followed the death of Germanicus is so striking, is
to the best of my knowledge so unparalleled in history, that I make
no apology for transcribing in its original form the pathetic description of the Roman historian :

> ' At Roma, postquam Germanici valitudo percrebuit cunc-
> taque ut ex longinquo aucta in deterius adferebantur, dolor,
> ira, et erumpebant questus. Ideo nimirum in extremas
> terras relegatum, ideo Pisoni permissam provinciam. . . .Hos
> vulgi sermones audita mors adeo incendit ut ante edictum
> magistratuum, ante senatus consultum, sumpto justicio,
> desererentur fora, clauderentur domus. Passim silentia et
> gemitus, nihil compositum in ostentationem ; et quamquam
> neque insignibus lugentium abstinerent, altius animis mœre-
> bant. Forte negotiatores, vivente adhuc Germanico Syria
> egressi lætiora de valitudine ejus atulere. Statim credita
> statim vulgata sunt. Ut quisque obvius, quamvis leviter
> audita in alios atque illi in plures cumulata gandio transferunt.
> Cursant per urbem, moliuntur templorum fores. Cuvat
> credulitatem nox et promptior inter tenebrae adfirmatio. Nec
> obstitit falsis Tiberius donec tempore ac spatio vanescerent.
> Et populus quasi rursum ereptum acrius doluit' (Aun. II, 82).

("After the illness of Germanicus became noised abroad in
Rome, and all its circumstances, like rumours magnified by
distance, were related by many aggravations, sadness seized
the people. They burned with indignation, and even poured
out in plaints the anguish of their souls. ' For this,' they said,
' he has been banished to the extremities of the Empire,
for this the province of Syria was committed to
Piso. . . . ' These lamentations of the populace were upon
the tidings of his death so inflamed, that without staying for an
edict from the Magistrates, without a decree of Senate, they by

general consent assumed a vacation ; the public courts were deserted, private houses shut up, prevalent everywhere were the symptoms of woe, heavy groans, dismal silence ; the whole a scene of real sorrow, and nothing devised for form or show ; and, though they forbore not to bear the exterior marks and habiliments of mourning, in their souls they mourned still deeper. Accidentally, some merchants from Syria who had left Germanicus still alive, brought more joyful news of his condition. These were instantly believed and instantly proclaimed ; each as fast as they met informed others, who forthwith conveyed their light information with improvements and accumulated joy to more ; all flew with exultation through the city, and to pay their thanks and vows, burst open the temple doors. The night, too, heightened their credulity and affirmation was bolder in the dark. Nor did Tiberius restrain the course of these fictions, but left them to vanish with time. Hence, with more bitterness they afterwards grieved for him, as if anew snatched from them." (Translation by Thomas Gordon, 1728.)

" The analogy which these words unconsciously suggest is one which anyone who runs may read."[1]

He found time, indeed, for a good deal of miscellaneous writing, in addition to his platform campaign. His article on the Conservatism of Young Oxford, referred to in chapter two, was written at this time, and in addition to his paper on Gordon, written for the *Oxford Review*, he contributed an Essay on the Conservatism of Tennyson to the same publication. A paper which he sent to Sir H. Howorth, M.P., for his opinion, was lent by the latter to a man by the name of Roby, and it is easy to picture George Curzon's chuckle of delight as he read that part of Sir Henry's letter of acknowledgment in which he introduced Mr. Roby as " a person whom you ought to know, although he is such a decided Radical. Muller made a very good joke about him when he moved a resolution for the abolition of the House of Lords. He said that the only peers Roby would tolerate would be Robespierres."[2]

[1] *Oxford Review* of February 25th, 1885.
[2] Letter from Sir H. Howorth, M.P., September 30th, 1884.

CURZON, 1885

As the session of 1885 wore on, it became clear that the days of the Government were numbered. Yet it is interesting to recall the fact that when defeat in the House of Commons came, it was neither Afghanistan, nor South Africa, nor Egypt, nor dynamite, nor the Phœnix Park murders, that was the occasion of it, but what in these present days of swollen Budgets and crippling taxation seems a comparatively trivial matter, namely, a proposed increase in the income tax from sixpence, at which it then stood, to eightpence in the pound, the raising of the duty on spirits by two shillings a gallon, and the beer duty, for the space of one year, by one shilling a barrel. In the division which took place on these proposals on June the 8th, the Government were beaten by twelve votes. Mr. Gladstone resigned, and Lord Salisbury formed an Administration with Lord Randolph Churchill as one of his most notable colleagues. He invited George Curzon to join him as an assistant private secretary—a mark of recognition which delighted the latter's friends. " I was so delighted to see that you had got into office. . . . It is the shadow before the substance, and I feel that I am only getting my hand in to congratulate you some day, when your shoulders will be considered broad enough and your head old enough to bear great responsibilities. Don't disappoint your faithful old friend, in whose heart you have become an immovable bit of furniture." [1]

The General Election took place in the late autumn, and long before the poll George Curzon realised the hopelessness of his task. The last months of the dying Parliament had been marked by the passage of a Franchise and Redistribution Bill which had completely altered the character of the constituency for which he was standing. In October he wrote to St. John Brodrick : " My electorate is 11,500, over 7,000 new voters. Of these, between 4,000 and 5,000 are colliers and manufacturers and I haven't a chance with them. They won't even hear me. . . . So certain am I to be beaten that I am planning a tour round the world, to commence in the spring of next year." Nevertheless, he stuck valiantly to his task. " I have now had thirty-nine separate meetings and have sixteen more before

[1] Letter from Lady Ribblesdale, July 24th, 1885.

I go round in the final agony to the principal places again."[1] And a fortnight before the poll :

> " I have been for three days canvassing among the collieries and potteries of my worst district. You have no conception of the tyranny which prevails. No shop-keeper dare admit he is a Conservative, for fear of losing his custom. Even the publicans have to pretend that they are Radicals . . . Some of the men won't so much as speak to me or look at me. . . . I had my forty-ninth meeting to-night and have fourteen more before the poll on November the 27th. It is my only chance, as the other man is not much of a speaker."[2]

His forebodings were well founded, for when on November the 28th the result of the count was made known, it was seen that George Curzon had been defeated by 2,090 votes in a poll of 10,280. It is quite possible that a less brilliant man would have proved a more suitable candidate for the division, for he was never an adept at speaking down to an audience of a low level of education and intelligence. It was said by one who claimed to have attended a very large number of meetings of both candidates, that the variety and freshness of his speeches day after day had been remarkable, but that in this respect his very abilities had told against him. " Had he been content to go on driving away at a few strong points all the time, as his opponent did, he might have advanced his chances as a candidate, but he would not have advanced his reputation as a man cut out for statesmanship."[3] Nor, it may be added, would he have been George Curzon, for to give less than his best was at all times an impossibility for him. Those who knew him well were conscious of this, and his old friend, R. W. Raper, of Trinity College, Oxford, wrote to him to express the hope " that you are at once taking steps to secure another constituency, this time, I hope, a town one, where I think you would find yourself better appreciated, because they are generally more intelligent."[4]

[1]Letter dated October 17th, 1885.
[2]Letter dated November 12th, 1885.
[3]A writer in the *Derby Mercury*, December 2nd, 1885.
[4]Letter dated December, 1885.

Defeat stimulated rather than diminished his interest in the political situation which had arisen as a result of the General Election; and closer acquaintance with some of the more notable personalities of the day caused him to revise the rather hasty judgments which he had at one time formed with regard to them. The first week in January saw him at Hatfield, where he found Lord Randolph Churchill in a rather distant and haughty mood. " I used to know him well and to be on familiar terms with him. But since he has become a swell he will scarcely look at his subordinates, and the barest civility is all that one can expect."[1] On the other hand, Sir Michael Hicks Beach, of whom he had once spoken as scornfully as he had admiringly of Lord Randolph, he now regarded as a first-rate man, for in the course of the debate on the Queen's Speech which he attended on January the 27th, he noted : " Beach had to get up later. . . . He is a capital leader of the House—self-possessed, clear, fluent and imperturbable. Everyone sees that he is the best man."[2]

But it was in the case of Lord Salisbury that his opinion underwent the most striking change. While at Oxford he had been so dazzled by the oriental brilliance of Lord Beaconsfield, that all other lights seemed to him to burn dimly by comparison. He then regarded him as the last of a line of statesmen including the names of Pitt, Fox, Canning, Peel, Russell, Derby and Palmerston, " which had shed an unbroken lustre on the annals of Parliament during a period of a hundred years."[3] It seemed to him that a legacy of statesmanship had been handed down from one generation to another, " till now the lineage in which it should descend seems on the verge of becoming extinct and the legacy itself of perishing."[4] He could detect no one amongst the Parliamentary personalities of the day who would be likely to prove worthy of the name of statesman. He admitted that Conservatives at large seemed to place great reliance on Lord Salisbury. " Many of them swear by him ; some regard him as a great statesman. . . . I fail to see what he has done that can in any way justify a claim to statesmanship."[5] And if Lord

[1]Notes made by G. N. Curzon in January 1886. [2]Ibid.
[3]From a paper read at the Canning Club, February 18th, 1879.
[4]Ibid. [5]Ibid.

Salisbury was not capable of carrying on the torch, still less were any of his colleagues.

> " When the figure of Lord Beaconsfield vanishes from the House of Lords and when that of Mr. Gladstone ceases to rise from the front bench on either side of the table in the House of Commons—the country will confess that its two greatest and only statesmen have gone. Parliament will go on as before, public business will be transacted, speeches made, policies challenged and vindicated, Budgets expounded, Motions brought forward, passed, rejected, but the pre-eminent importance attaching to the doings and sayings of a statesman will be wanting—and men will lament the degeneracy of the age." [1]

His brief personal contact with Lord Salisbury as his assistant private secretary had placed him in a very different light. As compared with the hauteur of Lord Randolph, he found Lord Salisbury's affability almost embarrassing. " He pays as much attention to the words of a boy of twenty-one as to those of a statesman of seventy. When I mentioned my willingness to do any work for him that he was good enough to give me, he expressed himself in terms of the warmest gratitude." [2] The task assigned to him was that of assisting Lord Salisbury in the compilation of his speeches, and George Curzon noted down Lord Salisbury's method of employing him. " I went down to Arlington Street and related the result of my researches. Lord Salisbury asked me questions and listened to my replies, taking no notes. He is a man of singularly powerful memory. At Newport (during the election of 1885) he delivered his famous speech, one and three-quarter hours long, without a single note from beginning to end. I was within five feet of him at the time and could see." [3]

From Hatfield he went on to stay with Lord Cowper at Wrest, and later to Knebworth as the guest of Lord Lytton. Of the former he noted, " he reads and writes a great deal and belongs to the large class of excellent Conservatives whose sole hobby is to persist in calling themselves Whigs " ; and of his host at Knebworth : " you

[1] From a paper read at the Canning Club, February 18th, 1879.
[2] Notes made by G. N. C. January, 1886.   [3] *Ibid.*

103

smoke everywhere, in all the drawing-rooms. I can believe that Lord Lytton smokes in bed. I am sure that he says his prayers—if he says them at all—with a cigarette in his mouth." [1]

The fall of Lord Salisbury's short-lived Administration was brought about on January the 27th by the division on the amendment to the Address, which came to be known as " the three acres and a cow " amendment, moved by Mr. Jesse Collings. George Curzon was present and noted down his opinion of the mover—an opinion which was coloured, possibly, by recollection of a heated passage of arms of a somewhat personal nature, which had taken place between them during his candidature for South Derbyshire. " Jesse Collings is a dull old twaddler, but has earned the right to speak on the subject by making himself and it a bore." [2]

The result of the division, though a foregone conclusion, caused him some regret. " I am sorry we are out, for there is an end of my work for Lord Salisbury for the present. He wants very little help when in opposition, being peculiarly self-dependent and personally industrious." [3] This brief spell was to lay the foundation, however, of a close and happy association later on.

CHAPTER VI

ENTRY INTO THE HOUSE OF COMMONS
1886—1887

WHEN it became known that Mr. Gladstone, who had assumed office on February the 1st, was contemplating a measure of Home Rule for Ireland, it was realised that a further appeal to the country at an early date was probable ; and George Curzon took steps to find a constituency where he would have a better chance of being returned to the House of Commons than from South Derbyshire. There was no lack of seats anxious to secure him as their candidate ; but there were many difficulties to be overcome before he was prepared to commit himself. He was no longer willing to fight a hopeless battle, and in the case of seats which offered a reasonable prospect of success the financial difficulty was an appreciable one.

It is sometimes forgotten that, until his marriage in 1895, George Curzon enjoyed none of the advantages that wealth confers. His father had succeeded as heir presumptive to an estate with a modest rent roll and considerable charges, including the upkeep of a palatial mansion. He had to make provision for the upbringing of a large family, and he was in no position to provide even his eldest son with anything more than a modest allowance. George Curzon himself added to this by his writings ; but the uncertainty of this source of income necessitated a strict supervision of his expenditure and a careful husbanding of his resources. The necessity for subjecting all expenditure to minute personal scrutiny thus imposed on him by circumstances became a habit which remained with him for life, and in later years often excited surprise at the time and trouble which one who entertained so generously devoted to the petty details of household economy. When Viceroy of India, surrounded by a large personal staff, not the least of whose duties it was to relieve the Head of the Administration of the tedium inseparable from the supervision of a large household, he embarked on a protracted correspondence—carried on as was his custom in his own handwriting—with a friend in England in connection with the engagement of a cook. The trouble which he took in setting forth in minute detail both the qualifications which he himself demanded in his cook, and the conditions of employment and prospects which he was prepared to offer him in return, deserved a better reward than it actually met with. A cook was duly engaged, sent out to India and installed in office. The temptations to one in his position were great ; his cupidity greater still ; but greatest of all was the vigilance of the Viceroy. The news of his downfall was communicated by the latter to the friend who had been instrumental in engaging him—" we caught him redhanded. He returned 596 chickens as having been consumed within a single month. We went to the tradesman who had the contract and found the figures were 290. . . . Result was that he left here at twelve hours' notice."[1] But in early life and, indeed, until he married at the age of thirty-six, a careful counting of the cost of every enterprise was a grim necessity. Not until he was twenty-seven years of age did he feel justified in engaging a valet, and he was much exercised in mind as to the wages he ought to offer for one. And when he entered Parliament he felt obliged to take up his abode in unpretentious lodgings. " I must seek some unambitious quarter near Piccadilly," he told St. John Brodrick ; " as you rightly indicate, I am a veritable pauper."[2]

His candidature for the Southport division of Lancashire was the subject of protracted correspondence, because, as he informed Sir W. Forwood, the chairman of the Conservative party there, the sums suggested as the contribution which the candidate would be expected to make towards the cost of the election and the maintenance of the party organisation were altogether out of the question. These had been put at £1,000 to meet the cost of an election, and thereafter from £150 to £200 a year to cover registration and other

[1] Letter to Sir Schomberg McDonnel, July 25th, 1900.
[2] Letter dated January 23rd, 1887.

expenses. As a result of a daily interchange of letters covering a fortnight, these figures were reduced to £600 and £50 respectively. And in the end the first of these was remitted altogether, the Executive Committee of the local Conservative organisation deciding by resolution on July 29th, 1886, to bear the whole cost of the election, including the candidate's personal expenses, in recognition of the spirit and resource which he had shown in leading the party to victory.

Even so he found the necessity of forwarding his stipulated contribution of £50 immediately after the election a source of embarrassment, and confided to St. John Brodrick that it would mean that he could not leave England before the next session—" which is a bore, as I wanted to get away." [1] And making up his accounts at the end of the year, he mentioned, almost with dismay, the expenditure for which his candidature had been responsible. " Southport has cost me since I was returned (what with subs. and railway fares) between £180 and £200." [2] But this is anticipating somewhat the course of events.

The fatal division on the Home Rule Bill had taken place on June the 7th, and Mr. Gladstone, beaten on a crucial question by a majority of thirty, made an immediate appeal to the country. Before the end of July the Conservative party was back in the House of Commons with a clear majority over all other parties of one hundred and eighteen. The Cabinet resigned, and Lord Salisbury formed an administration once more, with Lord Randolph Churchill as Chancellor of the Exchequer and Leader of the House of Commons. " So Lord Randolph has secured the object of his ambition. I hope he will use his great position wisely. I must confess to being a wee bit anxious as to how he will lead. A leader requires angelic temper—this, I fear, Lord Randolph has not." [3]

George Curzon's victory over the sitting member, Dr. Pilkington, by a majority of 461, was a personal triumph little expected by his opponent. Like other Conservative candidates, he derived considerable advantage from the split in the Liberal party over the Home Rule Bill. But against this had to be set the fact that he was a com-

[1] Letter dated September 15th, 1886.
[2] Letter dated January 23rd, 1887.
[3] Letter from Sir W. Forwood to Mr. Curzon, July 29th, 1886.

plete stranger to the Division, whereas Dr. Pilkington was a very strong local candidate. " The Rads were positively astounded at our majority, as they counted on winning by eighty. Their agent showed me his figures during the counting. I believe against any other candidate but Pilkington, whose local popularity is prodigious, I should have won by twice as many." [1]

His satisfaction at the result was obvious. He had at last set foot on the ladder which he had always meant to climb ; and he had no intention of lingering unnecessarily on the lower rung. Fresh from his triumph he proceeded to Bradford, where the meeting of the National Union of Conservative Associations was being held. Here he moved a resolution inviting the Conservative party to recognise " the supreme importance " of Imperial Federation and the desirability of its " universal adoption as an article of Conservative policy." He was well satisfied with the impression he created. " I have got on very well at Bradford. I moved a resolution at the conference about Imperial Federation, and I think the speech, though a short one, was a good deal talked about." [2]

Lord Randolph Churchill was at the zenith of his popularity and was attracting to the banner of the Progressive Conservatism which he preached, large numbers of the youth of the country. His eloquence, it was remarked, on the occasion of his visit to Bradford, " has touched the popular imagination as the eloquence of few men has ever done," [3] and before leaving he was presented with an Address of congratulation and confidence by two hundred and forty delegates amid the uproarious enthusiasm of a crowd of some four thousand people. But if Lord Randolph was the hero of the hour, George Curzon was equally hailed as a brilliant representative of the younger men who had enrolled themselves under his banner. " After Randolph had spoken, the people would not have Rollit, who was announced to second a resolution, but kept shouting my name till I had to get up and speak. It was the greatest compliment I have ever had paid me, especially considering I was a stranger to them all a day before." [4]

[1] Letter from George Curzon to St. John Brodrick, July 8th, 1886.
[2] Letter from George Curzon to St. John Brodrick, October 28th, 1886.
[3] The *Yorkshire Post* of October 28th, 1886.
[4] Letter from George Curzon to St. John Brodrick, October 28th, 1886.

His speech of the previous day had undoubtedly made a great impression.

" The most striking speech delivered in the council on Tuesday was, by general consent, the speech of one of the youngest men to be found in the House of Commons. . . . Speaking with plenty of dash, in a businesslike tone, and with a touch of cynicism, Mr. Curzon seemed at once to get on terms with his audience. . . . and this speech of Mr. Curzon at Bradford proves that in him the Conservative party possesses a debater of rare power, freshness and brilliancy, and if we congratulate the electors of Southport on their representative, we congratulate the Conservative party still more upon possessing in the member for Southport a man who promises in a year or two to take his place in the first rank of Parliamentary debaters." [1]

Invitations to speak poured in on him ; but there were just sufficient disappointments to remind him that success is not easily won. " Whatever be their opinion (that of the delegates at the Bradford conference) of me, it does not extend to the masses who will never go to hear an unknown man. Thus at Preston I was promised 4,000 and only got 1,500." [2]

On December the 23rd he read in *The Times*, with the same stupified astonishment as the rest of the world, the announcement of Lord Randolph Churchill's resignation, and wrote his feelings to St. John Brodrick the next day. " The outlook, as you say, is bad. Chamberlain's disgraceful speech makes it worse. I do not expect Hartington will move. Goschen may save us. I attach enormous importance to gaining the latter. . . . Anything better, or, rather, nothing worse than the promotion of any of our own men bar Smith, and I doubt if he could lead."

It is clear from Mr. Winston Churchill's account of Lord Randolph's resignation that while the ostensible cause of it was his inability to agree to estimates which, in the case of the army and navy, he regarded as excessive, the real difference between him and

[1] *Yorkshire Post* of October 28th, 1886.
[2] Letter from George Curzon to St. John Brodrick, January 23rd, 1887.

the Prime Minister was of a much more fundamental nature. His experience of the attitude of the majority of his colleagues in the Cabinet headed by Lord Salisbury towards the scheme of reforms set forth in the so-called Dartford Programme, brief though it had been, had convinced him that his political outlook differed profoundly from theirs. Almost from the beginning of their association in office it had been borne in on him that they represented " conflicting schools of political philosophy " ; that they stood for " ideas mutually incompatible." Quite early in November he had complained in a letter to Lord Salisbury that in the hands of the Cabinet the Dartford Programme was " crumbling to pieces every day," and he had concluded on a note of palpable disillusionment : " I am afraid that it is an idle schoolboy's dream to suppose that Tories can legislate—as I did stupidly. They can govern and make war and increase taxation and expenditure à merveille, but legislation is not their province in a democratic constitution."[1]

But in December 1886 these differences, if apparent to those within the Cabinet, were wholly unexpected by those outside its walls. George Curzon was himself an advocate of the Democratic Toryism that Lord Randolph preached—a political creed which seemed to him to be instinct with the spirit breathed into the dry bones of an obsolete doctrine by the genius of Lord Beaconsfield. He had declared at Bradford that to hear " the incisive eloquence and brilliant leadership of Lord Randolph Churchill " was like coming to " a positive oasis in the dreary waste of platitudes," and he asserted, after listening to him, that it must be clear to all that their party was no longer, if it ever had been, " a stagnant and reactionary party," but that it was, on the contrary, " instinct with life and fire," and that from it might be expected, under Lord Randolph's leadership, " measures of a reformatory and progressive character in accordance with the spirit of the age, and which would place the Conservative party upon that pinnacle of popularity which it so emphatically deserved."

Few men remain unmoved by the enthusiasm of a crowd. It is always exhilarating, and it is sometimes even a little intoxicating.

[1] The quotations in this paragraph are from Chapter XVI of Mr. Winston Churchill's " Life of Lord Randolph Churchill."

ENTRY INTO THE HOUSE OF COMMONS

George Curzon returned from Bradford more convinced than ever of the appeal which Democratic Toryism was capable of making to the rising generation of Englishmen. And with the Conference's plaudits for the Dartford Programme still ringing in his ears, he dipped his pen rather deeply in the democratic inkpot. In an article in the January issue of the *National Review* he stressed a burning zeal for reform as the distinguishing characteristic of Young Conservatism. In one or two rather florid passages he indignantly repudiated the charge levelled against the Conservative party of being unduly influenced by class interests.

> " Sir William Harcourt may conceive that he is uttering an epigram when he describes the Conservative party as a combination of all the prejudices of caste, all the interests of classes, and all the passions of party . . . . the country knows well enough that the Conservative party is no more composed of bloated aristocrats, or feudal despots, or grabbing land owners, or selfish monopolists . . . . than the Jockey Club is composed of jockeys or the Crystal Palace is built of crystal."

He concluded by uttering something that sounded almost like a threat to the Government, should it be found lagging behind the advance guard of the Tory Democratic army. The Conservative party in the new House of Commons, he pointed out, comprised an unusually large number of young men. Many of them had been educated together at the same public school or university, had discussed and exchanged opinions, and were prepared to act on a common basis defined by a generous interpretation of the aims and duties of the Conservative party. They were animated by "a hearty contempt for the sham distinctions of party titles, a healthy freedom from the shackles of old superstitions, an unfeigned sympathy with the struggles and aspirations of the labouring classes, and an active interest in the inexhaustible work of reform." To some of them it would not suffice that the National Institutions should be defended solely on the ground of merit, irrespective of any attempt to deal with recognised anomalies or abuses. Unofficial Liberals had quite recently been observed " successfully interpolating their own dogmas into authorised programmes and claiming almost to re-write the original text." In the same way it would be the duty of independent Conservatives to impress upon the Government the necessity of dealing boldly with certain questions which, "without the impulse of such pressure "—significant phrase—they might excuse themselves from taking in hand. " Of such a character will be the reform of the Church and of the House of Lords." The article, taken as a whole, certainly provided some excuse for the comments of a writer in *John Bull*, that if this was a true picture of Young Conservatism, it bore the strongest resemblance to the Old Radicalism. [1]

All this was written before Lord Randolph Churchill's resignation " burst upon the country like a thunderclap from a clear sky." And when the blow fell George Curzon had little difficulty in persuading himself that it must be attributed to a sudden fit of pique on the part of the Chancellor of the Exchequer, rather than to any difference in principle between him and his colleagues. " I was at Hatfield when it all came out," he wrote to St. John Brodrick on Christmas Eve. " I happen to know that Randolph Churchill did it not of premeditation, and, therefore, from a passing burst of temper. Two days before he wrote a letter which shewed that he had no idea of such a step." But if he was satisfied that Lord Randolph Churchill had not entertained any serious intention of resigning, he was equally sure that Lord Salisbury was profoundly relieved at finding himself in possession of his resignation. " His (Lord Randolph Churchill's) one great blunder was with Lord Salisbury," he told a correspondent many years later. " He did not know that the latter would be only too pleased to get rid of him. I was at Hatfield that night and I remember the thanksgivings and hosannas that went up." [2] And he found no difficulty in ridiculing the suggestion that there might be grounds for Lord Randolph's erstwhile supporters following him into the wilderness. " If there is a mutiny it has been of a solitary mutineer." [3]

In his *National Review* article he had gone to the extreme limit of

[1] *John Bull*, January 29th, 1887.
[2] Letter to Sir A. Godley, January 31st, 1901.
[3] Article in *England*, of January 1st, 1887.

his enthusiasm for Tory Democracy. Perhaps carried along on the wave of popular success on which he had been borne at Bradford, he had even overstepped the limit to which in moments of less elation he would have restricted himself. In any case, it was the foreign policy of the country that ordinarily loomed largest in his eyes ; and if the pursuit of a vigorous policy abroad proved incompatible with the prosecution of a comprehensive programme of reform at home, there was never any doubt in which scale his vote could be cast.

To those who passed from his Essay in the *National Review* to his article in *England*—the one written before and the other after the resignation of the Chancellor of the Exchequer had become known —it must have appeared that already some of the enthusiasm for domestic reform had evaporated. While the Dartford Programme was not for a moment abandoned, the claims of the Conservative party to the affections of the people were stated rather differently. The tradesman, the mechanic and the artisan, he here argued, had come to realise the benefits that he derived from a party of law and order and from a policy that left his individual freedom untouched while protecting him from the encroachment of his fellows. " The advantages of stable government, of a continuous policy with foreign Powers, of a regard for Colonial and Imperial interests, of respect for such institutions as reconcile a historic grandeur with an ability to meet the requirements of the age, and of a sensible endeavour to amend such old laws as have grown faulty, or to make such new laws as may be necessary without soaring into the empyrean of philosophic abstractions "—these were the considerations which had profoundly impressed the minds of the British working classes. And he felt sure that if it became a question " of granting to the Government the supplies believed by them to be necessary for the proper equipment of our military and naval forces and for the preservation of the befitting dignity and influence of Great Britain in the serious complications that are threatened abroad," there would not be an honest member of the House of Commons nor a loyal citizen in the country who would refuse so legitimate a demand. " Parsimony on such an ocasion would certainly be folly, and might be crime. If this is the ground, as alleged, of Lord

Randolph's resignation, he will stand self-convicted before his countrymen." [1]

At any rate, he looked forward to his first experiences as a member of the House of Commons with the keenest interest. "I look forward to six months' constant application and work. I have for the moment no hankering after society, of which I have had a good spell this winter." And he followed and commented on every move in the Parliamentary game. "Gerald Balfour is a capital selection for seconding the Address. For choice of Weymouth there is no excuse, as his father blackguards Lord Salisbury on every possible opportunity." [2]

His own chance came before the conclusion of the debate on the Address, and on the last day of January he rose to make his maiden speech. He dealt chiefly with the Irish situation arising out of the adoption of what was then known as "the plan of campaign"; but he also spoke critically of some parts of the speech delivered by Lord Randolph Churchill in explanation of his resignation. The speech was undoubtedly a good one. It was widely commented on and generally praised. It was referred to in a leading article in *The Times* as "a brilliant maiden speech." Elsewhere it was praised for its incisive vigour and logical acumen. [3] On one at least of those who heard it it made an immediate and ineffaceable impression, for, writing twenty-five years afterwards, he declared that he was so thrilled by its remarkable eloquence that he exclaimed to himself at the time "that man will one day become Prime Minister!" [4] It was witty, well-phrased, and fluent, cogent in its argument, spirited in its attack. It was admirably delivered. And yet, paradoxical though it may sound, it is difficult to resist the conclusion that it would have been an even better speech if it had not been quite so immaculately perfect. The speaker was so fluent that he found himself under no necessity of compressing his remarks. He was, consequently, a little long. On this point he received a friendly hint—which must have recalled the advice constantly given him by Jowett—from the

[1] Article in *England*, January 1st, 1887.
[2] Letter to St. John Brodrick, dated January 23rd, 1887.
[3] In the *Manchester Courier*, February 2nd, which devoted the greater part of a leading article to praise of the speech.
[4] Mr. Algernon Ashton, writing in the *Academy*, December 9th, 1911.

writer who at that time regaled the public with humorous descriptions of the proceedings of Parliament in the pages of *Vanity Fair*—" Rest of the debate commonplace except for capital maiden speech by youngster named Curzon. For my own part rather disposed to fight shy of lads all piping hot from Oxford Union ; but fancy Curzon has some grit in him. (Mem—Dangerously fluent, though, and must study art and mystery of condensation. Otherwise will perish miserably, like many other promising lads before.)" [1]

But it was, perhaps, the almost too faultless manner of its delivery that detracted most from the effect which it produced upon those who heard it. It was spoken with an ease seldom attained on the occasion of a first speech in the House of Commons. And it is human fallibility that kindles sympathy. A mechanical perfection, while it may excite the highest admiration of the intellect, is apt to leave the heart untouched. It may, indeed, have more than a merely negative effect upon the emotions. By the suggestion of superiority which it conveys it may excite feelings of active irritation. Here again it was by the half-humorous, half-satirical pen of a shrewd onlooker writing for the press that a hint that was worthy of attention was conveyed to the speaker. ' It was at once amazing and amusing to witness a very young man, who looks even younger than his years, calmly haranguing the House with a coolness, an assurance and a fluency which would have done credit to the most experienced and impassive Cabinet Minister of twenty years standing." And the writer went on to present his readers with a brief impression of the man. " As a rule he bears himself smilingly. . . but a sense of his own great destiny occasionally casts a lengthening shadow over his boyish face. . . But whether grave or gay, stern or smiling, he has, like the person in Labishe's delightful comedy, *toujours son petit air* of ineffable superiority. He has always the same appearance of being a distinguished historical personage sitting for his portrait—an appearance which is heightened by the fact that he is not a man of many gestures." [2]

His second speech, on March the 25th—also on the Irish question—more than confirmed the good impression created by his first, and

[1] *Vanity Fair* of February 5th, 1887.
[2] From an article in the *Observer* of February 13th, 1887.

elicited a note of warm approval from Mr. W. H. Smith, then leader of the House of Commons—" I heartily congratulate you. You have made a great success."[1] It was reported at length in *The Times*, and its ability was universally recognised. As in the case of his previous effort, criticism, where it existed, was directed at the personality of the speaker rather than at the matter of his speech : " he will, we feel convinced, pardon us if we tell him that there are moments when he is a trifle too priggish, a thought too petulant for the position at which he aims."[2]

Success in the House of Commons was all that was required to give George Curzon, young though he was, an assured position as a platform speaker. Henceforth he was regarded as an authoritative exponent of Conservative policy. This was demonstrated when early in April a vast crowd flocked to the Free Trade Hall in Manchester to listen to a speech by him on the Government's Irish policy. If we may judge by contemporary comment, the success of the meeting was, indeed, remarkable. " The Free Trade Hall has been the scene of many great and historic gatherings, and the foremost orators of the day have spoken within its walls ; but it is no exaggeration to say that few rhetorical efforts, even from that famous platform, have been more successful or have more thoroughly aroused the enthusiasm of the audience than did Mr. Curzon's eloquent and closely reasoned Address last night."[3] Preston, where he had been promised an audience of four thousand, and had had to be satisfied with one thousand five hundred, was a thing of the past. George Curzon had arrived, and talk of his stepping into the shoes left vacant by Lord Randolph Churchill's dramatic disappearance from public life became a commonplace of the newspaper paragraphs of the day.

During the remainder of the Session he preserved silence in the House of Commons, but spoke at a number of demonstrations in the constituencies, and when, in August, he started on his first journey round the world, he had created a sufficient impression to cause his absence from the autumn campaign organised by the

[1] Letter dated March 26th, 1887.
[2] The *Whitehall Review*, March 31st, 1887.
[3] The *Manchester Courier*, April 7th, 1887.

Conservative party in the country to be noticed and commented on. " The Hon. George Curzon, who attracted so much attention by his Addresses, has been silent since Parliament was prorogued. His admirers have noticed his absence from the platform, and wonder. It happens that he is on a voyage round the world, being at the present moment, I believe, at Yokohama." [1]

Before leaving he had worked hard with his pen, the output of which served the dual purpose of keeping his name before the public and of augmenting the funds required to carry him through his journey. The wide range of his interests is well illustrated by the diverse nature of his contributions to the monthly Reviews. Apart from his political articles, to which reference has been made, he contributed an article on " The Voice of Memnon " to the *Edinburgh Review* in July 1886 ; a graphic description of the scene which he had witnessed in the mosque of the Aissaouia dervishes outside the Tanner's Gate at Kairwan, when visiting north Africa in the spring of 1886, to the *Fortnightly Review* for August 1887 ; and a verse translation, in the metre employed by Tennyson in his "Palace of Art," of the " Myth of Er," to *Murray's Magazine* for September of the same year. This latter composition, which he described as an attempt to render in English verse " the most beautiful of the various myths or allegories by which the genius of Plato sought to illustrate his belief in the immortality of the soul," was republished at a later date in a volume entitled " War Poems," issued in 1915 ; and a slightly revised version of his article on "The Voice of Memnon " was included in " Tales of Travel," published in 1923.

[1] *Newcastle Daily Journal*, November 7th, 1887.

CHAPTER VII

FIRST JOURNEY ROUND THE WORLD

1887--1888

PARLIAMENT was still sitting when, on August the 4th, George Curzon started in the company of his old friend, J. E. C. Welldon, and the Rev. S. A. Donaldson, for Canada, which was to be the first stage in the journey round the world which he had long planned and had now determined to carry out. This desertion of the House of Commons before the end of his first Session had excited some qualms in his mind ; but the call of the road was ringing in his ears, and the summons was one which he found it beyond his powers to resist. " I feel quite guilty in having run away,"[1] he wrote a month after his departure, when he learned that the House had not yet adjourned. But as he left England further behind him and found himself in the congenial atmosphere of Asia, the ties of public life at home weakened and the grip of the East closed tighter upon him. From the waters of the southern China seas he wrote : " I am already flushed with the fever of desire to come again, I could come the same way round the world without seeing a single place or country twice over, save only Japan, and that I could not see too often."[2]

They travelled by Quebec, Montreal and Toronto to Niagara, and thence to Chicago, a huge and smoky town " absorbed in the worship of mammon in a grim and melancholy way."[3] But the aggressive materialism of Chicago was soon forgotten in the presence of the natural wonders of the Yellowstone Park. The Grand Canyon of the Yellowstone river possessed features which seemed to him to

[1] Letter to St. John Brodrick, dated September 10th, 1887.
[2] Letter to St. John Brodrick, November 14th, 1887.
[3] This and all other quotations in this chapter, unless otherwise stated, are from the diary kept by him during his first journey round the world.

118

render it not only marvellous, but unique ; and the hot springs of the upper and lower geyser basins excited his deepest interest and admiration. " We spent our last night in the Park, full of gratitude for the extraordinary success that had attended our little trip, and deeply regretting the termination of one of the pleasantest and most interesting experiences in our lives."

From the Yellowstone Park he proceeded to Salt Lake City, where he probed with interested curiosity into the theory and practice of Mormonism ; and thence to San Francisco and the Yosemite Valley. Here he found ample material for his ever-ready pen and a vivid description of the scenery appeared in due course in *MacMillan's Magazine*[1] under the title of " The Valley of the Waterfalls," and was rewritten at a much later date for the second volume of his " Tales of Travel," published posthumously in 1926 with the title " Leaves from a Viceroy's Notebook and Other Papers." The task served to while away a few idle hours on the Pacific Ocean, where the monotony of the journey acted as a stimulus to work. " I have just finished an article on the Yosemite Valley, which took me exactly twenty-four hours to write—the quickest work I ever did."

From Welldon, who was unable to accompany him beyond America, he parted " with sincere and more than ordinary sorrow."[2] But to George Curzon the new world had never been more than a stepping stone to the old. Asia, Ancient of Days, loomed large on the horizon of his consciousness and beckoned imperiously to him ; and with his arrival in Japan the sense of loneliness which had haunted him on the long uneventful journey across the Pacific was swept aside by the stream of new impressions that poured in on him from every side. During his first brief visit to the Island Empire he fell under the spell which she casts over every traveller from the West, and surrendered himself cheerfully to the business of sightseeing. His three or four weeks in the country on this occasion were responsible for a solitary article descriptive of Japanese wrestling, first published in the *New Review* for September 1888, and subsequently in a revised form in " Tales of Travel" in 1923. His deeper

[1] *MacMillan's Magazine* for July, 1888.
[2] Letter to St. John Brodrick, September 10th, 1887.

Study of the political problems of the Far East was postponed to a later date.

For the present he was too fully occupied absorbing new impressions and adjusting his outlook to a strange environment, to probe very deeply beneath the surface of fascinating but unfamiliar scenes. He approached each new country in turn—Japan, China, Malaya, Ceylon and India—with a fresh and sensitive mind ; and with a diligent and graphic pen he pinned down the fleeting pictures which presented themselves to him in bewildering succession, in five hundred and eighty octavo pages of closely written narrative and description. These first impressions possess an interest greater as an index to his personality than the maturer gleanings of a later time, and it is of his first, rather than of his second, journey round the world, therefore, that I propose to give a brief account.

He landed in Yokohama in that enviable frame of mind induced by anticipations which are wholly pleasurable. He marvelled at the natural beauty of the scenery, was delighted with the demonstrative politeness of the people, was mightily intrigued with the pristine simplicity of their attitude towards matters which in the more sophisticated countries of the West have become the subject of a rigorous conventional code, and was fascinated by the delicacy of their craftsmanship and the bizarre effect of the profuse ornamentation of their tombs and temples.

Tokio, with its immense open spaces, " a Paradise of gardens and temples varied by occasional streets in the ordinary sense of the word," was a revelation to him ; and he revelled in the shops, flat platforms raised about a foot from the street, with movable screens concealing, or more often revealing, the back part of the premises, where the family life is lived before the eyes of the world. " There is no false modesty because there is no shame. A people who are even now semi-nude and a few years ago were almost wholly so, and of whom both sexes bathe together naked in the public baths, do not know what indecency is." Of this he had a striking demonstration in a country village, where he encountered the inhabitants walking about freely in a state of nature in the streets. " I was astonished as I entered the single tiny street to run up against four naked men and two naked women. Here, I thought, must be a new rendering of the first chapter of Genesis, a reincarnation of the pristine innocence of Eden." They were merely poor folk afflicted by disease, strolling down to a neighbouring sulphur spring, in whose steaming water they sought a remedy for their complaint. Everywhere he found an elaborate civility of manners passing all belief. " Any two people meeting, bow almost to the ground. Your shopkeeper as you enter prostrates himself and touches the floor with his forehead. This is no veneer of manners, but the inbred gentlemanliness and gentleness of the people."

The combination of solemnity and superstition, of rich artistry dedicated to the creation of grotesque effects, which made of the temples museums of superstition in metal wood and stone, bewildered him. Outwardly they had the appearance of gigantic pagodas, their dim interiors, mysteries of huge columns with grotesquely carved capitals, housing a medley of votive offerings of every form, colour and variety of hideousness, glittering shrines and sculptured images and monsters. Yet he found something profoundly impressive in the dim light glimmering on the gold and bronze images, the burnished lacquer on roof and walls, the sombre magnificence of the whole display and the crowd of worshippers that kept streaming in. And when his gaze fell on the terraced hill at Nikko, with its ascending tiers of tombs and temples embowered in lofty cryptomerias, its balustraded flights of granite steps, its richly painted and sculptured archways and arcades, its great bronze lanterns, lamps and bells, its copper-plated roofs, its columns, friezes, cornices and figures encrusted with imperishable gilding and " an eccentric and barbaric mixture of colours," the whole crowned by a broad paved enclosure containing the burial places of two of the most famous of the Shoguns, his admiration knew no bounds. " No Sovereign, not even the Pharaohs of Egypt, had more glorious or worthy sepulchres."

His sense of the beautiful in nature found constant satisfaction. The " finished symmetry " of the great cone of Fujiyama, one of the few mountains that can be seen from base to peak, " unspoiled by a single intervening foothill or spur, a sheer thirteen thousand feet raised on end in the air," made a deep impression on him, as did the landscapes upon which he looked daily as he travelled over the country. Of the view which ſtretched away from the village of Nokendo, known as the Plains of Heaven, he wrote : " If Heaven be but a beautified and beatified earth, it may well resemble this particular outlook, for a more exquisite combination of all the elements that go to make up lovely scenery I have never seen."

Kioto, the ancient capital, possessed for him the same kind of attraction as Damascus, " a superb situation framed for a panorama, a hiſtory and traditions of myſterious antiquity, temples and buildings of great hiſtorical intereſt, ſtreet scenes and life of extraordinary variety—the fountain of pure orientalism bubbling from as yet untainted wells."

He had little time to give on this occasion to China, and travelled from Japan direct to Shanghai, whence he proceeded after a ſtay of two days to Foochow. From here he had intended making an expedition up the Min river to a famous monaſtery at Yuan Fu, situated in some of the moſt ſtriking and picturesque scenery in China ; but if the main goal of the journey—India—was to be reached in time to enable him to carry out the programme which he had mapped out for himself, before returning home for the meeting of Parliament, he had to adhere rigorously to his time-table, and since he found that a visit to Yuan Fu would necessitate missing out Canton, he decided that scenery muſt for once yield place to character, which could beſt be ſtudied in a great and populous Chinese city. He was able to make good part at leaſt of what he loſt through this decision by a visit to the monaſtery of Kushan in the neighbourhood of Foochow.

At Hong-Kong his pride in the might and preſtige of Great Britain was deeply ſtirred. " No Englishman can land in Hong-Kong without feeling a thrill of pride for his nationality. Here is the furthermoſt link in that chain of fortresses which from Spain to China girdles half the globe." But it was not merely pride of power that he experienced, for here he witnessed a spectacle which afforded ſtriking juſtification of the " passionate loyalty to the English name," which he had placed so high in the articles of his political creed when wooing the electors of South Derbyshire. This was the celebration of Queen Victoria's Jubilee by the indigenous population, a demonſtration " altogether remarkable both in itself and in what it proved." The rejoicings, which lasted two days, included an immense pantomimic procession of revellers, stretching over a space of more than a mile, and illuminations which far excelled in beauty and effectiveness anything that he had seen in London on Jubilee night. From a launch in the harbour he gazed on " as fairy-like a sight as was ever pictured in the Arabian Nights." But striking as was the display itself, it was the significance of its spontaneity that at once impressed him. The two hundred thousand native residents had collected among themselves two hundred and forty thousand dollars with which to celebrate the reign of a Queen of an alien race, and he could not but see in the voluntary giving and spending of so large a sum in a small British Crown Colony a very remarkable tribute to the English name and to the success of British rule in Asia.

A visit to Canton excited lively interest. As he threaded his way through " the tortuous intricacies of its myriad alleys and lanes," he was bewildered by the variety of sights and sounds—" by the bustling, shouting, ant-like crowd, by the gaudy shops with their exposed wares, by the huge perpendicular and painted sign-boards almost blocking up the streets, by the unexampled mixture of squalor and magnificence of destitution and wealth." In every shop he found a shrine to the god of wealth, with incense smouldering upon the altar—a key to the character which he had come to study. He was disappointed in the temples, which, though numerous, were in shocking repair, and were filled with images which were for the most part " grim, grotesque and grinning." In the temple of the five hundred gods he found one image with a low crowned hat and black beard, which was variously reported to be Marco Polo and a shipwrecked English sailor.

One can appreciate the feelings with which he examined the buildings in which were held the triennial literary competitions—" an endless succession of brick stalls, each separated from the other and all opening on to a passage patrolled by guards," to prevent possible fraud. He ascertained that when the candidates from all parts of the Empire, sometimes numbering as many as thirteen hundred, were safely locked up in their cells, the subjects for themes, essays and compositions were given out, and that thereafter the competitors were kept in isolation until their task was finished the time taken varying from twelve to forty-eight hours.

A monotonous week at sea on an Austrian Lloyd steamer between Hong-Kong and Singapore drove him back upon his pen. His visit to the monastery of Kushan near Foochow had suggested an intriguing subject for literary treatment. In a country where the worship of ancestors was the corner-stone of popular belief and the raising of a family, consequently, a religious necessity, even more than a civic duty, monasticism must, surely, be a profound anomaly. How, then, had this outstanding feature of Buddhism become rooted in so unpromising a soil? " I think it will make a good subject and is capable of interesting treatment," he noted in his diary. He was quick to discover a key to this apparent mystery in the success with which the Buddhist monk had metamorphosed himself into the family priest and made himself indispensable in the due performance of the rites which popular belief demanded. And as his pen slid smoothly over the paper it left behind it in its track sentence after sentence punctuated with the paradox which he loved. Because of his renunciation of family life the Buddhist monk was derided and despised ; because of the part which he played in essential rites associated with the solemn moments of life and death, he was not only tolerated but maintained by voluntary contributions. The peculiar sanctity of the family relations was the cause both of his ostracism and of his employment. " They are needed to discharge on behalf of others the very obligations which they have renounced themselves. Expelled from the world because they have ignored the family, they are brought back into it to testify that the family is the first of all earthly ties." And Buddhism in China was, consequently, an oddly altered creed. " The beautiful teaching enshrined in the sacred writings as they came from India, the precepts that made white lives and brought tearless deaths, that almost Christianised idolatry and might have redeemed a world," had faded out of sight. Strangest transformation of all, it was now a creed "whose apostates are enlisted as its prophets and whose perverts become its priests."

The article first appeared with the title, " The Cloister in Cathay," in the *Fortnightly Review* for June 1888 ; the greater part of it was incorporated in the most successful of all his books, " Problems of the Far East "; much of it made a third appearance in the second volume of his travel tales, " Leaves from a Viceroy's Note-Book," in 1926. In its original form it is a delightful and characteristic piece of writing which interests to-day, not so much on account of its subject matter, nor because of any great depth of thought which it displays, but because the reader who is familiar with George Curzon's personality becomes conscious as he reads of the intense enjoyment and satisfaction with which the author plied his pen.

A break in the journey at Singapore made a welcome change. " Singapore marks a very bright little spot in the radiant circle which I am describing round the world." A short halt at Penang and a longer stay of ten days in Ceylon made equally pleasant interludes.

In the latter island he found much that appealed strongly to him. To begin with, there was a mystery to be unravelled—the mystery of the shadow of Adam's Peak, " about which a great deal of vapid theorising has been indulged in." And nothing gave George Curzon greater satisfaction than a chance of laying to rest the pretentious theories that, for some reason or other, always seem to hover round any problem, however simple, upon which no authoritative judgment happens to have been pronounced. So the traveller spent a toilful night groping his way to the summit of the mountain. And as the sun rose he was rewarded with a clear view of the shadow " thrown in a perfect isosceles triangle over the misty land to the west, with its apex rising against a bank of fleecy clouds on the horizon." The phenomenon was striking, but there was no need for " abstract scientific phrases to explain it." It was merely a case of " ordinary shadow thrown by a dark object with a light behind." The reason why it appeared to stand up instead of lying flat was equally simple ; it was due to the mist wreaths being drawn upward by the sun's rays, so that it was against them as upon a wall that the shadow was cast.

He gave himself no rest. From Adam's Peak he went to Kandy and from there embarked upon a long journey mainly by road to the famous buried cities in the lowlands. His diary here is interspersed with very human touches. " Dear me, how tired I was when I at last got to bed " ; and describing a night journey in a bullock cart : " I had to curl up like a caterpillar with a stomach-ache. Not a wink of sleep ; jolt, jolt, jingle, jingle, mixed with the most diabolical noises from the driver."

His love of historic ruins was kindled by the sight of " the jungle-buried cities, which were mighty capitals when Rome was only a village on a hill " ; and as was his custom, he took a keen delight in fitting them into their proper places in the map of time and the calendar of fame. Anaradhapura, " the metropolis of Buddhism as well as of monarchy, the Rome of that mysterious faith which, introduced from India three hundred years after the time of Buddha, has survived the extinction of its parent branch by one thousand years," with its splendid palaces, temples, monasteries and baths, must have rivalled Assyrian Babylon or Egyptian Thebes. The huge topes built by famous kings as reliquaries or shrines were the only structures in the world which could be compared for bulk and solidity with the pyramids of Egypt. On the summit of Mihintale, a hill one thousand feet in height, scaled by a spacious flight of more than one thousand eight hundred granite steps, stands a famous tope. " Here the royal missionary Mahinda, son of the great Bud-dhist Emperor Asoka, alighted when, like St. Augustine, he came to convert a remote island and made his first convert of a king." From that time the city had become a famous centre of Buddhist culture. It had been the recipient of Buddhist relics, conferring upon it a sanctity far surpassing that of " Venice with the bones of St. Mark, or Damascus with the head of St. John the Baptist."

But what struck him more than all was the discovery in these old Singhalese structures dating from before the Christian era of the most graceful and perfect of classic designs. On all sides of him he saw " Greek pillars, cornices, capitals and even foliation, with just such modification as would be dictated by the different genius of the East." What was the explanation ? Had Greek art, which reached Northern India in the track of the armies of Alexander, filtered down as far south as Ceylon ? Or was the style indigenous and had Greece herself borrowed not only from Egypt but from India ? The riddle was one to which he confessed he was unable to find the answer.

From Ceylon he crossed to the mainland and experienced a

feeling almost of disappointment at his first contact with the soil of India. Though tropical in character, it seemed to him that southern India lacked the rich luxuriance of Ceylon. And he found difficulty in adjusting his æsthetic standards to the bizarre and unintelligible features of Dravidian art. The workmanship of the temples was everywhere " a miracle of elaboration and prodigy of ugliness." He appreciated the natural advantages of the rock at Trichinopoly, but was disappointed at the poor use which had been made of it. " I was reminded, by its shape and relation to the town, of the Acropolis at Athens, and would fain have seen on this impressive summit the white marble columns of a second Parthenon. Instead there is only the barbarous dirt and decay of the least attractive style of architecture I ever remember to have seen."

A new train of thought was set in motion by an interview with Colonel Olcott, then head of the Theosophists at Adyar, near Madras. The latter stoutly defended Mme. Blavatsky, asserted his belief in her miraculous powers and narrated several instances, " which I sceptically declared might be accounted for by the more reasonable theory of skilful charlatanry." He showed messages from Mahatmas, spirit paintings and other queer things, which, " in his eyes, were evidences of faith ; in mine, insinuations of fraud." On reflection however, he decided that he was not disposed wholly to condemn this aspect of Theosophy as necessarily false or fraudulent, " being one of those who hold that a miracle is only an exception to certain laws believed to be fundamental and immutable, but only really so within the imperfect boundaries of human experience."

From Madras he proceeded to Calcutta by sea, and here the pride of race which had been so deeply stirred by his first sight of Hong-Kong received fresh stimulus. " Calcutta is a great European capital planted in the East. The sight of these successive metropolises of England and the British Empire in foreign parts is one of the proudest experiences of travel." The splendour of this eastern capital seemed to him to lie in the vast open space known as the Maidan and in the river crowded with ships and sparkling with life, rather than in the streets and buildings. But at Government House he looked with special interest, " for it was erected by Lord Wellesley upon the model of my own home, being a complete reproduction of the design which Adam contemplated, but fortunately never succeeded in finishing, at Kedleston."

He was flattered at the reception accorded to him by Lord Dufferin—" Prince and Paragon of diplomatists "—who talked to him of his work, of the Indian land system, of the rapid increase in ability and influence of the educated Indian and of much else. But George Curzon was still bent on sightseeing, and after a brief stay in the capital he went to Darjeeling and thence by Benares to Agra and Delhi. Neither at Darjeeling nor at Agra, the one providing a panorama of mountain scenery reputed the finest in the world, the other containing a building at once the most famous and the most beautiful of all the monuments made by the hands of men, was he disappointed. Rather was he rendered all but speechless by the overpowering majesty of the one and the ineffable loveliness of the other. In a chilly room in the hotel at Darjeeling he sat up till 1.30 a.m., trying to put on paper a record of his sensations. Perhaps the following extract will indicate sufficiently the nature of his feelings : " long did we stand and stare and wonder, gloating over our extraordinary privilege and building up bricks of glowing recollection into the fabric of our future lives."

As he approached Agra his eyes caught sight of the object of their desire and rested upon " the pure swelling dome and spear-like minarets of the pearl of fabrics, the gem of man's handiwork, the most devotional of temples, the most solemn of sepulchres, the peerless and incomparable Taj." No building had ever stirred the emotional depth of his being in quite the same way. " I stood there and gazed long upon the entrancing spectacle, the singular loveliness of it pouring in waves over my soul and flooding my inner consciousness till the cup of satiety was full, and I had to shut my eyes and pause and think." In the case of all the most famous buildings he had hitherto seen—St. Marks at Venice, St. Peters at Rome, the cathedral at Seville—there had been something to criticise, " some apparent violation of an artistic canon or conflict with one's own esoteric standards of taste." Here the voice of criticism was completely silenced. " I could not find it in me to devise wherein, even according to my own faulty notions of beauty and style, it was imperfect or capable of improvement."

He was charmed with all the Moghul buildings, and especially with those of Shah Jahan, " whose genius seems to have compassed the whole gamut from the colossal to the minute," in justification of which he quoted as examples the Pearl Mosque at Delhi, " the most exquisite little private chapel in the world," and the Jumma Masjid, whose superb scale and proportions entitled it, all things considered, to be regarded as " the most regal mosque in the world."

It was not until he reached Delhi, the most northern point of his projected tour, that he was seized with a desire to see the North West Frontier. The knowledge to be acquired in the course of visits to Peshawar and Quetta might well prove useful in the future, and in any case would be " of greater practical value than an exhaustive acquaintance with even the most beautiful saracenic mosques and tombs." Such a tour would necessitate a brief postponement of his departure for England ; but this was of no great consequence. " I shall not be home as soon as expected, having decided on a bold stroke. To-morrow night I start for Peshawar, six hundred and twenty-four miles. And from there shall ride as far up the Khyber as they will allow me. Then I shall go south and make my way through the Bolan by the new railway to Quetta. You will agree with me that it is worth the grind—which will be stupendous—and that the knowledge may come in useful." [1]

The interest of the Khyber pass lay in its historical associations and its strategic value. After the feast of beauty which he had been enjoying he found its physical features repellent. " For sheer repulsiveness I would compare it to the valley of the tombs of the Kings at Egyptian Thebes." And, after seeing as much of it as he was permitted, he retraced his steps to Lahore, and from there travelled by Multan and Jacobabad to Sibi, and so, through the Bolan pass by the railway " hastily and imperfectly constructed in the war scare of 1885," to Quetta. The difficulties of some sections of the line had induced the authorities, " who were laying the line in a wild hurry (characteristic of the never-in-time Gladstonian party), to construct a narrow gauge line " over a distance of ten miles in the worst part of the pass. This he was glad to find was being converted to a broad gauge, for he was quick to realise the supreme importance of this line of communication in the event of war.

From Quetta he was conducted by Sir R. Sandeman to Chaman, on the Afghan frontier, camping for the night just below the spot at which a two mile tunnel was about to be driven through the Kojak range. The view which he saw the next day from the summit of the range was one which roused his dramatic instinct. "We were on the apex of the ridge that is the rampart of England's Indian Empire on the West, and all below us was Afghanistan." The character of the landscape was in keeping with the hard realities of life on these inhospitable marches. "More than three thousand feet below stretched the great Kadanai plain—a vast ocean of yellow sand rolling to the horizon, broken only by rocky ridges which rose up like islands out of the sea, and bounded in the distance by loftier mountain ranges." Here lay the key to the whole of southern Afghanistan—the nerve ganglion from which, if necessary, the long arm of Great Britain would shoot forth and clutch at Kandahar. "I felt a thrill of satisfaction at being for the moment on the very uttermost verge, the Ultima Thule, of the Indian Empire."

He pondered deeply on the problems with which this long, rugged and turbulent frontier bristled : and it was on this account, perhaps, that the sight seeing which he did on his way south to Bombay seemed to have lost something of its earlier attraction. He commended the wisdom of the Sikh Guru, Ram Dass, who built the Golden Temple at Amritsar in 1581, for utilising the taste and the materials of his day and erecting a building which was purely Saracenic in style. But of Jeypore and its ruined capital at Amber, and later of the caves of Elephanta, he was critical. He was obviously surfeited with sightseeing, and his palate had become jaded. At Amber he went about everywhere enquiring for the Mardana Gateway, which Edwin Arnold had declared was "the finest portal to any palace in the world," and finally discovered that he had already passed through it more than once "without noticing anything beyond the inferiority of the material and poverty of the decoration." He was even more irritated by a statement of Bishop Heber, that he had never viewed a scene "so strikingly picturesque and beautiful as that which is presented from the vast and gorgeous palace of Amber."

He thought that either the Bishop must have travelled with his eyes shut or he must have been in " the same state of mental dogmatism and waywardness" as when he wrote of Ceylon that only man was vile. He was not prepared to concede more than that, without deserving " the childish encomiums of the prelate," the landscape was pretty.

He thought that the merit of the cave temples on the island of Elephanta, off Bombay, had been " grossly exaggerated." Had he recalled what he had himself once said of travel in Greece, namely, that the man who was familiar with his Herodotus enjoyed sensations which no one else could possibly share, he would perhaps have been less scathing in his condemnation, for he would have realised that the man who was familiar with the symbology of Hindu philosophy and religion would see in the sculptury of the temples much that was not apparent to the uninstructed eye.

He reached England on the eve of the meeting of Parliament, in February 1888, and there is no doubt that, looking back over the six months of his absence, he was well satisfied with its results. These were due in no small measure to the possession in high degree of what he himself once described as " middle-class method." It was a quality on which he always prided himself. Many years afterwards when, as Foreign Secretary, there was a possibility of his going to the Washington Conference of 1921, he was vehemently attacked in the columns of *The Times*, then under the direct control of Lord Northcliffe, on the score of " business incapacity." He was grievously hurt by the accusation. "As you say," he told his brother, who had written in very natural indignation at the extraordinarily violent language employed by *The Times*, " if I am anything it is a man of business, and the Foreign Office has never been so much up to date as now. That attack I did resent. The personal abuse leaves me unscathed."[1] He certainly employed this quality to great advantage upon his travels. It was once said of Sir Charles Dilke that no question of foreign or colonial policy could well come up in the House of Commons about which he was not able to say : " I know the place ; I know the conditions ; I know the men."[2] The same thing might have been said with equal truth about George Curzon.

[1] Letter to the Hon. F. N. Curzon, dated July 17th, 1921.
[2] By Mr. Justin McCarthy.

131

Not only the names of the men whom he met when travelling, but his impressions of their characteristics and abilities were duly noted. A careful list of the books read on any particular journey was compiled. The names of all the hotels at which he stayed were tabulated with terse descriptive notes appended. A detailed record of distances and expenditure was kept. Thus, an entry shows that the *per capita* cost of the seven days' trip to the Yellowstone Park was worked out at $60\frac{1}{3}$ dollars or £12 11s. 4d. A table containing eighty separate entries shows that on this first journey round the world he covered 31,561 miles. A comparison of the figures compiled on his two journeys round the world affords a striking illustration of the possibilities of " middle-class method." The first journey occupied a hundred and ninety-one days and cost in all £336 5s. or an average of £1 15s. a day. The second journey, in 1892-3, lasted two hundred and three days and cost £353 19s. 6d., or an average of £1 14s. 10d. a day. With the same methodical care facts of all sorts were collected, sifted, tabulated and stored for future use.

Except in one or two cases, he was chary of drawing definite conclusions from his experiences on this first journey. It had been a reconnaissance rather than a detailed survey. That was to follow. And where he ventured to draw tentative conclusions he sometimes found occasion to revise them in the light of further study. In his estimate of the relative value of the forces at work in the Far East he was misled by the superficial gaiety of the Japanese and underestimated the strength and tenacity of purpose that lay beneath the surface. Similarly, he attached too great weight to the solid virtues of the individual Chinese. He concluded that the reserve of forces, " moral as well as material," in the Chinese Empire was prodigious, and that the alliance of China was " a factor of first rate importance in the East." [1] But when as a result of these opinions he wrote : " in the event of a war between China and Japan, I fear the latter would be beaten out of the field," he had omitted to take into account the corruption and incompetence of the Chinese official classes. The deeper study of China and Japan which he made during his second Journey round the world in 1892-93 caused him to modify this opinion—so much so that an outstanding feature of the

[1] Letter to St. John Brodrick, November 14th, 1887.

book which he eventually wrote on the Far East was his prediction of the collapse of China and the triumph of Japan.

Apart from providing him with a good deal of useful first-hand information, the journey was important from another point of view, for it exercised a determining influence on his future course of action. If it be true that it did not actually implant in his mind certain definite ambitions, it is certain that it gave to them a much clearer and more concrete form. He returned to England with his belief in the civilising mission of Great Britain enormously enhanced and with a high opinion both of the men who represented her in foreign lands and of the greatness and worthiness of the task which they were privileged to discharge. He thought the representatives of his country whom he had met in the course of his journey, "as able and enlightened a body of men as ever carried or sustained a con-quering flag in foreign lands." Good administration, good buildings roads and wharves, order and decorum he had expected to find. Over and above these things he had found something of infinitely greater significance—"a satisfied and grateful acquiescence in our domination." He recalled the fact that the popularity and prestige of the Roman Empire had rested upon the capacity of its consuls and proconsuls. Such was the case with Great Britain also. And not the least vivid of the impressions left upon him by his journey was a sense of the splendour of the opportunities for Imperial service which the Eastern possessions of Great Britain offered to those among her sons who were conscious of the high purpose of her mission and the greatness of her Imperial destiny. It was imbued with such ideas that he penned the dedication of the book which he subsequently wrote on the problems of Eastern Asia. He dedicated it to all those who believed that Great Britain was, under Providence, the greatest Instrument for good that the world had seen and who held with him that its work was not yet accomplished.

From now onwards Asia laid her spell upon him; stirred the idealism latent in his nature; intrigued him; fascinated him; filled his mind. Journey followed journey with a single object in view— the study of the multifarious problems which she presented. His journey round the world in 1887 was, indeed, an eventful and a fateful enterprise.

CHAPTER VIII

HIGH POLITICS AT HOME AND ABROAD

1888–1890

THE session of 1888, though protracted, was uneventful and was occupied mainly with the Local Government Act creating County Councils, and with Mr. Goschen's Conversion Scheme. Opportunities for supporters of the Government in the House of Commons were, consequently, few, and George Curzon described himself at this time as a member of " the great silent brigade in the House of Commons that sat mute amid a universal babble." On the few occasions on which he spoke he fully sustained the reputation which he had already won, and notably on the occasion of a Motion by Mr. Labouchere in favour of abolition of the hereditary principle in the constitution of the House of Lords. This excursion provided him with an opportunity early in the Session of showing that while he wielded a keen-edged and agile rapier in attack, he was very far from underestimating the importance of the subject, and had devoted to the problem of the Upper House the thought necessary to enable him to approach it with a constructive mind.

The speech was characterised as his first deliberate challenge of the opinion of the most critical assembly in the world. No one disputed its ability. Some thought that its length detracted a little from its effect—that " had it been fifteen minutes shorter, it would have been twice as good a speech."[1] But apart from criticism on this ground it was regarded as a very distinct success.

The question of the reform of the House of Lords was one with which from now onwards George Curzon was constantly concerned.

[1] The *Observer* of March 11th, 1888.

With all his sympathy for the ideals of an enlightened Tory Democracy, he foresaw the approaching peril of a clash between the interests of the classes and those of the masses, and the threat held out to the former by an extended franchise and a growing attraction for those into whose hands power was thus being transferred, of radical methods of dealing with the social inequalities and the increasing disparity in the distribution of wealth, inherent in the organisation of a modern industrial state. The sole safeguard against the tyranny of government by mere numbers in the future was a Second Chamber sufficiently strong to discharge adequately its functions of revision and delay. He was convinced that no Second Chamber constituted on an almost exclusively hereditary basis would prove capable of doing so, and with characteristic energy and courage, he led a crusade in favour of its reform.

It seemed to him that the time was ripe for action. A peer of independent views who had held office under Lord Salisbury—Lord Dunraven—had brought forward a Bill dealing with the question. A Liberal peer, Lord Rosebery, had moved for the appointment of a Committee to enquire into the matter ; and though his Motion had been defeated it had extracted a promise from Lord Salisbury that he would consider carefully any definite scheme which might be submitted to him. George Curzon accepted Lord Salisbury's challenge with alacrity, and in collaboration with St. John Brodrick drew up a scheme which was given publicity in two successive issues of the *National Review*.[1] His two articles constituted something more than a mere Essay in constitution mongering ; they contained passages which gave them almost the appearance of a manifesto—an impression which was heightened when, in a third number of the same periodical, there appeared a formidable list of names of the eldest sons of peers then sitting in the House of Commons, who professed their belief in the importance and feasibility of the reform proposed. And the manifesto began and ended with a pretty plain intimation to the House of Lords that in their own interests they had better not delay in putting their house in order, and to the Conservative party in general that, " by a prudent acceptance of the desirability of reform," it had now a favourable opportunity of arming

[1] The *National Review*, March and April 1888.

itself with the moſt powerful weapon for resiſting "the cynical insolence of revolution."

He declared himself unable to see in the hereditary principle any sacrosanct element in the composition of the House of Lords as a legislative body. Hiſtory showed that, far from any such principle having been designedly included in a British Senate, the Senate, like every other great and noble inſtitution that we possessed, was in its exiſting shape an accident, "evolved out of heterogeneous elements by that providential dispensation which has ever seemed to watch over the deſtinies of the Anglo-Saxon race, converting their errors into blessings, extraƈting salvation from their sins, inveſting the freaks of chance with the ſtately consequences of design, and by mild and merciful processes of change averting the tempeſtuous throes of revolution." There was, therefore, no real reason why the conſtitution of the Upper House should not be so altered as to furnish the country with a Second Chamber which should be in deed, as well as in name, a co-ordinate branch of the legislature and which should unite with "the adminiſtrative efficiency of the Senate of Republican America the superb preſtige of the Senate of Republican Rome."

The defeƈts of the exiſting body were then examined. They were its unwieldy size, absenteeism on the part of a large proportion of its members, except on special occasions when they were urgently summoned to vote down Radical legislation, and the inequitable privilege which such black sheep as there might be within the ranks of the peerage shared with its moſt diſtinguished members of exercising great powers which carried with them corresponding responsibilities. Not that he thought that in praƈtice the performances of the Upper House had shown the taint of these defeƈts. On the contrary, it had discharged its duties with method and ability. It had been singularly free from whim or caprice. It had rarely been called upon to repent its own vagaries, because it had rarely committed them. It had seldom been romantic and never ridiculous.

Nevertheless, its defeƈts laid it open to legitimate attack and, consequently, impaired its usefulness. Moreover, its composition on an almoſt exclusively hereditary basis had been a source of weakness from another point of view. For it had resulted in an uneven distribution of representation between the various interests in the life of the nation which ought to find a place in any properly constituted Senate, if it was to be qualified to discharge its most important function—that of safeguarding against the decisions of mere numbers the interests of minorities. The Lower House being an assembly representative of the masses of the people, might be expected to give prominence to the requirements of the industrial and labouring classes. In the Upper House, therefore, expression should be given to those interests—property, wealth, culture, administrative efficiency and Imperial advantage—which could not enforce their claims by the imperious sanction of numbers, but which must always be controlling factors in the Government of any well-regulated State. Property and wealth, it was true, found adequate representation in a hereditary Chamber. Culture and administrative experience were doubtless, incidentally, represented ; but such representation was accidental rather than devised. Intellectual distinction might well be represented of right, as might also administrative experience from the bench, the fighting forces, the diplomatic and civil services.

How was provision to be made for the due representation of all these classes ? In the second article a scheme was tentatively put forward. It rested on the distinction between " a lord " and " a Lord of Parliament"—already observed in the case of Scotch and Irish peers—and required that no heir to a peerage upon succeeding to the dignity should be entitled to a writ of summons as a Lord of Parliament unless he had qualified in one of a number of categories, such as membership of the House of Commons or public service of distinction in various specified walks of life. In other words, heredity alone would not qualify a peer to serve in a legislative capacity. To the qualification of birth must be added the qualification of proven service. Nor should membership of the Second Chamber be obligatory on a peer, even though he was qualified. He should not be compelled to apply for a writ of summons as a Lord of Parliament. It should be open to him, if he preferred it, to stand for election to the House of Commons. Both the peer who was not qualified to sit in the Second Chamber and the peer who was qualified but was unwilling to do so should share the privileges of commoners in this respect.

By these means the positive defects of the existing Second Chamber would be overcome. There remained the desirability of securing representation of the other interests to which reference had been made. This could be done partly by nomination by the Crown and partly by election. Fifty life peers might be appointed, and a similar number of peers might be elected by the House of Commons for a term of years, and with the object of better enabling it to discharge its Imperial obligations, a further number by the Legislatures of the Colonies. He thought it desirable, both on historical grounds and on grounds of expediency, that representation of the State Church should be retained, though on a somewhat reduced scale. A Senate constituted on these lines would consist, consequently, of four main elements—qualified hereditary peers, life peers, spiritual peers and elected peers.

While he offered his scheme as a concrete contribution towards the solution of the problem, he declared that he was not wedded to its details, but pleaded for acceptance, if not of his specific proposals, at least of the principles on which they were based. And he concluded as he had begun, by urging upon the House of Lords the adoption of reform without delay. They alone—short of a revolution—had power to act. Reform could not be imposed upon them from without. They were the masters of their own fate. They could initiate and carry through a measure of reform from which they would emerge with renewed youth and increased vitality. On the other hand, they could, if they chose, " stand stiff till the crack of doom "—though it would be with the grim conviction that they had " accelerated its terrible tocsin."

He could not know then that a day would come, less than a quarter of a century later, when he would find himself the spokesman of a still unregenerate House of Lords, faced with the humiliating duty of advising his fellow peers, against their own judgment on the merits of the case submitted to them, to bow the knee to a Radical Government and, under a threat of force majeure, to submit, not to a reform of their constitution, but to a drastic curtailment of their powers. But had a vision of the tragic scene of 1911 been vouchsafed to him, he could not have pleaded for reform more earnestly or with more conviction than he did.

The list of supporters of the scheme published in the May issue of the *National Review*, was not secured without energetic canvassing, and owing to an enforced absence from London on the part of George Curzon, this task fell almost entirely on the shoulders of St. John Brodrick. " I have worked like a slave over the list and have felt your loss terribly."[1] His efforts met with gratifying success and the published list contained the names of twenty-four eldest sons sitting in the House of Commons, headed by Lord Hartington who were prepared to urge reform of the House of Lords as desirable and feasible.

It must not, of course, be supposed that there was behind this campaign anything remotely resembling a spirit of iconoclasm. Very far from it. George Curzon was by temperament and tradition a convinced upholder of an aristocracy. Had he believed in the possibility of a communistic organisation of society, he would still have viewed any attempt to introduce communistic principles into the life of the State as fraught with mischief and doomed to irreparable disaster. He never doubted that an aristocratic order founded on the English model had been, and would remain, of priceless value to the British people. " As a moral and social power, as a *primum mobile* in the internal evolution of the State, the English nobility has, partly by its constitution, but mainly by its conduct, acquired a position without parallel in any foreign country." But he drew a clear-cut distinction between the peerage as a social order and the peerage as a piece of legislative mechanism.

The movement attracted a great deal of notice. *The Times* devoted to an examination of the scheme a long leading article, which, if critical, was certainly not hostile, and concluded by welcoming it as a contribution " full of significance in respect of the source from which it comes, towards the discussion of a very important subject."[2] And in due course it published and commented approvingly on the declaration of the eldest sons. " *The Times* treats us well," wrote St. John Brodrick to his collaborator, on April the 27th. Nor was the campaign without its effect upon Lord Salisbury, who made what the same paper regarded as " a very important statement"

[1] Letter from St. John Brodrick to George Curzon, April 20th 1888.
[2] *The Times* of March 28th, 1888.

in the course of the debate on the second reading of Lord Dun-raven's Bill. He informed the House that since opposing Lord Rosebery's Motion for a Select Committee the Government had been considering the question, and while anxious to avoid creating an impression that they would undertake any large reform, they thought that a measure for facilitating the entrance of life peers into the House was one which would be useful and which they ought to propose. On which St. John Brodrick wrote, " I think Lord Salisbury's start is a good one—inadequate, of course, but expansible."

For the time being there was little more to be done in this direction and George Curzon turned his thoughts to the other subject which was taking a steadily increasing hold upon his mind, that is to say, the problem presented by the unique position which Great Britain had acquired in Asia. He was most anxious to speak in the debate on the Indian Budget, and was exasperated by his failure to catch the Speaker's eye. " This is what comes of trying to speak in an Indian debate. I sat in the House from six-thirty till twelve, and rose every time and was never called once. . . This is the second entire evening that I have spent in the House vainly trying to fire off a speech on Indian affairs."[1] This disappointment was soon banished from his mind, however, by the prospect of an early visit to the Russian terri-tories in Central Asia on the northern borders of Persia and Afghanis-tan, where he hoped to see for himself to what extent that Power was busying herself on the far side of the Indian frontier, which he had visited earlier in the year.

He had already begun to write on the frontier question, his first article, which was published in the *Nineteenth Century* for June, with the title, " The Scientific Frontier an Accomplished Fact," having been suggested by the spectacle of the House of Commons being asked to condemn a frontier policy as unwise, " by persons who required themselves to be informed as to where that frontier was." It was in the main descriptive, being designed to give an account of the steps which had recently been taken—and particularly since the Penjdeh scare of 1885—to put the defence of India on a satisfactory basis. Something was said of the railways, the bridges and the

[1]Letter to St. John Brodrick, August 9th, 1888.

tunnels that had been and were still being constructed, since it was against these that criticism in the House of Commons had been directed ; and a good deal of space was devoted to a description of the Bolan pass, to an insistence on the strategic importance of Quetta and to commendation of the foresight which had been displayed by the Government of India in acquiring it and the surrounding country from the Khan of Kelat. " The entire history of British interference in Kelat may be quoted as a triumphant answer to those who decry British interference anywhere and extol the odious theory of sedentary and culpable inaction." The article concluded with a spirited defence of the expenditure—admittedly heavy—which was being incurred ; and with a glowing tribute to Lord Dufferin, whose term of office was about to expire, for the courage and sagacity of his frontier policy. ". . . the new frontier alone is a magnificent monument to his Viceroyalty, and when the history of India comes to be written it will be said of him—and a prouder epitaph could not be desired by a statesman—that he found an Empire in peril and left it secure. At this moment I venture to assert that the solid character of his achievements is better understood at St. Petersburgh than it is in London."

The article attracted notice in high places and from the India Office he received a complimentary letter from Mr. Clinton Dawkins, then serving as private secretary to Lord Cross. " It is certainly the clearest and ablest exposition of the Frontier position which has yet been given to the public, and it is up to date in almost every particular." [1]

Before starting on his projected journey he visited his constituents at Southport where he found " exuberant enthusiasm." He then embarked once more for Asia, leaving England on September the 6th, assailed with but one regret. His absence during the Parliamentary recess meant giving up the country house parties and the congenial company which he loved so well—" a large slice out of the happiness of a year. But I think I am right." [2]

His experiences during his tour more than confirmed him in this opinion. " Looking back on the past eight weeks, I am positively

[1] Letter dated June 11th, 1888.
[2] Letter to St. John Brodrick, September 5th, 1888.

amazed at all I have seen and learnt. St. Petersburgh, Moscow, Tiflis, Baku, the Caspian, Askabad, Merv, Bokhara, Samarkand and even Tashkent. The thing has been a marvellous success. . . . I met all the interesting people too. Komaroff, Alikhanoff, and stayed with the Governor-General at Tashkent. This railway makes them prodigiously strong, and they mean business."[1] Throughout the journey he made good use of his amazing powers of work. " I have been working like a Trojan at the articles—thirteen out of sixteen already completed—2,400 words apiece, which will give you some idea of the labour involved. They are to appear from now in a syndicate of six principal provincial newspapers, and I shall prob-ably republish them afterwards."[2] They formed the basis of his first important book, " Russia in Central Asia in 1889," published a year after his return.

Its pages were permeated with the rich colouring of a varied and picturesque romance, for which these ancient lands had for so long provided an appropriate setting. But a change was fast coming over them. " The era of the Thousand and One Nights, with its strange mixture of savagery and splendour, of coma and excitement, is fast fading away, and will soon have yielded up all its secrets to science. Here, in the cities of Alp Arslan, and Timur, and Abdullah Khan, may be seen the sole remaining stage upon which is yet being enacted that expiring drama of realistic romance."[3] And his own interest in them was frankly of a political character. He viewed them in the main as " a theatre of Imperial diplomacy, possibly—*quod di avertant omen*—as the threshold of international war."[4] And it was from this point of view that he addressed himself to the public of Great Britain.

In the interval between his return and the publication of the book he applied himself to the study of what he called the Anglo-Russian Question with the concentrated energy which was alike one of his most marked characteristics and most valuable assets, which was, indeed, an outstanding feature of all his work in life and the source whence he derived a large part of his success. If, as he told his readers, he did not start upon his journey without having

[1]Letter to St. John Brodrick, October 25th, 1888.   [2]*Ibid.*
[3]From the Preface.   [4]*Ibid.*

made himself thoroughly acquainted with the researches and opinions of previous writers, he did not complete his own work without " subsequent study of every available authority." The main purpose of the book was to warn his country of the gravity of the menace which Russian ambitions constituted to the Imperial position of Great Britain in the East, and to appeal to her statesmen not to drift before the oncoming tide, but to meet every fresh move made by Russia with a counter move of her own. There were two goals which Russia kept steadily in view. By stabbing at us in India she sought to disable us from preventing her grip from closing finally upon Constantinople ; and by steadily eating into the heart of Persia she hoped in time to secure the warm water port which she coveted on the shores of the Persian Gulf.

It is generally supposed that it was at this time that George Curzon first formed the view which dominated his outlook when circumstances placed him in a position of power and responsibility, and which was one of the causes of the disagreement which grew up between him and the Cabinet and ended in his resignation of the Indian Viceroyalty. It is true that the opinions put forward in this and in his later book on Persia remained unaltered, and formed the basis of the policy which, when Viceroy, he constantly urged on the Government at home. " In 1888 I wrote a chapter in my book on Russia in Central Asia, upon Anglo-Russian relations and the future that lay before them in Asia, and although that chapter is eleven years old, I do not think that there is a statement of opinion in it that I would now withdraw or a prediction that has so far been falsified." [1] But the main contention running through both books was based on a view of Russian policy in Central Asia formed at a much earlier date. The case provides, indeed, a striking illustration of the early maturity of mind and the fixity of his opinions, which have been spoken of so often in these pages as one of the outstanding characteristics of the man. On May the 7th of the year 1877 the members of an Eton house debating society assembled for discussion at Wolley Dod's. The question debated under the chairmanship of George Curzon was : " Are we justified in regarding with equanimity the advance of Russia towards our Indian frontier?"

[1] Letter to Lord George Hamilton, May 3rd, 1899.

CURZON, 1889

And in the Minutes of the proceedings which have been preserved occurs the following—

> " The President expressed the opinion that the policy of Russia was a most ambitious and aggressive one. It dated its origin from the time of Peter the Great, by whom the schemes of conquest had first been made. He did not imagine for a moment that the Russians would actually invade India, and were they to do so we need have no fear of the result ; but . . . a great question of diplomacy might arise in Europe in which the interests of England were opposed to those of Russia. It might then suit Russia to send out an army to watch our Indian frontier. In such a case as this England's right hand would obviously be tied back."

There was added as a postscript to the above Minute the following note—" The President said a good deal more about the importance of Persia and Afghanistan and the recent advance of Russia on Khiva, but want of space forbids him to commit it to writing."[1] Here in a nutshell was the argument which twelve years later was elaborated in four hundred pages of print.

The book brought him many letters of congratulation from experts both British and foreign and many gratifying reviews. *The Times*[2] devoted two columns of warm approval to it ; the *Saturday Review*[3] asserted that it was the best book which had yet appeared in England on the subject, and the *Spectator*[4] applauded the candour and moderation with which the author submitted his opinions no less than his bright and sometimes eloquent style. The general opinion of the work was succinctly summed up by Mr. Schomberg MacDonnell, whose position at the Foreign Office brought him into touch with many who took more than an academic interest in its subject matter.

> " Every one is loud in praise of it, and this, too, from all points of view. The experts praise it as being, beyond doubt,

[1] Journal Book of the Rev. W. Dod's House Debating Society.
[2] *The Times* of October 10th, 1889.
[3] The *Saturday Review*, November 16th, 1889.
[4] The *Spectator* of November 16th, 1889.

144

the most valuable contribution to the existing literature on the subject which has appeared in this country for a long time. The literary men say that for style it is excellent, far superior to anything you have hitherto produced. And society (for whose opinion you probably don't care a damn) likes it because it is smart, amusing, and because it gives them a good deal of information upon a subject of which they know very little in an entirely new shape."[1]

Even newspapers which were not in the habit of smiling upon any coming man in the ranks of the Conservative party, and least of all upon George Curzon, wrote cordially of the book. The *Daily News*[2] admitted that the author showed himself a traveller and observer of merit and mettle ; and a reviewer in the *Star* wrote : " Not for a long time have we read so forcible a description of the life of other peoples and of other lands," and concluded with what was doubtless intended to be a high compliment : " Had Mr. Curzon devoted as much time and trouble to the social problems of his own land as he has done to the less momentous problems of the East, we can hardly doubt but that he would be found in the ranks of the party of progress."[3] All this was very pleasing. " Even the *Star* has blessed my book—a second Balaam. Wonders never cease."[4]

[1]Letter from the Hon. S. MacDonnell, February 8th, 1900.
[2]The *Daily News* of December 4th, 1889.
[3]The *Star* of November 30th, 1889.
[4]Letter to St. John Brodrick, January 6th, 1890.

CHAPTER IX

PERSIA AND THE PERSIAN QUESTION

1889–1892

THE next three years were to play a decisive part in determining George Curzon's future career. With a Conservative Government still in power there was little scope for the younger members of the party in the House of Commons, and he found himself free, consequently, to devote himself whole-heartedly to the study of those Eastern problems which had taken so firm a hold upon his imagination.

Opportunities for speeches in the House of Commons occurred now and then, chiefly in connection with academic discussions on matters brought before the House by private members on the days allotted to them at the beginning of each session. In March 1889 he spoke strongly against the payment of members, and in that and the following year he replied to Mr. Labouchere's annual motion for the abolition of the House of Lords. In the press he was still spoken of as destined to play the part of Elisha to the Elijah of Lord Randolph Churchill ; and each fresh rumour of change in the composition of the Government was accompanied by predictions of the offices which he was about to fill. But George Curzon had now definite ideas of his own on the subject, and made light of the predictions of the political prophets. " *Pall Mall* assigns me to Under Home Sec., I see, *vice* C. Wortley. What next ?"[1]

During the spring and summer of 1889 he was busy with his book on Central Asia and upon articles on the defence of India for the

[1]Letter to St. John Brodrick, dated November 13th, 1889.

Reviews. In the *Nineteenth Century* for February he followed up his article on the Indian Frontier which had appeared in the June number, with a corresponding article descriptive of the Russian frontier, his object being to make it clear that while in our own case a permanent frontier had been adopted, in the case of Russia the frontier was still in a state of flux, and that in the movements observable in it from time to time, particularly in the neighbourhood of Afghanistan, Great Britain had " a direct and commanding interest arising from its vital bearing upon the integrity and peace of the Indian Empire." The conditions—geographical, ethnological, historical and political—which rendered some part of this section the least stable were carefully examined, and the British public was prepared for its early repudiation. On the vital question of Russian policy he stated his considered opinion—one from which he never departed until the situation underwent radical alteration eighteen years later as a result of the Anglo-Russian Agreement of 1907. " Russia does not retreat ; she may say, ' J'y suis, j'y reste.' But neither can she stand still. She may also say, ' J'y suis, je n'y reste pas.' Ambition, policy, necessity, Nature herself, call her on ; and she is powerless, even if she be willing, to resist the appeal." And these being the plain facts of the situation, he stated with even greater emphasis the policy which, it was clear to him, Great Britain must adopt. " Instead of nervous anticipation of an advance which we do not mean to prevent and petulant protests when it is accomplished, let our statesmen make up their minds what they mean to hold and what they are prepared to abandon. . . Let a responsible Government declare : ' Thus far and no farther. Short of that point, let England and Russia, so far as it is possible, co-operate. . .' But once it has been passed, let the Foreign Office clerks dry their pens and the historical ' Krieg mobil ' be flashed from Whitehall."

A controversy waged in the pages of the *Fortnightly Review* by two military writers as to our true policy in the event of a Russian advance against Afghanistan provided him with the occasion—of which he availed himself in the March number of the *National Review*—for stating his view of what we ought to hold and what we ought to be prepared to abandon. The follies of the rash offensive advocated by one of the two combatants were ruthlessly exposed ;

the undue caution of the other was suitably condemned ; the golden mean between the two contending views was carefully laid down.

"Let England by all means, in response to Russian aggression, assume the offensive in Afghanistan, as recommended in principle by ' An Indian Officer.' Let her simultaneously either by herself, or through allies, operate against other and not less vulnerable quarters of the Russian dominions as recommended by Colonel Maurice. But, as she is wise, do not let her go on a wild goose chase into the Khanates of Central Asia as suggested by the first. Neither, as she is strong, let her sit twiddling her thumbs upon her Indian threshold as hinted by the second."[1]

In these views George Curzon had the satisfaction of knowing that he carried an appreciable section of informed military opinion with him, for General Sir C. Brownlow wrote: "Your article on our true policy in India is the best exposition of the subject that I have yet read. Since I saw you I have met Brackenbury, and I told him that I thought you knew more about the whole question than any man alive, soldier or civilian."[2]

For the rest he was busily occupied with his book on Central Asia and with plans for a journey to Persia which for a second successive autumn was to deprive his friends of his society. "I am grieved, but not surprised, at your preference of Persia to Scotland ... But I know that there is no use in preaching to you. Travelling is worse than drinking. Take my blessing and come back without another book in embryo. Authorship is killing work."[3]

This was advice which George Curzon had not the smallest intention of following. The whole object of his journey to Persia was, indeed, the collection of material for a more ambitious literary venture, and he threw himself into his preparations for it in a fever of expectation. "I am now making arrangements which are nume-

[1]The "Indian Officer" was, I believe, Sir F. (afterwards Lord) Roberts, Commander-in-Chief in India at the time. At any rate the views set forth were those which Sir F. Roberts was known to hold.
[2]Letter dated April 23rd, 1889.
[3]Letter from A. J. Balfour, dated September 9th, 1889.

rous and complicated. This is my thirty-third letter to-day. I have seen Buckle and am going to send them about one dozen letters, £12 10s. each."[1] He found it impossible to deal adequately with the subject within these limits, and between November and April *The Times* published in all seventeen articles from his pen. They attracted wide attention. From the Foreign Office Schomberg Mac-Donnell wrote, "We are devouring your letters in *The Times*. I was amused a few days ago by receiving a letter from a Scotchman who wrote to beg me not to miss the Persian correspondence in *The Times*, as it was, he thought, the best thing of the kind he had ever seen."[2] But I anticipate.

The traveller reached Constantinople on September the 28th. This was to be the jumping-off point for his journey, and being armed with a red courier's passport from the Foreign Office, he had hoped that he would find the Turkish authorities, if not actively helpful, at least not deliberately obstructive. The Turks had, perhaps, never read Pope's Odyssey ; at any rate, they did little either to welcome their coming or to speed their parting guest. At the very outset the Customs officials snapped their fingers at his vaunted red passport. " They are so proud of having a railway terminus now that they insult every foreign arrival and put him through indescribable tortures in the custom house."[3] It was no doubt all very annoying at the time, but he worked off his irritation in a letter, from the writing of which he derived, we may be sure, a satisfaction which must have made his exasperation, when once over, seem well worth while. "They tore out all my things packed for Persian travel ; they swore the saddle was a new one ; they crashed into my Liebig soups ; they ravished my chocolate ; they made me pay special duty on my Waterbury watches, taken out to conciliate respectable Persian Khans. They made me swear, anathematise, curse, blaspheme, condemn them to a thousand hells of eternal fire ; and after over an hour of this they let me go panting, lacerated, foaming, unsubdued. As I think of it now I still consign them in my choicest vocabulary to the concentrated flames of a thousand Gehennas."[4]

[1]Letter to St. John Brodrick undated.
[2]Letter from the Hon. S. MacDonnell, dated February 8th, 1890.
[3]Letter to Miss Margot Tennant, September 28th, 1889.   [4]*Ibid.*

The Turkish dogs were no more considerate than the Turkish officials, and they shared with them the visitors' full-mounted and comprehensive denunciation—" Those damned Constantinopolitan dogs that litter the streets are howling and barking like fiends outside. How is one ever to sleep ?"[1] These and such as these constituted the petty annoyances of Eastern travel to which he was to become inured before he completed a journey of five months duration, which included some two thousand miles on horseback over the inhospitable post and mule tracks of Persia. " The long desolate rides used sometimes to be odious—4 a.m. till 5 p.m.—vile horses, bad roads, weary bodies."[2] But the bodily fatigue can hardly have been greater than the mental exhaustion. From Tehran he wrote : " I have been resting a fortnight here, if one can describe as rest perpetual audiences and interviews, and note taking and argument and transcribing and all the laborious adjuncts of a journalistic life."[3] But his never failing sense of humour helped to lighten the labours of the cities and the trials of the roads. " Had a parade of the troops in my honour. Commend me to that for a droll situation ! George, the incorrigible and unmitigated civilian, seated on horseback at saluting point by the side of General, evolving discreet comments out of the deep resources of his ignorance and praising the worst army in the world."[4] On the post roads the stolidity of the Persian post-boys was a never failing source of surprise. " Not once in postal rides of over twelve hundred miles did I receive the faintest sign of acknowledgment from any one of these individuals whose stolidity is proof even against the agreeable emotion of receiving a tip, and who never deviate even by accident into an expression of gratitude."[5]

When the chronic weakness in his back is taken into consideration, his Persian journey bears eloquent testimony to his fortitude and strength of mind. When he wrote that the first few strides on each new mount as he sallied forth from each new posting stage provided a moment of acute suspense and that within a few hundred

[1] Letter to Miss Margot Tennant September 28th, 1889.
[2] Letter to St. John Brodrick, November 13th, 1889.
[3] Letter to Miss Margot Tennant, November 18th, 1889. [4] Ibid.
[5] " Persia," Vol. I, page 31.

yards he knew whether the next three or four hours were to be "a toleration or an anguish," there was more behind his pen than a mere semi-humorous recalling of the petty discomforts of eastern travel; and it must have been the realisation of a formidable task successfully accomplished that led him to present to the museum of the Royal Geographical Society " the long Persian whip of twisted leather " which had been his constant companion on his long and arduous journey. At any rate he had only been back in England a short time when he was ordered abroad by his doctor.

The autumn of 1890 was spent partly at Southport, where he took up his residence for some weeks in order that he might devote himself to his constituency, and partly in London, where he set to work on the book which he had planned on Persia. To obtain the undisturbed quiet which he required for this task he took lodgings in Church Road, Norwood, and here he settled down to his work with undiluted satisfaction. "Here I grind, grind, grind, morning, noon and night. I love it. Never was in better health or higher spirits. Row in a boat in the afternoon on the Crystal Palace Lake; have become a thorough and acclimatised cockney. I think of living here permanently in total isolation from the world. There is such a furious exhilaration about one's own society." [1]

The writing of the book entailed strenuous reading and a vast correspondence, for, as he told Sir F. Goldsmid, he was striving to make a book that should be authoritative. He had a great respect for the latter's knowledge, and asked to be allowed to submit the MS. of some parts of his work to him for revision. " For the opinions expressed or inferences drawn I am, of course, responsible and everyone will not be found to agree. But I would not like to be convicted of unsound data." [2] A little later he wrote asking his opinion on a matter of considerable political and strategical importance—" are you in favour of a Quetta-Sistan railway, or do you think it fantastic?" [3] In this correspondence he wrote his mind with complete freedom. "I always anticipate that the next Anglo-

[1] Letter to Miss Leiter, October 13th, 1890.
[2] Letter to Sir F. Goldsmid, October 15th, 1890.
[3] Letter to Sir F. Goldsmid, November 9th, 1890.

Russian row, or an Afghan commotion arising out of the death of the reigning Amir, ought to result in the proclamation of an English protectorate. It is the only method of saving Herat from the Russians. Then and then only we could afford to join our respective railway systems."[1] Reflection seems to have suggested doubts as to the prospect of this solution meeting with favour in responsible quarters, and he added a little naively, " but I fear this consummation may after all be frustrated by indecision at home."

The sense of well-being of which he had written early in the autumn was unfortunately short lived. The strain of his dual task coming on top of the exhausting journey of the previous winter, was overtaxing his strength, and in January 1891 an inspired paragraph in the local press prepared his constituents for a further absence abroad. It was pointed out that travel in the realms of the Shah could only be undertaken with impunity by men of robust health, that Mr. Curzon was not to be reckoned among them, that he had never thoroughly recovered from his exertions of the previous winter, and that he had, consequently, been ordered to spend the remainder of the cold weather out of England.

Enforced residence at St. Moritz did not deter him, however, from his self-imposed labours, and he had not been there long before he was writing delightedly of the progress which he was making. " Vol. I is just about finished, and is going into print. I have written five hundred pages of print since October. Think of that as a manual exercise apart from the composition."[2] And at the end of March he wrote to St. John Brodrick : " I have long ago finished the first volume of my book and have broken the back of my second, and the MS. which I am bringing home would excite an emotion even in a Civil Service clerk."

The tonic effect of the keen, dry air of the Swiss highlands was apparent from the tone of his correspondence, which was soon sparkling with his usual high spirits. At one moment he was making fun of the gaieties of hotel life. " They dance here and act and perpetrate every conceivable frivolity that can accelerate the tomb."[3] At another he was employing his pen to depict the society

[1] Letter to Sir F. Goldsmid, November 16th, 1890.
[2] Letter to Miss Leiter, February 3rd, 1891.   [3] Ibid.

behalf of your utterances that they are *true* is quite inadmissible. in which he found himself. There were some whose sombre taciturnity defied his most ardent attempts at intercourse. " You might be with them in Charon's boat or Elijah's car, and they would never utter." But he found others ready to respond to his own hilarious spirits, and on the whole he found life at St. Moritz " not merely tolerable, but in many respects comic and in some exhilarating." He was, as usual, the moving spirit. " I confess I think I have been rather like a stone thrown into placid waters, for I have ruffled them a bit. Our table at dinner became a centre of rollicking hilarity, while the others combined could barely muster a co-operative smile. We had fun fast and furious, local jokes risible though atrocious, weekly rhymes, sallies and excursions in the newspaper ; comic speeches at smoking concerts and other jests that passed the time, tickled the participants and scandalised the residuum." [1]

During the summer the claims of the House of Commons, of society and of his constituency made large inroads on his time, and work on the book had to be suspended. But the autumn recess saw him hard at work again amid the peaceful surroundings of Norwood, —" And now back to old Persia," he exclaimed with something like a sigh of relief, " with his panorama of mingled splendour and squalor, the superb oriental medley of dignity and decay." [2] A month later he was able to write, " I have been making good progress with the book, of which only two more chapters now remain to be written," [3] and finally, on November the 5th, " the book is all written bar one chapter, upon which I am now engaged. The whole thing will be out of my hands long before the Session begins, and will be in those of the public soon after." [4]

In the meantime mild excitement was caused in political circles by the promotion of Sir James Fergusson from the Under Secretaryship for Foreign Affairs to the office of Postmaster-General, and writers in the press were unanimous in their choice of George Curzon as his successor. To the surprise of most people and to the

[1] Letter to St. John Brodrick, dated March 26th, 1891.
[2] Letter to Miss Leiter, dated September 6th, 1891.
[3] Letter to Miss Leiter, dated October 10th, 1891.
[4] Letter to St. John Brodrick.

indignation of George Curzon's friends, the post was offered to Mr. J. W. Lowther—now Lord Ullswater. " When Fergusson was made P.M.G. all the papers with one accord (I saw no exception) appointed me Under Secretary for Foreign Affairs in his place. . . . It is a bore to lose one of the few things for which I have combined taste and qualification, as the chance may not recur. But I honestly think my friends were more disappointed than I."[1]

He was not to wait much longer for official recognition. On November the 10th, Lord Salisbury wrote to him as follows :—

" Gorst's migration to the Treasury has left vacant the Under-Secretaryship for India. Are you disposed to undertake it ? It concerns matters in which, without any official obligation, you have shown great interest in a very practical way, and it carries with it duties in the House of Commons which some-times involve important issues."

His appointment raised an awkward question, namely, the expe-diency of his publishing as a member of the Government what he had written concerning another country with the freedom of a private individual. Lord Salisbury was doubtful and asked to see the proof sheets of his chapters on international policy and on the Shah of Persia. His verdict was ominous. " I am bound to say that I think the part concerning the Shah cannot properly be published by a member of the Government. It is more severe than I expected when I spoke to you and I have no doubt it would give the deepest offence."[2] But George Curzon was not prepared lightly to forego the fruits of three years strenuous labour, and he promised Lord Salisbury that he would make it clear that the book had been written before he became a member of the Government, and when Lord Salisbury remained unmoved by this concession, he urged that all that he had written was indisputably true. To this Lord Salisbury replied on November the 30th. " I am afraid your feelings to me cannot be those of charity. You must be saying, like Mr. Puff— ' The pruning-hook ! Zounds, Sir, the axe !' But your plea in

[1]Letter to Miss Leiter, October 10th, 1891.
[2]Letter from Lord Salisbury, November 27th, 1891

That is precisely the circumstance that will make them intolerable to the Shah." It was then agreed that the chapter on the Shah should be re-written and the book as a whole referred to an Indian Office referee. " I am much obliged to you for accepting my suggestion in so kindly a spirit and allowing yourself to be Bowdlerised without resistance. I trust Sir Alfred Lyall's mutilations will not be barbarous."[1]

George Curzon had already realised that there were passages which required modification, and on November the 29th he had written : " Here I am tied by the leg and engaged (this is private) in smoothing down all the startling things in the book that might otherwise provoke a splutter. This will retard its appearance, and February will be the earliest date."[2] It was fortunate, perhaps, that the chapter on the Shah had been re-written in what George Curzon called " a lower key," for even the revised version excited comment —" Mr. Curzon's picture of the Shah is no less correct than unpleasant—a callous barbarian in a state of childhood with all the caprice of childhood."[3]

The process of Bowdlerising postponed the publication of the book till May ; but when it did appear it certainly created a stir. *The Times* devoted nearly four columns to it.[4] The *St. James' Gazette* declared that it would at once rank as the standard work on the subject and would greatly add to a high and growing reputation ; *The Spectator* found everyone of its thirteen hundred pages worth reading ; and the verdict of the *Athenæum* was that from its lucid and straightforward introduction to its closing word of caution as to our future dealings with the Shah's Government, Mr. Curzon's latest work might honestly be recommended as a trustworthy, instructive and interesting book. With these and many other notices written in a similar strain before him, George Curzon had every reason to be satisfied ; but when he wrote that the English reviews had been extraordinary in the unanimity of their praise,[5] he was to some extent overstating the case.

[1]Letter from Lord Salisbury, December 5th, 1891.
[2]Letter to Miss Leiter, November 29th, 1891.
[3]The *Echo* of June 2nd, 1892.
[4]*The Times*, May 19th and June 11th.
[5]In a letter to Miss Leiter, July 22nd, 1892.

CURZON, 1892

There was a perfectly natural disposition in some quarters to regard the amount of time, labour and, finally, of print, which he had devoted to Persia as excessive. "Thirteen hundred pages, nearly seven pounds weight of solid print are more than any man without Mr. Curzon's appetite for statistics has the courage to try his intellectual digestion with."[1] And scattered over the book were passages which recalled the assumption of superiority which irritated in the case of his speeches. "Mr. Curzon seems to be under the impression that he has discovered Persia, and that having discovered it, he now in some mysterious way owns it."[2] Moreover, by the claims which he made for the book he definitely challenged criticism, and it was not everyone who was prepared to accept the verdict of the *St. James' Gazette* that the book must necessarily rank as a standard work. "We can admire Mr. Curzon's industry and accept his work with gratitude, duly acknowledging its weight of pages and its wealth of information. But it does not reach the idea of a standard work. The political chapters are generally excellent, and if the whole had been conceived and composed in the same form, Mr. Curzon might have realised more closely his not vainglorious hope."[3]

George Curzon knew quite well that its length must militate against it, and he was as ready as any one to poke fun at its monumental proportions. He wrote to Miss Leiter, who had taken a keen interest in the writing of the book, to inform her that he was sending her a work "whose two ponderous tomes will stagger across the sea and require a truck to convey them to Dupont Circle and a dining table to support them when they get there"; and a little later, ". . . I suspect that while librarians order the work as in duty bound the number of readers who attack those two inordinate tomes is prudently small. Still, the thing is not so much that people should read the book as that they should say that it is a classic— which, after all, is easily done, while perusal is little removed from penal servitude."[4]

[1]*Daily Chronicle*, May 19th, 1892.
[2]The *Sunday Sun*, June 5th, 1892.
[3]Mr. Arthur Arnold in The *Academy* of June 11th, 1892.
[4]Letter dated July 22nd, 1892.

He had from the first discounted criticism on the score of an undue solidity. " I am not writing this book for ephemeral popularity or a good sale," he told his publisher, who was inclined to doubt the prospects of the venture as a business proposition. " It is not a work of travel. It is to be an authoritative work (I trust) of permanent value, which will be read and referred to, twenty, fifty, and perhaps more years hence, when lighter productions that sold well in their day are forgotten." [1] And of the many letters of congratulation which he received he was particularly proud of one from Thomas Hardy, of literary fame. " You have been much in my mind since we met. I had not then seen your monumental work on Persia—which I have done since. The amount of labour and enterprise it represents and the value to investigators of the facts acquired put some of us scribblers to shame." [2]

[1] Letter to Mr. Longman, dated February 20th, 1891.
[2] Letter undated, but with postmark of June, 1892.

CHAPTER X

SOCIAL INTERESTS

HERE on the threshold of his official career we may pause for a moment in the narrative to look a little more closely at the man himself. The years which had elapsed since his Oxford days had been full indeed. Great academic successes had been garnered; strenuous political battles had been fought, lost, and finally won; a recognised position in the ranks of the Conservative party had been gained as the reward of combined brilliance and industry in speech and writing; a comprehensive programme of educative travel had been carried through. And it might well be thought that to such a record there could be little else to add. Unless, however, what has been written of his character and personality in an earlier chapter has failed altogether of its purpose it will have been realised, for reasons there set forth, that a picture based solely on the activities of his public life must provide not merely an inadequate, but a misleading portrait of the man.

"Long before leaving Oxford," wrote a member of the Government in 1891, "the name of George Curzon had become a household word in London society, and for ten or twelve years past he has been a welcome guest in the best literary, political and social circles."[1] No one, certainly, lived more abundantly than did George Curzon, and "no one could turn with more elasticity from work to play."[2] And it was at play and in his intercourse with his many friends when the restraints which always seemed to hamper him in public were cast aside, that his individuality found more ample scope for its

[1] In the *Whitehall Review* of November 21st, 1891.
[2] Lady Oxford in "The Autobiography of Margot Asquith."

expression. Much may be learned, consequently, by watching him at play.

About the time that George Curzon left Oxford there was noticeable a movement away from the rather staid and rigid grooves along which society in the nineteenth century for the most part travelled, and in the direction of the association of men and women on a basis of intellectual comradeship. In 1881 Rennell Rodd had written to him complaining bitterly of the dull materialism of the day. " The last month in London has set me more than ever à l'outrance with the spirit of to-day. . . Of what use is it to gather a society round one of people whose dullness and deadness make the evenings spent with them absolutely barren ?"

But there were already the stirrings of better things, and early in 1886 George Curzon noted in one of his sporadic jottings—made at uncertain intervals, mainly, it would seem, for the pleasure of using pen or pencil at moments when more serious work was lacking—" A. J. Balfour is as usual cynical and charming. He is one of the most attractive men in society, and society just at present is passing through the phase of worshipping intellect." Into this movement George Curzon threw himself with zest, and was quickly recognised as one of its leading spirits. An annual gathering of some of the rising men of the day—H. Cust, Lord Houghton (now Lord Crewe), G. Wyndham, G. Leveson-Gower, Godfrey Webb, Lord Elcho (now Lord Wemyss) and George Curzon among others—which was held at Crabbet, the country seat of Wilfred Scawen Blunt in Sussex, and was known as the Crabbet club, was captured by this new spirit, and became the centre of a sort of dilettante intellectualism which in its turn percolated to a wider circle, infusing an unwonted brilliance into the staid society of the Victorian era.

It was only in the later years of a somewhat chequered existence that the Crabbet club had undergone this striking metamorphosis. In the early eighties it had been a gathering of intimate friends fond of good cheer and indifferent lawn tennis. It had crashed when the majority of its members, who were Tories, had been incensed by the revolutionary activities of their host, first with regard to Egypt, and then in connection with the Irish Home Rule agitation, and finally, in the words of Wilfred Blunt himself, " it was all but submerged by my imprisonment at Galway." A reconstruction of the club after this cloud had blown by was accompanied by a change of orientation. Its new members were for the most part young Oxford men, largely with Home Rule sympathies and with more intellectual tastes than their predecessors. After-dinner speaking and a verse competition with the election of a poet laureate for the year were added to tennis handicaps. The political bias which it had now acquired was discounted by the introduction of new blood in 1889, when George Wyndham, grasping the intellectual possibilities of such a circle, brought in a number of new members with George Curzon prominent among them. The character of the club in this, its final phase, may be gathered from a letter written by George Wyndham to Mr. C. T. Gatty, in the summer of 1890, and from the published pages of Wilfred Blunt's diary. " They (the members) meet to play lawn tennis, the piano, the fool and other instruments of gaiety. To write *bouts rimés* sonnets and make sham orations. . . . You will find young Radicals and Tories, amateurs of poetry and manly sports. The President presides at dinner in the costume of an Arab Sheik, and produces sonnets and shrewd observations on man and nature." The host noted in his diary that the meetings were really brilliant " with postprandial oratory of the most amusing kind," and added that they were productive of " verse of a quite high order."

The club song, sung to the tune of " The Vicar of Bray," is typical of the spirit of light-hearted camaraderie which was the keynote of its meetings :

> " The world would be a weary place
> If wise men had their way, Sir,
> And every tortoise won the race,
> And only fools might play, Sir,
> Against such doctrines we protest
> And vow to live and laugh our best,
> And so we say
> That, come what may,
> Our life shall be a holiday.

SOCIAL INTERESTS

" The lilies of the field are fair,
  They toil not neither spin, Sir,
But foolish man is still in care
  Of what his work shall win, Sir.
This folly needs our loud dissent
In this our club and Parliament,
        And so we say
        That, come what may,
        Our life shall be a holiday.

" Then leave ambition to the schools,
  'Tis good wit gone astray, Sir.
The most of all the world are fools ;
  We will not be as they, Sir.
From all such weakness we dissent
And call on you, our President,
        To move and say
        That, come what may,
        Our life shall be a holiday."

The host's part in these meetings, which, as he confessed, " were essentially convivial," was that of chairman and President, " an anomalous one, seeing that I was a teetotaller, but which yet worked well." His guests played tennis, made speeches and competed for the laureateship. There is nothing in the records of the club which has survived to indicate that the epic of which the following are a few stanzas was judged worthy of a prize, so that it is quite possible that Wilfred Blunt's estimate of the merit of some of the verse for which the club was responsible was correct.

CHARMA VIRUMQUE CANO

Charms and a man I sing, to wit—a most superior person,
Myself, who bears the fitting name of George Nathaniel
  Curzon,
From which 'tis clear that even when in swaddling bands I lay
  low,
There floated round my head a sort of apostolic halo.

CURZON, 1889

At Oxford I made speeches which might well provoke a fit
In persons jealous of the name and fame of William Pitt ;
And if the school's examiners deprived me of a First
It was because with envious spleen those blinking owls were
    curst.

'Tis true that when a seat I fain would win in Parliament
My native county did not smile upon that just intent ;
But when they gave me notice in emphatic terms to ' off it,'
I smiled and quoted from St. Luke a phrase about a prophet.

For me no mean ignoble stage—give me the whole wide
    world—
The seas of either hemisphere must see my sails unfurled.
I have furrowed many an ocean, I have trodden many a land
From Chinquapin to far Cathay, from Fez to Samarkand.

Stanley in Darkest Africa may mix with dusky broods ;
Give me the mystery of the East, the Asian solitudes ;
Ten thousand readers fall to sleep o'er Stanley's turgid pages.
Mine, though uncut, will light a fire for unbegotten ages !

That I am most remarkable there cannot be a doubt,
Although no one remarks it when he once has found me out ;
The only fear to which I own is lest some ass should blab it,
And I should nevermore be asked to lose the prize at Crabbet.

But the Crabbet club was confined to one sex, the revolt against the drab formality of the age was not. George Curzon, as in other things, admired beauty in women with all the ardour of his artistic temperament, and he courted their admiration in return. Not that good looks alone gave entry into the brilliant circle of society men and women which during the last quarter of the nineteenth century sprang up like a rich exotic flower on the arid soil of a stiff and conventional age. Men and women with tastes in common and a mental horizon that extended beyond the restricted world of day to day existence discovered a new zest in life in meeting and exchanging ideas on a wide range of subjects. A number of such persons fell into the habit of meeting frequently at dinner tables in London, at country places from Saturday to Monday, and at certain well-known country houses in the winter. No more formal link than that of mutual enjoyment in each other's society and common affection bound " the Souls," as they came to be called, together.

No one seemed to know for certain who it was who first applied the sobriquet to those who thus foregathered. The credit was sometimes given—and with some probability—to Lady Randolph Churchill. There is, however, no doubt as to the occasion which confirmed them in their title. Ever since his Oxford days George Curzon had been a favourite with those who formed this circle. From them he had received constant hospitality in town and country and as a bachelor he had found little opportunity of making any return in kind for the entertainment which he had so frequently enjoyed. By way of doing something to redress the balance he conceived the idea in the summer of 1889 of inviting a number of his intimate friends—sometimes, though not universally, known as " the Gang "—to a dinner party at the Bachelor's club. It was just at this time that he learned that he and his friends had been christened " the Souls," and that others outside their own circle who were said to resent the claims to a superior culture which " the Gang " were supposed to make, had dubbed themselves " the Bodies." High spirits were not the least of the characteristics of " the Gang," and George Curzon, ever ready with his pen, sat down to write a series of rhymes, in which he sang the praises of each member of the party in comic strain. The opening lines of this rollicking doggerel may be said to constitute the copyright of the erstwhile " Gang " to their new title.

The verses were printed and were fairly widely circulated at the time ; and they were subsequently published by Lady Oxford in her autobiography. The opening stanzas ran as follows :

> " Ho ! list to a lay
> Of that company gay,
> Compounded of Gallants and Graces
> Who gathered to dine,
> In the year '89,
> In a haunt that in Hamilton Place is.

CURZON, 1889

" There, there were they met,
And the banquet was set
At the bidding of Georgius Curzon ;
Brave youth ! 'tis his pride,
When he errs, that the side
Of Respectable licence he errs on.

" Around him that night—
Was there e'er such a sight ?—
Souls sparkled and spirits expanded,
For of them critics sang
That, tho' christened the Gang,
By a spiritual link they were banded."

Then followed a number of stanzas extolling the merits of each of those who had been invited, whether absent or present, and the lay concluded with the following lines :

" Now this is the sum
Of all those who had come
Or ought to have come to that banquet ;
Then call for the bowl,
Flow spirit and soul,
Till midnight not one of you can quit.

" And blest by the Gang
Be the rhymster who sang
Their praises in doggrel appalling.
More now were a sin—
Ho, waiters begin—
Each *soul* for consommé is calling."

After dinner the party repaired to number 40, Grosvenor Square, the home of Sir Charles Tennant, whose daughters were among the most brilliant of those who led the crusade against what a writer subsequently described as " all the solemn pretences that too often make English society a weariness." Here, according to Mrs.

164

Humphrey Ward, who, though not herself of them, was a sympathetic onlooker at their revolt against the tyranny of a too rigid
conventionality, "people were dancing, or thought-reading or
making music as it pleased them." [1]

A similar dinner party was given the following year :

> " A second time these friends are met,
> Again the festal board is set,
> The envy of a world to whet.
> Again 'tis George N. Curzon,
> The author of the original crime,
> The minstrel of a former time,
> Who mounts his Pegasus of rhyme
> And claps his rusty spurs on."

This was more than sufficient to feed the rumours which were
beginning to obtain credence, that in the midst of London society
had sprung up a secret society with esoteric rites, pledged to a
revival of culture based on Greek philosophy. Gossip of this sort
was sufficiently widespread to percolate through to the London and
provincial press, with the result that the dinner party of July the
9th, 1890, obtained a notoriety which must have raised smiles on the
faces of host and guests alike.

" Mr. George Curzon was the most privileged host of last week,
for on Wednesday he entertained that select circle best known as
' the Souls ' at dinner at the Bachelor's club. This highest and most
aristocratic cult comprises only the youngest, most beautiful and
most exclusive of married women in London. Its high priest is
Mr. A. J. Balfour, and its Egeria is Lady Granby. . . Very few have
been initiated into its mysteries. . . Certain intellectual qualities are
prominent among ' the Souls,' and a limited acquaintance with
Greek philosophy is a *sine qua non*." [2]

But "the Souls" were not out for advertisement, and the tinge
of acidity which began to creep into the comments of the press may

[1] A letter from Mrs. Humphrey Ward to her Mother published in her book " A
Writer's Recollections."
[2] The *World* of July 16th, 1890.

be attributed, perhaps, to the disappointed hopes of the baffled reporter. "Despite soulful endeavours to live up to their name, they have failed. The intellects have tailed off, leaving a substratum of fad and fancy."[1] Their alleged claim to intellectual superiority lent itself readily enough to satire—"They are just a little inclined to pose for having invested to a unique extent in the kingdom of mind, and when asked their *raison d'être*, arrogate to themselves as a divine right refinement and intellectual aspiration."[2]

The absurd rumours which thus played around the doings of "the Souls" gave them a notoriety which was neither desired nor deserved. Their tastes were largely literary, and found expression in their activities both grave and gay. A favourite pastime was a game called Styles, which must have been responsible for a prodigious output of humorous doggerel. The rules were simple. Each player was given a piece of paper and a pencil and half an hour in which to compose a poem or piece of prose in the Style of any well-known writer. The resulting rhymes or essays, as the case might be, were then read out, and the winner acclaimed by the votes of the competitors. George Curzon's parody of one of the best known of the poems of Edgar Allan Poe, composed in the course of a game of Styles at Stanway in 1886, must surely have been awarded a prize:

> "I sing of the attractions of the Belles,
>   London Belles,
>   Society Belles.
> Of the manifold allurements of the Belles:
> Oh, what rhapsodies their charm deserves;
> How delicious and delirious are the curves
>   With which their figure swells—
> Voluptuously and voluminously swells—
>   To what deeds the thought impels.
>   How their image in me dwells
>   And inspires the inmost cells
>   Of my agitated brain;
>   Till it whirls and whirls again

[1] The *Birmingham Gazette*, November 3rd, 1892.
[2] The *Queen* of April 14th, 1894.

SOCIAL INTERESTS

With the captivating vision of these Belles,
Country Belles,
Stanway Belles ;
With the vision of these most seductive Belles ;
But most of all they capture,
And with fiery warmth enrapture,
The vulnerable bosoms of the Swells
London Swells,
Society Swells ;
The palpitating bosoms of the Swells,
Country Swells,
Stanway Swells ;
The wild and wanton bosoms of the Swells.

But for all their love of gaiety, they were no idlers, for most of them were ordinarily engaged in serious occupations, such as politics and the law, and they found in one another's society the recreation required to add zest to the business of life. They delighted in wit and repartee, and they talked literature and morals and philosophy and flirtation with equal facility and enjoyment. In such an atmosphere George Curzon was in his element. " There is a *diablerie* about Mr. Curzon's dialogue," declared a contemporary writer, " and a disregard for the personal sensitiveness of others, which sometimes brings upon him the rebukes of his fellow souls " ;[1] and along with " a ready pen, a ready tongue and an excellent sense of humour," with which, with complete justification, he was credited in private life, he displayed " an intrepid social boldness."[2]

He was sometimes accused by his friends of giving too little time to reading. He certainly does not seem to have cared particularly for light literature, even as a boy. " You never read novels, or I could mention some good ones."[3] Neither did he read at all steadily, nor, generally speaking, for the mere pleasure of reading ; but he read voraciously at times, and particularly when he was engaged upon some task—the Oxford History examinations for example—

[1] In *England* of November 19th, 1892.
[2] Lady Oxford in her Autobiography.
[3] Letter from St. John Brodrick, March 10th, 1879.

that necessitated the acquisition of information. When half way round the world in 1887, he mentioned in a letter to St. John Brodrick that he had done a great deal of reading, " mainly of a light though useful character, having read about forty different books." And a carefully compiled list of the actual books read during this journey comprises between fifty and sixty volumes by an astonishing medley of writers—Carlyle and Voltaire, Thackeray and Goethe, Milton and Horace, R. L. Stephenson and Gaboriau, Macaulay and Marco Polo, George Eliot and O. W. Holmes, Charlotte Brontë and Fenimore Cooper—a list which shows, moreover, that his rule excluding novels from his intellectual fare was not without its exceptions. He did, indeed, occasionally come across a novel from the reading of which he derived genuine recreation. "'Monte Cristo' is a wonderful book," he once told Lady Curzon ; " the only novel of inordinate length that I ever read through from beginning to end. I read it daily at dinner time at Norwood while writing my book on Persia." [1] And in after years he found solace during frequent periods of inaction forced upon him by physical suffering, in books. " I wonder if you are well enough to read ?" he asked a friend on one occasion. " If so, even sickness has its consolations."

When he was writing his own books he read as few men could have done. " Of the works, between two and three hundred in number, which have been written in European languages on Persia during the last five centuries, I have either read or have referred to nearly everyone myself " ; [2] and he told Sir Frederic Goldsmid that in addition to the books he had also gone through the whole Proceedings of the Royal Geographical Society, through the Journal of the Royal Asiatic Society and of the Bengal Asiatic Society, of the R.U.S.I., and of the old Bombay Geographical Society. [3] And his reading, when the subject was one that interested him, was done with the most painstaking care. He would settle down with pencil and paper in hand, making notes and criticisms as he read ; and many an author must have been astonished at receiving from him long letters, setting forth not merely his general opinion

[1] Letter to Lady Curzon dated March 15th, 1899.
[2] " Persia," Vol. I, p. 8.
[3] Letter to Sir F. Goldsmid, October 15th, 1890.

of some volume they had written, but minute corrections of textual errors and comments on statements both of opinion and of fact. In 1900, when he was hard at work in India, Lionel Cust had occasion to thank him for a favourable opinion of a small book which he had written on Eton. " As you have been kind enough to *review* my book in private to me, I take the chance, etc."[1] And I can speak from experience, for shortly before his death he sent me, quite un-solicited, some notes which he had made on a book which I had recently brought out on India. His notes embraced references to no less than thirty-six of the three hundred odd pages of which the volume consisted.

But if he was sometimes accused of reading too little, no one would ever have thought of suggesting that he was indolent with his pen. A taste for letter-writing, acquired at Eton and cultivated at Oxford, took so firm a hold upon him that to the normal tale of correspondence which, in the case of most people, is tolerated only to the extent to which it is necessary, he voluntarily added a vast volume of letters of a purely conversational type. From his earliest entry into society he had acquired a habit of corresponding freely with his personal friends, both male and female. And if such inter-course was often concerned with trivialities it was seldom brainless, and beneath much badinage was often to be detected a rich vein of seriousness. Books and politics were discussed equally with persons and personalities. With the talented members of the Tennant family in particular he maintained an animated correspondence. And nowhere is the real man so apparent as in this voluminous written interchange of feelings and ideas. " You were so kind and bright, so easily entertained," wrote Laura Tennant of his first visit to them at The Glen, their country home in Scotland, " that you won a large place in the heart of the everlasting hills."[2] A little earlier she had written to him to tell him of their life at The Glen—"I get up at eight and I read Gibbon before breakfast. I write, yes I write for hours and hours, and seem never to have finished. And I walk. . . . But I must read in this life—that's why I've embarked on Gibbon. Are you horrified that I have never read him ? I suppose it's shock-

[1]Letter from Mr. H. L. Cust, dated February 13th, 1900.
[2]Letter dated September 28th, 1884.

ing. . . . I have read very few novels, but any speculative reading I love. My soul hankers after philosophy and poetry. I am not like you for history, however interesting, sometimes bores me—which is awful, and not to be uttered." [1] And Margot Tennant wrote—" I'm in the last volume of Consuelo, which I've no doubt you know, I like it ever so much. Albert le bon bores me à perir, he's so noble and devoid of humour and so conscientiously refined " ; [2] and on another occasion—" I am reading Ruskin and Dostoievsky's ' Crime et chatiment ' ; beyond that Je n'en sais rien, and my country life, smelling of boots, agriculture and bone manure would not interest you." [3]

His frequent absences from England were deplored—" We all miss you and have come to the conclusion that you *never* must go abroad again. Bring me home an idol of some sort. . . all I can get for you here is love, but so much from "—here follow the names of a number of his friends—" that the envelope would split if I sent it all." [4] And he was equally demonstrative. From Constantinople he wrote : " my heart is bubbling with warmth and bursting with a generous affection for far distant ones, for those I am leaving behind, for the inmates of The Glen. . . ." [5] And a little later from Tehran : " my thoughts strain homewards over the long leagues, and I think of the delicious country house parties, the fun and talking and wild delight." [6]

And never, surely, have the essentials of friendship been put higher than they were in this illuminating correspondence.

> " I am sure that unless a man and a woman's friendship is built on more sure foundation than the appreciation of a good story in common, or a kiss, or a sitting out under the chaperonage of a half palm-hid Venus, or even the love of a poet or a novel, it will not stand—it will fall and sink, or cease to exist. So our friendship must be built on one Faith, one Hope, one

[1] Letter dated August 5th, 1884.
[2] *Ibid.,* August 18th, 1884.
[3] *Ibid.,* March 17th, 1887.
[4] *Ibid.,* September 25th, 1887.
[5] *Ibid.,* September 28th, 1889.
[6] *Ibid.,* November 18th, 1889.

Love. The Faith in the perfectability of Man, the Hope of that Perfectability and the Love of it. Unless we are baptised into that church it is not much good imagining one's friendship will be a blessed one." [1]

It is impossible to draw from the correspondence, of which it has not been possible to give more than a few fragmentary extracts, a picture of anything but a generous, warm-hearted man, eminently companionable, essentially lovable, the very antithesis of the proud and disdainful figure, haughtily reserved, cut off by invisible but none the less real barriers from the generality of his fellow men, which to the public George Curzon appeared to be. Nor was the circle of his personal friends by any means a restricted one. The wide range of his interests brought him into personal touch with men and women in many walks of life. In these days of which I am at present writing he courted the society of men and women in the world of letters. His admiration for the poetry of Tennyson aroused in him a strong desire to make the acquaintance of the poet. And among the many fragmentary jottings which he preserved with his private papers is a vivid description of a day and night spent with the Tennysons at their home near Haslemere in the summer of 1884.

The party was an intimate one of five—the host and hostess, the latter "lying like a pale saint upon her invalid sofa," Eleanor Tennyson, wife of Lord Tennyson's second son, a daughter of Locker Lampson the poet, and afterwards Mrs. Augustine Birrell, and last, but not least, Laura Tennant. After an afternoon in the open spent lazily on a heather-clad hilltop, where the time was passed in desultory talk and in reading " Evelyn Hope " and " Porphyria's Lover," the party assembled for an early dinner. During the meal their host " talked a good deal in a strange gruff voice, told stories and laughed." At nine p.m. Lady Tennyson went back to her sofa and Lord Tennyson to his study, to read or work, the guests remaining downstairs. " How well I remember it—Laura playing to us in the darkness, her little fingers dancing like lightning over the keys." At ten p.m. the party reassembled to drink tea, " and then the real pleasure of the evening began," for Lord Tennyson took up

[1] Letter from Laura Tennant to George Curzon, December 3rd, 1884.

a book of his poetry and read part of " Maud," " Blow, Bugle,
Blow," and " Come down, O maid from yonder mountain height."
" Never shall I forget the last two lines—

> " ' The moan of doves in immemorial elms
> And murmur of innumerable bees.' "

" His reading was a guttural, solemn chant in a rolling resonant
monotone. In one of his own poems he describes it exactly where he
makes a young poet recite his verses ' mouthing out his Hollow
o'es and a'es, deep chested music.' "

The dramatic excitement of the evening was crowned by Laura
Tennant, when for an hour or more " that brilliant child acted to
us, one thing after another of Sarah Bernhardt, with perfect imitation
of style and gesture and, above all, voice."

Among novelists he knew Ouida and Amelie Rives—afterwards
Princess Troubetzkoy—the latter intimately. He was fully conscious of the weaknesses of the former, but gave her credit for one
great strength—pathos. He thought that no one in the world could
read " A dog of Flanders " without crying. He had read Amelie
Rives's " The Quick and the Dead " before he met her, and had
speculated on the character of the writer. This and other of her
books were disfigured, he thought, by sensuous phrases and morbid
turns of thought ; yet he found her innocently unconscious of the
interpretation placed on them by her readers. He described her as
sensitive and highly strung, but talented both with pen and brush—
" she drew exquisitely with a fine pencil point, and her oil paintings
showed character and originality "—and, above all, the purest
minded and least suspicious woman he had ever met ; one who was
shocked by the slightest breath of impropriety. What she lacked
and what she required was a stern literary censor ; and on one
occasion, at least, George Curzon assumed the rôle, for in 1890 she
placed all her poetry in his hands and agreed to abide by his decision
as to whole or partial publication or suppression. He decided on the
latter.

CHAPTER XI

THE WRITTEN AND THE SPOKEN WORD

WE have now seen George Curzon both at work and at play. In the portrait of the man which we draw from the material thus placed at our disposal there stands out a strongly marked characteristic which throughout his life played a strangely determining part in shaping not merely his career, but all his thoughts and actions—a characteristic, therefore, which calls for special consideration. I refer to an intense love of language, which led him to attach unusual importance to the written and the spoken word. He had fallen under the spell of words while still at Eton, and his infatuation had grown with the passage of time, extorting, as we have seen, frequent admonitions from Benjamin Jowett.

The pleasure which he derived from speech and writing made of him a great master of language; but it tended to broaden rather than deepen his mind. He absorbed knowledge rather than evolved it. This need cause no surprise, for it is not necessarily the greatest masters of language who are the profoundest or most original thinkers. George Curzon made no claim to the possession of originality, and was well aware of the direction in which his own strength lay. " I have never claimed the merit of the first discovery in anything that I have attempted in this country," he declared in a speech in India, on February the 12th, 1903. " Wiser brains have started the ideas long ago. . . But at least let me drive the machine a few laps forward in my time." More striking still is an admission contained in a note which he made of his life at Eton. " I particularly excelled in writing Latin verses; not, I think, because I had the least vein of poetry or the smallest imagination, but because I had great facility and command of words." And looking back over the extraordinary record of success which marked his public school career—he won more prizes than had ever been carried off before by a boy at Eton—he came to the conclusion that he must have had "an extraordinary gift for assimilating the contents of books, committing to memory precisely what was wanted and writing just what an examiner required." This would certainly be the verdict of some at least of those who were in a position to form a considered judgment. One who coached him for his final schools at Oxford, while struck by the tremendous power of assimilation which he displayed, did not regard him as a man of any originality of mind[1]—a view which is supported by the weakness in philosophy to which he himself confessed;[2] and a contemporary who was in close touch with him throughout the greater part of his life once told me that his reverence for language was so great as to lead him to doubt the existence of thought which was incapable of being expressed in words.

Yet this estimate of him is certainly not wholly true. Despite his own denial, he did undoubtedly possess the imagination which is so often found in association with highly strung natures. How far it was the outcome of emotionalism and how far the product of processes of thought may be left to the psychologist to determine. But without imagination he could never have developed his overwhelming sense of the romance of Empire ; neither could he have displayed the foresight which enabled him, in the sphere of international affairs, to figure in the rôle of a successful prophet as he did when war broke out between Japan and China, and to frame policies to meet situations which were still veiled in the uncertainties of the future. " I am always looking ahead in India," he told Lord George Hamilton on one occasion. " There is not a day of my life in which I do not say to myself ' What is going to happen in this country twenty or fifty years hence?' "[3] Nor, again, could a man devoid of all imagination have planned enterprises on the vast scale which appealed so strongly to George Curzon. The concep-

[1]Professor Alexander.
[2]See back, page 53.
[3]Letter dated August 29th, 1900.

tion of a great Ceremonial Durbar, unsurpassed in magnitude and unparalleled in splendour, to mark the accession of King Edward VII, was his. He it was, likewise, who planned and supervised and guided to its completion the erection in Calcutta of a noble memorial to Queen Victoria, which took a quarter of a century in the building. But all this is scarcely germane to my present argument, that love of language for language's sake was a striking feature in George Curzon's intellectual make-up.

The delight which he took in highly polished phrases was the outcome, in part at least, of a catholic love of beauty, from which he derived a deep admiration for the Arts. With his emotional temperament he worshipped freely at the shrines of all the Muses ; but his own offerings upon the altar were dedicated more particularly to Calliope and Erato. And as in the case of all passions too freely indulged, from being the servant it sometimes tended to become the master. He knew well the danger of a man allowing himself to succumb to the spell of mere words, and on one occasion at least he adjured others to be on their guard against it. "The first temptation that you should avoid," he told the graduates of the University of Calcutta, when addressing them as their Chancellor at the Convocation held on February 15th, 1902, " is that of letting words be your masters instead of being masters of your words." But knowledge of the existence of a particular pitfall is not always sufficient to prevent a man from stumbling into it ; and George Curzon was himself sometimes accused of allowing his love of language to take charge of his processes of thought. " Mr. Curzon is too apt to follow a rhetorical phrase or an attractive dissyllable. The feeling that he often lets his long words lead him is not one that inspires confidence."[1] When describing the kaleidoscopic scenes of the Orient he certainly delighted in covering his palette with the richest colours. Street life in Pekin, for example, he pictured as " a phantasmagoria of excruciating incident, too bewildering to grasp, too aggressive to acquiesce in, too absorbing to escape."

But quite apart from the criticism to which passages such as this gave rise, that he was sometimes more concerned with his

[1] The *Spectator* of August 25th, 1894.

language than with his ideas, there were certainly times when his passion for composition became an exacting taskmaster, goading him to incessant and excessive labour with voice and pen. To the art of writing he always devoted an astonishingly high proportion of his day. His restless pen, when not engaged in more serious tasks, was the almost constant companion of his leisure hours. He appeared, indeed, to derive positive satisfaction from the mere physical act of writing. From his earliest years, encouraged by his Mother, he took especial pains to cultivate the art of clear and rapid penmanship. " I have been looking through your letter and I have just seen what you say about my *t's*; I will try and make them longer."[1] How well he succeeded may be seen from the diaries which he kept when travelling, for they were invariably marvels of minute calligraphy. Until he became Viceroy of India he had never once employed an amanuensis. " This is my first experiment in dictating a letter," he told the Secretary of State in the opening sentence of his first communication to him after assuming the reins of office, "and I cannot, therefore, say whether it will be a success. You must attribute to the novelty of the experiment any want of cohesion or clearness in what I say."[2]   And all through his life the tremendous and unceasing output of his pen—Despatches, Minutes, Essays, books and letters—was the amazement of all who came in contact with him. He always maintained that by the time a letter or Dispatch had been dictated, transcribed, submitted for correction, corrected and returned for signature, he could have written it twice over in his own hand. And he remained quite unmoved by the comment on this particular idiosyncrasy dropped by a colleague who was taking over an office which he himself had just vacated, that as the business men of England, France, Germany and America—" I do not know about Italy "—dictated letters, he could not believe that they were all wrong—" and George was right." Even during the exacting days of the European War and the even more exacting days of post-war peace, when he occupied positions in the Cabinet entailing unceasing application to official business, it was always with hesitation and misgiving

[1]Letter to Lady Scarsdale, February 13th, 1873.
[2]Letter to Lord George Hamilton, January 12th, 1899.

that he had recourse to the adventitious aid of a stenographer. A perfectly intelligible, but none the less unfortunate, slip in the opening words of a vitally important Despatch to a Foreign Government which, in view of the urgency of the case, he had been persuaded to dictate, did nothing to reconcile him to the employment of such assistance. " His Majesty's Government entertain the sanguinary hope———," he read when the document was submitted to him for approval.

Endless examples could be given of the almost incredible extent to which he burdened himself with wholly unnecessary labour in this respect. When in office nothing exasperated him more than to be asked to append his signature to an indifferently written Despatch. Of one of his subordinates when Viceroy of India he declared —" His efforts at composition have caused me hours of additional labour and moments of agonised despair." [1] And it is impossible to compute the amount of time which he devoted annually throughout his Viceroyalty to re-writing drafts which fell short of the standard of composition which he demanded. In this respect he never altered. The astonished secretary of an important Committee of which George Curzon was chairman when the stress of war— it was in 1916—placed an almost intolerable burden upon all in authority, declares that when taking a draft to him for approval he felt, in spite of his forty years, much like a schoolboy taking a piece of Latin prose to his form-master for correction. You could almost see the gown and mortar-board. Any mistake in grammar, any flaw in good English, was instantly detected and amended. Certain words were forbidden ; sentences that began " last January" were changed to " In January last." [2]

More amazing still, amid the heavy toil of his Indian Administration, he found time one day in February 1905 to write with his own hand a letter of sixteen large quarto sheets to a friend in England, whose assistance he desired in a project for replacing the existing gates into the grounds of Government House with others which should be " worthy of so fine a building as this,

[1] Letter to Lord George Hamilton.
[2] Mr. Clement Jones, C.B., who served as secretary to the Shipping Control Committee established in January, 1916.

11

worthy of their situation and worthy of the official residence of the representative of the Crown in India." These sixteen pages constituted merely the covering letter to a parcel containing three duplicate sets of photographs and papers, which included " a ground plan of Government House compound (as we call it), drawings, elevations and measurements of the deficient gates and gateways, photographs of the same and photographs of the house from different aspects." But the matter did not end here. Later during the same day it seems to have occurred to him that some explanation was, perhaps, desirable of his reason for writing to arrange for the purchase and despatch of the new gates in this unofficial manner, and he thereupon penned a second letter explanatory of the first—" In another letter I have sought your assistance about some new gates for this place. A perhaps more ordinary method of procedure would have been to do, or try to do, the thing through the India Office. In this case there would have been a long wrangle as to whether we ought to have gates at all. This would have gone on for a year. Then there would have been . . ." and so on for four more pages. [1]

What are we to think of such performances ? As examples of incorrigible industry they compel admiration ; yet admiration is inevitably tempered by impatience at the spectacle of a great servant of the State gratuitously wearing himself out by insisting on doing with his own hand work which should so obviously have been delegated to someone else.

This strange delight which he took in travelling over reams of paper with a swiftly moving pen was the outcome partly of unusual industry, partly of a marked distrust of the capacity of others for doing a thing precisely as he wished it done, but partly, also, of his extraordinary love of language. The sound and rhythm which, under the manipulation of a master hand, words and phrases could be compelled to yield, appealed irresistibly to him. Speaking on one occasion of a famous traveller, he said, " One of the great merits of Mr. Doughty is that not only did his journeys provide us with the main authority on the geography of Arabia, but they also presented us with a classic in literature. Mr. Doughty must be tired

[1] Both letters to Sir Schomberg MacDonnell are dated February 16th, 1905.

of being told that his style is reminiscent of the Elizabethan age. I will only say this, that some of his phrases seem to be hewn out of the sheer granite, and when the blow is struck one can almost see the sparks fly forth."[1] And with him the act of writing was complementary to the art of composition. A sunset on an otherwise uneventful day on the Indian Ocean was sufficient to set his pen in motion. "I should not be taking up my pen to write anything about two absolutely uneventful days, were it not that one of them provided a sunset of surpassing grandeur ;"[2] and he set to work to compose a word picture in the pages of his notebook, going over the description with the critical eye of the artist, altering a word here, and the turn of a phrase there, subjecting it to the lapidary work with which he credited Tennyson, whom he pictured " chiselling and polishing " the language which provided his poetry.

" Some of these sunsets on the placid bosom of the Indian Ocean are sights to be remembered. On this occasion the wonder of it did not arise until the fiery ball had already vanished, staining, as it sank, the league-long galleries of the West. Then, as each minute slipped by, some new tint appeared upon that glorious sky-palette which shone with unknown and indescribable colour. Above the remotest sea line, momentarily deepening from azure to turquoise and from turquoise to sapphire and from sapphire to indigo, hung a curtain of saffron that from being pale primrose soon grew yellow as a crocus. Above this the great bulk of clouds were rolled together as though they had been mustered in squadrons and drilled in platoons to do honour to some parting commander. Stately and solid were their ranks, rich and gleaming the panoply, and the upper edges thereof were broken like a storm of penons fluttering in a calvary charge. But the glory did not cease here. For high above their heads floated a whirlwind of colours like silken banners streaming in the sky ; folds of crimson and purple and orange and gold superbly shining upon

[1]Speech at the Annual Dinner of the Royal Geographical Society, May 20th, 1912.
[2]A diary of a journey round the world in 1887-88.

a background of opaline blue and ever fading, ever dying green. Too soon the procession had passed and the pageant was no more."

The high place which he accorded to the art of composition is further illustrated by his Rede Lecture, delivered at Cambridge University in 1913, on the subject of modern Parliamentary eloquence. As he traced the changes which had come over the character of Parliamentary speaking he made clear his regret at the disappearance from it in modern times of classical quotations—" one of the most hallowed and effective implements of oratory "—and of " the imagery, metaphor, antithesis, alliteration, trope," which had been at one time the popular adjuncts of the rhetorical art. He paid his tribute to the intellect and dialectical skill of speakers such as Arthur Balfour, who, he felt sure, had " never consciously cultivated a single rhetorical art," and who could never, except by mistake, have " strayed into a peroration." But he showed unmistakably that while admiring the intellectual gifts to which Arthur Balfour could lay claim, he did not agree with the view which he attributed to him, that it was the thought behind the words that was all important and that the form being accidental, temperamental and secondary, might very well be left to look after itself. His obvious preference was for the studied eloquence of Lord Rosebery, with his great oratorical gifts, his voice " flexible and resonant rather than melodious, gestures bold ,and dramatic, perhaps even at times histrionic, a diction both chaste and resplendent, an exhaustive knowledge of all that is pertinent in literature or history, an exuberant fancy, great natural wit, a gift of persiflage, sometimes almost too generously indulged." His speeches might lay claim to be " both oratory from the effect produced on their audiences at the time, and literature, to judge by the enjoyment with which they may be read afterwards."

He was deeply moved by the mere music of well-chosen words sonorously declaimed, and spoke with admiration of the glowing periods of which Lord Hugh Cecil was capable when the fire of eloquence was ignited on his lips, and the House of Commons was " hushed to silence " as it listened to words that combined " the charm of music with the rapture of the seer." One of the features of a great building that always arrested his attention was its acoustic properties. Overwhelmed though he was by the pure beauty of the Taj Mahal at Agra, he did not fail to take note of its remarkable echo. "The feeblest utterance of the voice is taken up and passed on and swollen in the smooth concavity of the dome by a rolling and musical murmur. . . . A loud note goes echoing on through the gloom overhead, in delicious wave upon wave that eddies round the hollow vault, beginning with the peal of an organ till it dies away in thrills of faint and far off melody." Conversely inattention on the part of a speaker to the requirements of rhythm and sound constituted in his eyes the greatest of rhetorical crimes. He once described a speaker to whose oration circumstances obliged him to listen as " gabbling off his uninteresting and unemotional statement with about as much melody of utterance as a steam roller crushing in the flints on a new road." And on another occasion he said of a colleague—" His statements are of the baldest and most uninteresting description. He never makes ' these dead bones ' live ; but only rattles them together as though he were digging with a pitchfork into a dust heap."

He modelled his own speeches on the style of the ancients rather than of the moderns. Some of his Indian speeches were translated by an enthusiastic admirer into classical Greek,[1] and they lent themselves admirably to this treatment, for the resulting productions were declared by so competent a scholar as Professor S. H. Butcher to contain much that was Demosthenic in idiom and rhythm.[2] On one occasion he regaled—and possibly bewildered—the House of Lords by introducing into a speech of his own a Greek quotation from Herodotus.[3] And there were occasions when his Cabinet Minutes

[1]The translator was Mr. F. T. Richards, a remarkable man employed in the Agent's office of the Great Indian Peninsular Railway at Bombay, who devoted his leisure hours to Latin and Greek composition. He was an excellent scholar, who had read widely and minutely and who kept himself abreast of the best classical works of the day.

[2]In a letter to George Curzon, September 4th, 1906.

[3]κροῖσος "Αλλυν διαβὰς μεγάλην ἀρχὴν καταλύσε. These words were those used by the priestess of Delphi to Croesus before he embarked upon the enterprise which ended by destroying his kingdom. They were applied by Lord Curzon to Mr. Asquith in respect of his cryptic utterances on the intentions of the Government

CURZON

challenged comparison with the work of classical writers. Those
who served in the Cabinet during the war will perhaps remember a
scholarly Minute in which he dealt with the proposed evacuation
of Gallipoli—a piece of prose which must certainly have recalled,
if it was not actually modelled on, the writings of Thucydides in their
original tongue.

His love of language is further illustrated by his passion for poetry.
One[1] who was present at a small dinner at the House of Commons
in 1887, at which books and poetry formed the staple of conversation, describes how George Curzon " boomed out the lines—

'All night have the roses heard
The flute, violin, bassoon.' "

Fifteen years afterwards these lines were still ringing in his ears, and
in a brief moment of leisure in India he jotted down his explanation
of the " extraordinary beauty " of the second line, which so captivated his senses. It was compounded of the labial in flute, the
v in violin and the resonant last syllable of bassoon. He found a
similar charm in the neighbourhood of the *v* and *l* in other lines
from " Maud "—

" In violets blue as your eyes,"
and
" The valley of Paradise."

And he wondered if any one had ever sufficiently noticed the subtle
effect of the letter *v* in poetry, which always produced an effect that
required analysis.

Here again it was the music that caught his ear—the beauty of the
garment in which the message of the poet was clad—more than the
message itself that arrested his attention. He would not himself
have admitted this. Rather did he claim to belong to that school
which neither exaggerating the importance of matter nor idolising
beauty of form, believes that the highest art consists in a harmonious
combination of the two, and that " the greatest poet is he who con-

with regard to Home Rule for Ireland in the course of a debate in the House of Lords
on February the 12th, 1914.
[1]Miss Balfour, afterwards the Hon. Mrs. A. Lyttelton, D.B.E.

veys the profoundest moral lesson in the most perfect artistic shape "—the school which holds that all true poetry " is both intellectual and emotional, the expression of truth as well as the utterance of feeling." And on one occasion at least he definitely dissented from the view put forward by De Tocqueville that poetry was the search and the delineation of the ideal, and that its object was not to represent what was true, but to adorn it and to present to the mind some loftier imagery. [1]

Nevertheless, it was to his emotional nature rather than to his intellect that poetry ordinarily appealed. He discussed such matters freely with his intimates at Oxford—notably with Rennell Rodd, the founder and editor of " Waifs and Strays " ; and on one occasion entered into correspondence with the latter on the subject of a poem on which that cultured undergraduate happened to be engaged. George Curzon had suggested the employment of a richer and more arresting style. The poet had dissented—" I may write on a wrong principle, but I write as I can. . . . Some poems, like those in ' The Earthly Paradise,' are dependent on their story and a certain smooth, picturesque flowing treatment ; others are dependent on the language and certain grand pictures presented one after another to the mind. Such a one is ' Endymion,' which you quote. The story of it is nothing at all, absolutely nothing ; one hardly feels a story is being told. . . . Where the story is so much as I mean mine to be one would hardly be justified in employing such a style in words as would cause you to lose sight of the story." [2]

And George Curzon's comments on poetry were almost invariably concerned with the style as distinct from the matter of the poem. He thought Clough's hexameters unworthy of the name, for the reason that he was constantly making vowels short where they preceded two, three, or even four consonants. In the line ending—

" towers and pillars and domes,"

for example, he thought it atrocious that he should twice make *a* short ; first before *ndp*, and again before *ndd*. Longfellow struck

[1]His profession of faith was made in an article entitled " Poetry, Politics and Conservatism," published in the *Nationnl Review* of December 1885.
[2]Letter from Rennell Rodd to George Curzon, December 1881.

him as being an even greater sinner in this respect than Clough. He stood aghast at the lines from " Evangeline "—

> " This is the forest primæval,
>   The murmuring pines and the hemlocks."

" Look at the horror of *e* short in forest before *stpr*," he exclaimed. Not even the rather slovenly pronunciation and elision of consonants so common in English could justify such violations of the laws of sound. In his view Tennyson alone amongst English poets had faithfully copied the Latin metres. Other imitators were merely trifling with metres of which they ignored the elements. For Tennyson, consequently, he entertained an immense admiration. He took a special delight in his lyrics, which he thought must last, " as long as the English language is spoken and as beauty in diction appeals to the souls in men." He was captivated by the pealing grandeur of—

> " Blow, bugle, blow,"

and the flawless beauty of—

> " Come down, O Maid ! from yonder mountain height."

And he gave a gathering at the British Academy in 1909 a graphic description of Tennyson's own reading of his poems. " The greater part of the recitation," he explained, " was made in a low rolling monotone, which occasionally rose in the middle of a line and fell with almost uniform regularity at the end of the stanza or phrase. It was like some Norse king's funeral dirge."

Another poet from whom he derived infinite satisfaction was D. G. Rossetti, some of whose phrases reminded him of " Tennyson's lapidary work as he chiselled and polished ' The Dream of Fair Women.' " Indeed, of all the poetry with which he was acquainted, it was Rossetti's " Blessed Damozel " that exercised the most subtle and sensuous influence over his mind. He committed it to memory at an early age, and acquired a habit of reciting it to himself during his lonely wanderings over the trackless spaces of Asia—during solitary rides over the plains of Persia, through the hills of Korea, amid the solitudes of the Pamirs. And its appeal was in no way lessened by his realisation of the fact that it was a case, not of artless, but of highly studied perfection. The metaphors employed seemed to him to be magnificent—notably that contained in the lines—

> " And the souls mounting up to God
> Went by her like thin flames."

Here again it was the successful manipulation of words that excited his enthusiasm—" the onomatopœic force describing the upward movement of the words ' went by her,' and, again, ' thin flames,' and the sense of swift motion of flight produced by the aspirate at the beginning of ' her.' "[1]

He was familiar with the two main versions of Rossetti's picture of the " Blessed Damozel," one of which he had seen at the Manchester exhibition in 1887—on the occasion, possibly, of his visit to that city which did so much to establish his reputation as a brilliant platform speaker. His affection for the poem caused him to covet the picture, and on his departure for India in 1898 he left instructions for its purchase, should it ever come into the market.

This fine appreciation of the capacity of language gave to his speeches rare charm and distinction, and great facility in giving expression to his thoughts. Lord George Hamilton once mentioned in a letter to him a conversation which he had had with Edward Clarke, in the course of which the latter paid a great compliment to George Curzon's powers. " I alluded to Pitt as the man who was supposed to be able to dictate offhand a Queen's speech without a moment's preparation. Clarke replied : ' There is a man now in the House of Commons who could do the same,' mentioning you."[2] It is doubtful if he was ever much attracted by the commoner arts of the demagogue ; in later life he made little effort to win success as a popular speaker. But faced with a cultured audience anxious to hear him on some subject in which he was interested, he at once became a commanding figure. The least impressionable soon realised that he was in the presence of no ordinary man. He once said that it

---

[1]The pencil notes from which this is an extract were written on sheets of note paper some time during his residence in India as Viceroy.
[2]Letter from Lord George Hamilton to Lord Curzon, January 5th, 1900.

was his ambition, no matter what he was doing, always to lift it on to a plane above the normal. Few would deny that in the matter of his speeches this ambition was one in which he was frequently successful. There were often passages in them to whose appealing beauty no one could possibly be insensible. This was particularly so in the case of the speeches which he delivered before leaving England to assume the Indian Viceroyalty. To these passages attention will be called in due course. In the meantime we must return to his first official connection with that country in the less exalted position of an Under Secretary.

CHAPTER XII

UNDER SECRETARY FOR INDIA AND SECOND JOURNEY
ROUND THE WORLD

1891—1893

LORD SALISBURY's choice of a new Under Secretary for India was widely discussed. It was not unnaturally resented by those who had hoped to fill the post themselves ; and in such quarters it was hotly denounced as an object lesson for Members of Parliament who, while the favoured individual was holiday making abroad, had been assiduous in their attendance at the House of Commons and had made it a part of their religion to vote straight and hold themselves at the beck and call of the party Whips. It afforded others who had come under the lash of his tongue an opportunity which they were not slow to take, of paying back a little in kind. Prominent among these was his old opponent in the House of Commons, Mr. H. Labouchere. " When I say that Mr. Curzon is about one-tenth as clever as he thinks himself I am paying him a very high compliment indeed " ; and his good wishes took the form of an acid piece of advice. He should carefully eschew his present mode of speaking and realise " that he is not a divinity addressing black beetles when he has to explain the Indian policy of the Government." [1]

But opinion generally regarded the appointment as one of those obviously fit and proper arrangements which so seldom take place in the crooked world of conflicting interests and ambitions ; and the subject of these diverse views found little reason to complain of the reception which he was accorded. " On the whole, the press have been marvellously kind to me, though some killing things

[1] *Truth* of November 19th, 1891.

have been said."[1] The contrast between the real man and the man as he appeared to the public, which has been continuously emphasised in these pages, was brought out by one who knew him, in a letter to the *Pall Mall Gazette* : ".... in one matter may I venture a criticism ? Your article appeared to suggest that Mr. Curzon belonged to the class of academic prigs. . . . I think that opportunity is alone demanded to show that the new Under Secretary for India is not merely an authority on Eastern questions whom men of the highest military position are not ashamed to consult, but a man of delightful and boyish generosity and of bright and daring humour."[2]

Apart from the comments of the press, he received a host of congratulations from men in many walks of life. Jowett wrote— " I have never been more pleased at a political appointment than at yours."[3] Professor Vambery, the Hungarian Orientalist, expressed keen satisfaction. " Lord Salisbury has again shown his great capacity to select the proper man in the proper place . . . . In fact, there was rarely a man more fit for that position than yourself."[4]

Of George Curzon's own feelings of satisfaction there was never the smallest doubt. To have his fingers at last on the keyboard of contemporary events delighted him. " I have so much work that I know not which way to turn. The office interests me enormously, and the old boys there, who were authorities and swells before I was born, treat me with amazing affability. I believe they expected me to walk in and pull their noses, instead of which they meet with ingenuous deference and an almost virginal modesty."[5]

It was not long before he was called on to defend his Department in the House of Commons, for on February the 12th, 1892, Mr. Swift McNeill moved an amendment to the Address, condemning the attitude of the Government towards the employment of Indians in the Public Services. The debate was of small importance, and the new Under Secretary had no difficulty in showing that the mover's information was inaccurate and his deductions, consequently, unsound. It interested the House chiefly because it enabled

[1]Letter to Miss Leiter, November 29th, 1891.
[2]*Pall Mall Gazette*, November 19th, 1891.
[3]Letter dated November 23rd, 1891.
[4]Letter dated November 19th, 1891.
[5]Letter to Miss Leiter, November 29th, 1891.

it to see how the new Minister conducted himself. It was not left long in doubt. "He advanced to the box on the table in front of Mr. Balfour and leaned on its lid as carelessly as if he had been accustomed to stand there all his life ; he even slapped the box with the familiarity of an old friend."[1] He concluded his education of Mr. McNeill with a statement that it would be his privilege before long to introduce a Bill for the reorganisation of the Legislative Councils in India, under whose provisions the number of Indian members would be considerably increased.

But before the opportunity for the introduction of the Bill came he was again challenged by Mr. Swift McNeill, who moved the adjournment of the House on March the 10th to call attention to the alleged inadequacy of the measures being taken by Government to cope with the famine then raging in Madras. The Under Secretary's reply was replete with figures and facts, all of which explained why it was that the charges preferred by the mover were unsupported " by one scintilla of evidence." The motion was withdrawn.

On March the 28th, George Curzon rose to introduce the promised Indian Council's bill. It proposed to enlarge somewhat the existing Legislative Councils in India, and to give to their members an annual opportunity of ranging over the field of administration by means of a general discussion on the Budgets, Imperial and Provincial, and the right of addressing questions to the Government on matters of policy and administration. It was not claimed for it that it was " a great or an heroic measure," but that it was a step in advance which, without impairing the efficiency of Government, would promote the interests of India. It received the blessing of Mr. Gladstone, who went so far as to suggest that an amendment moved from the Liberal benches in favour of a mandatory application of the elective principle in the constitution of the legislative bodies should be withdrawn, a course which was agreed to, though reluctantly, by its sponsor. Thus the Bill received its second reading. " I have had to make a few speeches, but not very many. Still, there is always the office work, which is entrancing. I believe I am the only official who ever said so, and my originality is rarer in not being purchased at the cost of truth. It will be too heart-rending if

[1] *St. James' Gazette* of February 13th, 1892.

they go and turn us out."[1] The Committee ſtage and Third Reading of the Bill were got through without difficulty. " I have so far been lucky in my Parliamentary work, particularly with a Bill called the India Councils Act, which I had to introduce and pilot through the House of Commons."[2]

A General Election was at hand ; but George Curzon could face the future with equanimity. *The Times*, in its review of the Session, had written that as Under Secretary for India he had made a reputation in Parliament quite above the common level attained by subordinate officials ; and he viewed the prospect of an appeal to his conſtituents without apprehension. " I think my seat at Southport is fairly safe. I judge so from the extravagant denunciation of the radical paper, whose laſt number accuses me of brag, bluſter, blatancy, bombaſt, buffoonery, foppishness, malignity and other political virtues."[3] And if his party were to meet with defeat and he were to be deprived of office, there was always the consolation of travel, which the greater freedom of Opposition would permit. " If we are turned out—one laſt gorgeous frolic in the remote and untamed Eaſt."[4]

Matters turned out much as he expected. Parliament was prorogued at the end of June ; the General Election followed in July. George Curzon was returned for Southport by a majority of 604 over Dr. Pollard, the local Liberal candidate ; Lord Salisbury met the House of Commons on Auguſt the 4th, and on a vote of want of confidence moved by Mr. Asquith, was defeated by a majority of forty. On the 13th of the same month George Curzon left England for New York on his second journey round the world. He fled so precipitately that he was up till six a.m. packing, reſted for one hour only, and left London at nine a.m., reaching New York on the 20th. Here he heard of Mr. Asquith's appointment as Home Secretary—" sudden, unsuspected, agreeable to his friends (we sent off a telegram of congratulation) but scarcely deserved, and Labby's exclusion, which afforded me infinite delight."[5]

His friends had fitful news of him, sometimes from an article in

[1]Letter to Miss Leiter, dated March 22nd, 1892.
[2]Letter to Miss Leiter, undated.   [3]*Ibid.*   [4]*Ibid.*
[5]From a diary kept during his journey round the world 1892-93.

The Times, in a series of which were recorded the political results of his wanderings and studies ; sometimes from a hurried letter. " I am just tearing myself away from the fascinations of Japan for the rugged embrace of Korea ; one of the dirtiest and most repulsive countries in the world."[1]

From Korea he went on to China, visiting Peking and other cities. In the reading room of the European club at a small Chinese seaport he came across the October number of *Blackwood's Magazine,* in which he found an article on his book on Persia—" the best and most complete book on any Asiatic State in our language, not even excepting our Indian Empire."

During his travels and enquiries in Korea and China he was accompanied by his old Oxford friend, Cecil Spring-Rice, " the best, cheeriest, most unselfish, most amusing of travelling companions," from whom he parted at Shanghai with unfeigned regret. " For nearly two months we have been together at most hours of the day and night and have not exchanged one jarring word."[2]

His objective was now French Indo-China and Siam, where he found both politics and archæology of absorbing interest. Throughout the journey he made his usual elaborate notes of all that he saw and heard. But he also possessed the art of compassing much in a few terse sentences, and while at Saigon he dashed off, much in the style in which Mr. Alfred Jingle of No Hall Nowhere was in the habit of imparting information to Mr. Pickwick and his friends, a rapid but illuminating outline of all that he had accomplished.

" Oh ! it has been an amazing tour ; all new ; Korea, Peking, Tonking, Annam, Cochin China, Cambogia ; visits to fading oriental courts ; audiences with dragon-robed emperors and kings ; long hard rides all the day ; vile, sleepless, comfortless nights ; excursions by sea boat, by river boat, on horseback, pony back and elephant back ; in chairs, hammocks and palanquins."

He then referred to his articles in *The Times* and declared that,

[1]Letter to Miss Leiter, dated September 29th, 1892.
[2]Diary kept on his journey round the world, 1892-93.

" what with reading, writing and making notes, I doubt if I have ever been harder worked in my life." Finally, he spoke of the famous ruins of the great Khmer Empire, mouldering in the heart of the Siamese jungle. " I have just been up in the interior of Siam to some amazing ruins, the finest in the world. It is a place called Angkor, and there a race that has since perished came some 1,700 years ago from India, founded a mighty empire and built palaces and temples that rival those of Nineveh or Karnak. Now they are buried in a tropical forest, and one has to cut a path with a billhook to see their ruins." [1]

From Siam he travelled direct, making brief calls at Singapore, Penang, Colombo and Aden only. " In six days I shall be in the mill again, and the East will have sunk below the horizon into the fairyland of memory and romance." [2] He reached Brindisi on March the 1st, broke his journey for a day in Paris, and was back in London on March the 5th.

For long the lines of his future career had been acquiring ever clearer definition. It was no longer the Democratic Toryism of Lord Randolph Churchill that filled his mind and absorbed his energies. His enthusiasm for great programmes of reform at home had reached its climax at the Bradford Conference in 1886. With his contact with the lands of Eastern Asia in 1887 a different goal had risen above the horizon of his mind, and from that day onwards he had directed his steps towards it with steady determination and with ever increasing delight, until now it loomed large before him, limned in vivid outline against the background of his life. " Rightly or wrongly," he told his constituents on his return in 1893, " it appears to me that the continued existence of this country is bound up in the maintenance—aye I will go further and say even in the extension of the British Empire." In glowing sentences he proudly proclaimed himself the convinced and fervent apostle of a new Imperialism. When in some distant future Great Britain stood at the bar of history, upon what, he asked, would she be judged ? It seemed to him that the answer to that question could never be in doubt. She would be judged, not by her achievements in the domain

[1] Letter to Miss Leiter, January 14th, 1893.
[2] Letter to Miss Leiter, February 29th, 1893.

of domestic legislation, but by the mark which she had left upon the peoples, the religions and the morals of the world.

"It is remembered of Ancient Greece, not that she invented demagogues and murdered Socrates, but that she taught the first lessons of liberty to the ancient world. It is remembered of Rome, not that her people went to see gladiatorial combats in the Colosseum or that she produced Nero, but that she bequeathed her language and literature to the West of Europe. It is remembered of the Jews, not that they were the most disagreeable and turbulent people upon the shores of the Mediterranean, but that they were the first people to preach to the ancient world the creed of a single God."

So, surely, would Britain be judged and remembered by the manner in which she had exercised the power, " for some peculiar and inscrutable reason entrusted to her by Providence," over the many races which had become the subject to her sway. It was in Asia, consequently, that the burden of her destiny lay. And it was because he held this to be so that for the past six years there had been scarcely a minute of his spare time during which " Asia, its peoples, its politics, its religions, its pursuits," had not been the uppermost thought in his mind.

"It is only when you get to see and realise what India is— that she is the strength and the greatness of England—it is only then that you feel that every nerve a man may strain, every energy he may put forward, cannot be devoted to a nobler purpose than keeping tight the cords that hold India to ourselves." [1]

There was nothing in his daily life to suggest that his many interests had become less. His activity was as great, his versatility, if anything, greater than before. He had not been back in England many days before he became involved in wordy warfare, both in the House of Commons and in the press, with Mr. Bryce, then Chan-

[1]Speech at Southport, March 15th, 1893.

cellor of the Duchy of Lancaster, over his appointments to the
Southport bench. And no sooner had he finished with Bryce than
he found other lists to enter, " My row with Bryce being over, I
am involved in various other buccaneering pursuits—ungallantly
denouncing Lady Geographers in *The Times*, picking a bone with
Edmund Gosse, the critic, on a point of Egyptian archæology in the
Athenæum, and demolishing French claims to absorb Siam in the
nineteenth century." [1]

But such things tended more and more to become side issues,
while the main stream of his desires flowed in ever-increasing
volume in the direction of service in the wider fields which the
Empire offered. And there were times when he girded fiercely
against the constant demands which Parliamentary life made upon
his time and energies. " Oh ! you can't imagine the weary, weary
strain of daily letters. I cannot afford a secretary sufficiently intelligent to be of real use, and every day I have to sit down to some
three hours of weary plodding. . . Thus, next week I have got to go
away making long speeches in the country. And all this while I
have four or five articles on hand for magazines, lecture for the
Royal Geographical Society ; business of boards, and the Lord
knows what." [2]

It would have been futile to point out to him that much of the
work of which he complained was of his own making. He could no
more change his nature than the leopard his spots. His passion, not
merely for work, but for the thorough and detailed discharge of
every task that his restless fancy seized upon, pursued him with the
relentless tenacity of the Eumenides.

From his earliest days he had viewed with real apprehension a
growing tendency to break down the natural barriers between the
two sexes. And he opposed on principle any step which he
suspected of leading in that direction. " The Terrace of the House
is as crowded with women as the Royal Enclosure at Ascot," he
complained, " and the encroachments of the sex fill me with indignation which no blandishments can allay." [3] When, therefore, it

[1]Letter to Miss Leiter, June 4th, 1893.
[2]Letter to Miss Leiter, dated March 26th, 1893.
[3]Letter to Miss Leiter, dated June 21st, 1893.

was proposed to admit women to membership of the Royal Geographical Society, it was inevitable that he should throw himself heart and soul into a campaign against so sacrilegious a suggestion. In this matter he still stood precisely where he did when as an undergraduate he had opposed the admission of women to the library of the Oxford Union. In some of his letters to the press he was not a little contemptuous of the powers of women. He contested *in toto* their general capability " to contribute to scientific geographical knowledge." He was convinced that " their sex and training rendered them equally unfitted for exploration " ; and he regarded " the genus of professional female globe-trotters with which America has lately familiarised us as one of the horrors of the latter end of the nineteenth century."[1] But at the special General Meeting of the Society, which was held on July the 3rd to consider Lord Mayo's proposal for the admission of women on the same terms as men, he based his opposition chiefly on the ground of principle. Any success gained by the movement which sought to break down sex distinctions would prove, not so much injurious to men as disastrous to women. Voting on the question was close, but Lord Mayo's motion was defeated by a majority of fourteen.

> " I have pulled off my combat against the ladies at the Royal Geographical Society successfully, having won at the second and final meeting by a vote of 172 to 158. All the papers are very much down on me since ' woman's emancipation ' is the fashionable tomfoolery of the day. The funny thing is that I won it by argument, as I made a sensible speech, while the other people with far the easier case to defend, failed deplorably."[2]

In the meanwhile public attention was being drawn to parts of the world from which George Curzon had recently returned and in which he was profoundly interested. By the demands for territorial concessions which France was making on Siam she succeeded in arousing serious apprehensions in Great Britain ; and George Curzon, fresh from his study of the question on the spot, was in

[1] Letter to *The Times* of May 31st, 1893.
[2] Letter to Miss Leiter, dated July 9th, 1893.

much demand as a writer. " Siam has turned up as the question of the hour, and inasmuch as I am the only man in England who has been to all the countries concerned . . . it gives me a position of authority which questions in the House, letters in *The Times* and articles in the magazines assist to fortify, and which procures me even the notice and denunciation of the Parisian press." [1]

In the *Nineteenth Century* for July he explained the facts of the problem, and in August the same publication accorded pride of place to an article from his pen, setting forth the nature and gravity of the issue as it affected Great Britain. In its broad outlines the question was a simple one. Just as it was essential that Afghanistan should stand as a buffer between India and Russia on the west, so was it of the highest importance that Siam should serve the same purpose between France and the Indian Empire on the east. There was something sinister in the coincidence that while the Cossack was patrolling the Pamirs on the north-west, French gun boats were threatening Bangkok on the south-east. For this startling display of force on the part of France was the final assertion of claims which she had been industriously pushing to territory owned by Siam. Though her lawful boundary lay well to the east of the Mekong river, she was claiming that river and all the territory east of it as her own. " To support this patriotic theory maps have to be specially constructed, history re-written and political jurisdiction invented, processes from which the French imagination is the last in the world to recoil ; although it is unfortunate for the success of the design that among these constructive artists no two agree in their palimpsest, either of history or geography." [2]

The question, however, was not so much one of the methods by which the French Colonial party sought to justify the claims which they advanced as of the steps which the British Government were prepared to take to protect British interests. The need for definite action was imperative.

" It is serious enough that we should now be spending millions to counteract a Russian aggression on the one side

[1] Letter to Miss Leiter, dated July 24th, 1893.
[2] *Nineteenth Century*, for July 1893.

which our predecessors were blind enough and ſtupid enough
to deny. It would be criminal to repeat the error by a like
indifference to French aggression on the other side, againſt
which we are thus fully and early forewarned. The maintenance
of Siam as a buffer State is essential in the intereſts, not merely
of that country nor even of the Indian Empire, but of the peace
of the entire eaſtern hemisphere." [1]

It is a not unwarrantable assumption that Lord Rosebery's
Government were as anxious to ſtave off the peril as their critics. At
any rate, on July the 31ſt a Protocol was signed between Great
Britain and France, in which the principle of a buffer State was
accepted, and at a point north of Siam, where French territorial
claims brought her into direċt contaċt with the Burmese frontier, the
creation of a small neutral State decided on. But the assent of France
had been secured only at the expense of large concessions by Great
Britain—the price of what George Curzon regarded as the ineptitude
if not the positive apathy of the Liberal Cabinet. " The Siamese
tragedy is now, I suppose, over. I raised a debate about it in the
House yeſterday. France has behaved criminally, England weakly,
Siam foolishly ; and when folly, weakness and crime are in competition, it is the laſt named, as a rule, that wins." [2] And he did not
hesitate publicly to accuse the Government, not merely of declining
to interfere, but by their apathy of aċtually encouraging France in
the course upon which she had embarked.

Before the conclusion of the Protocol of July the 31ſt he had
urged that no weak concession to sentiment nor fear of decisive
aċtion should induce the British Government to acquiesce in, much
less to precipitate, the approach of France to the Indian frontier.
After he had become acquainted with its terms he declared that the
French, owing to apathy on the part of the British Government,
had got far more, not only than they had a right to, but more than
they had ever expeċted to get, and far more than their leading men
on the spot had imagined that the British people would acquiesce
in their obtaining. The result had been that " British preſtige—and

[1]*Nineteenth Century*, for July, 1893.
[2]Letter to Miss Leiter, dated Auguſt 3rd, 1893.

it is upon prestige that Empire depends in the East—has suffered greatly in these regions ; grave peril has been inflicted upon the interests of British commerce, and we have been brought by so much the nearer into approximate contact with the great Power whose interests in the East are, as in many other parts of the world, antagonistic to our own." [1]

CHAPTER XIII

THE PAMIRS AND AFGHANISTAN

1894-95

On the prorogation of Parliament George Curzon turned with relief to the book which he had planned on China and Korea. " I have begun writing my book on the Far East," he told Miss Leiter. " But there is no way to do it properly except absolute retreat as at Norwood. . . . In London one can never get two consecutive hours."[1]

He very soon become absorbed in the work. " I have been sitting tight, Oh ! so tight, working sometimes ten to twelve hours a day. No dinners out, no society, no pleasures but the greatest of all—solitude."[2] As he progressed he found it inconvenient to treat the whole of the countries of which he wished to write in a single volume ; and he decided to bring out in the summer or autumn, as a first series of the problems of the Far East, a volume on Japan, Korea and China, to be followed later by a second series embracing Tonking, Cochin China, Combojia and Siam. On March the 11th, he wrote, " I have finished my book, ' Problems of the Far East,' first series." It was unfortunate that circumstances prevented him from ever completing the second series which would have dealt with countries less well known than those which formed the subject matter of the first. For some years he clung to the hope that he would find time to write it, but eventually gave it up. " I am afraid my ' forthcoming volume on Tonkin ' will never forthcome at all," he informed Mr. Colles who at that time acted as his

[1] Letter to Miss Leiter, November 12th, 1893.
[2] Letter to Miss Leiter, February 4th, 1894.

literary agent. " Not a line of it is written nor, 1 fear, now ever will be." [1] Some small part of the material which he had collected for it formed the basis of a chapter on the capital of Annam in the posthumous volume entitled " Leaves from a Viceroy's Notebook," published in 1926. But except for this and the articles which he wrote on the Siamese question at the time, both the material which he collected and the thought which he gave to it were lost to the public.

The volume which he succeeded in completing certainly made its appearance at a most opportune moment. War had just broken out between Japan and China over Korea, a convulsion which immediately focussed the attention of Europe upon the three countries with which the book dealt. *The Times* which had published a series of articles from his pen while his journey was in progress, at once threw its columns open to him as an admitted authority on Far Eastern questions and the appearance of his own book was heralded by two long letters to that journal in which he set forth the underlying causes of the conflict and discussed the probable course of the war and its consequences. The picture which he painted of the Government of Japan confident in the newly acquired efficiency of her military forces, ambitious and aggressive, engineering an adventure abroad which, by reviving dormant historical memories, would appeal to the patriotism of her people and distract their thoughts from political difficulties at home, excited lively interest. His rehearsal of events up to the moment of writing, fortified by such definite statements as that ten thousand Japanese troops had been despatched to the scene of action—" one soldier to protect every Japanese resident in Korea"—created confidence in his knowledge of what was happening; and his judiciously balanced assertion that while the Japanese forces both naval and military were greatly superior in effectiveness to those of the Chinese, the resources of the latter were illimitable and her patience profound, stimulated a desire for further and more detailed information.

When, therefore, the book appeared a few days later, it was seized on with avidity and was discussed at length both in the daily press and the weekly Reviews. The widespread interest which it

[1] Letter dated April 8th, 1897.

excited was not altogether due, however, to the circumstances attending its publication. That it was the outcome in part at least of the personality of its author is apparent from the nature of the reviews themselves, for it is impossible to read the extraordinarily conflicting opinions which it elicited without suspecting that some at least of those who were ostensibly reviewing a book were in reality dissecting an individual. The member for Southport had in fact become so dynamic a figure in Parliamentary life that in the eyes of many people George Curzon the writer on Imperial questions was tarred with the same brush as George Curzon the puissant knight of the party arena. And even where party bias was absent his personality obtruded itself in his writings and excited the same strong feelings of attraction and repulsion that it did in the many other fields of public activity in which he engaged. A reviewer in the *Literary World* wrote in a strain of high praise of the style and matter of the introductory chapter ; a critic in the *Daily News* dismissed it contemptuously as unnecessary histrionics, though " not altogether out of keeping with the unrelieved commonplaceness of Mr. Curzon's literary manner."[1]

Those who differed from his views but devoted their comments to the book rather than to its author arrived at a much juster estimate of its merits. A writer in the *Westminster Gazette* found the volume both picturesque and philosophical and freely forgave the author " the touch of the Corinthian in his style for the numerous merits which his travel record " possessed. He found a little too much of the Imperialistic spirit in Mr. Curzon's writings ; but apart from his views on questions of high policy, he confessed that his books showed " so much knowledge, industry and close observation that the carping critic " was fairly disarmed.[2] It was precisely the Imperialism from which the *Westminster Gazette* dissented that appealed most strongly to *The Times*. " Faith and pride in the British Empire are, indeed, predominant in Mr. Curzon's book, as they must always be in the hearts and minds of all who know of Great Britain's work in the East." And it seemed to the reviewer that he

[1]The *Daily News* of February 20th, 1896. The two reviews here referred to were written of the fourth edition of the book, issued in 1896.
[2]*Westminster Gazette*, August 21st, 1894.

was not only " an adventurous traveller with a keen eye for all that is interesting and picturesque and a skilful descriptive writer," but that he was endowed with the far rarer faculty of " insight into the political and social conditions of the countries he visited."[1]

The same striking differences of opinion were noticeable in the comments of the weekly Reviews. The *Saturday Review* saw in the book a marked advance on his earlier work on Persia. " There is, for one thing, much less of the controversial matter, which was a somewhat tiresome feature of that work. Our attention is more exclusively directed to the matter in hand and less to Mr. Curzon's unique and meritorious knowledge of it."[2] The *Spectator*, on the other hand, was both patronising and critical. Mr. Curzon was no doubt " a diligent collector of facts," but he did not possess " that instinctive appreciation of international affairs which is requisite for those who undertake to diagnose the conditions of three such kingdoms as Japan, Korea and China." And having thus disposed of his pretensions to form a judgment of any value, the writer proceeded—unwisely as it turned out—to devote the greater part of his article to combating one of the main contentions running through the book. " Mr. Curzon's view of China is that though China has a great deal of latent strength she is in no sense the formidable Power she has been represented." This view was then, with the aid of a quotation from Lord Wolseley, dismissed as being little worthy of consideration. " Mr. Curzon infers that the Chinese are a very unwarlike people. The world will, we think, prefer the verdict of a soldier who has met the Chinese in battle to that of a civilian who has done little but sniff the evil odours of Pekin and, as he would doubtless be the first to admit, has nothing that can be called first-hand knowledge of China."[3]

On the whole the public showed a truer appreciation of the merits of the book than some of its reviewers. St. John Brodrick wrote to him in India, giving him the impressions of the book which he had been able to gather. " I think it has put a finishing touch to the conviction that you are a master of Eastern affairs and

[1] *The Times*, August 20th, 1894.
[2] *Saturday Review* of August 25th, 1894.
[3] The *Spectator* of August 25th, 1894.

PLATE VI GILGIT, 1894, *en route* FOR THE PAMIRS

Col. N. Chamberlain. Hon. G. Curzon M.P. H. A. Lennard. P. N. L...

raised your already high reputation to the pinnacle which endures."[1]
From the other side of the world he received equally gratifying
testimony. "I will tell you about your book here," wrote Cecil
Spring-Rice from Washington. "It has been continually open in
the U.S. State Department as well as quoted in the papers."[2] And
these indications of its success were confirmed by the demand for
it on the part of the public. It quickly ran through three editions,
and when two years later George Curzon had the satisfaction of
learning that a fourth and revised edition was called for, he had the
additional satisfaction of appearing before the public in the rôle
of a successful prophet. He would have been more than human if,
in these circumstances, he had refrained from making use of the
opportunity with which fate had furnished him, of a polite retort to
his previous critics. After reminding his readers of the central
theme of the book when first published, namely, the utter rottenness
of Chinese Administration and the certainty of military disaster in the
case of conflict with a well-equipped foe, and recalling the scepticism
with which these views had been received in some quarters, he
permitted himself the following comment : " Somehow or other
the evil odours of Pekin seem, after all, to have left a correct impression upon my civilian nostrils ; and so fair-minded a critic as the
Spectator will not, I am sure, grudge to a writer who has dared to
prophesy the rare satisfaction of success."[3]

A writer in the *Academy* had said, when the book first came out,
that it would not be the author's fault if it did not keep its place
permanently among standard authorities upon the peoples and
politics of the Far East. It may certainly be said to have done so,
for there is in George Curzon's handwriting a note of the royalties
which he received on it which shows that its sale continued steadily
year by year for ten years from the date of its first publication to
1903, when the fourth edition was presumably exhausted.

These references to " Problems of the Far East " have carried us
into the future, and we must now return to pick up the thread of the
narrative where we dropped it in the Spring of 1893.

[1]Letter dated, October 8th, 1894.
[2]Letter dated March 1st, 1895.
[3]Preface to the fourth edition.

CURZON, 1891-1894

George Curzon's whole outlook at this time was dominated by a determination to visit the Pamirs and Afghanistan. He was obsessed with the idea that failing such a journey the elaborate programme of Asiatic travel which he had mapped out for himself would be incomplete. And to leave any task unfinished was to George Curzon little better than to fail altogether. This explains the sacrifices which he made in order that he might carry it through, and the stubborn determination which he displayed in breaking down one by one the obstacles which kept cropping up in the way of its accomplishment. For years past he had been gathering information concerning the Pamirs and on a day of comparative leisure on an Atlantic liner in 1892 he had collated the material which he had collected. "I have done a lot of work," he noted in his diary, "having gone through and annotated all my Pamir notes and extracts accumulated for the past six years." And as far back as the beginning of 1891 he had written to Lord Lansdowne, then Viceroy of India, informing him of his desire to visit India the following winter with the ulterior object of making his way "as a private and unofficial tourist," into Afghanistan. The reply which he had received had not been very encouraging. As a Member of Parliament he could not hope to figure in the eyes of the Amir as a private traveller; and in any case experience had shown that the Amir's unwillingness to admit any Englishman into Afghanistan was not likely to be easily overcome. The Viceroy had added that he was himself most anxious to see some departure from the attitude of aloofness which that potentate had adopted, and with this object in view was hoping either that the Amir would consent to pay a visit to India, or, alternatively, that he would be willing to receive a Mission from the Indian Government in his own country.

In face of these difficulties George Curzon had given up his idea of visiting India in 1891. But he had kept both the Pamirs and Afghanistan constantly in mind, and having successfully carried through his second journey round the world, had determined to concentrate his energies on bringing off this final expedition. There were now, however, in addition to local difficulties in India, the uncertainties of the political situation at home. "People say," he wrote in June 1893, "that we are beginning to make some impression on the Government. . . . Their majority is dwindling and the spirit of their followers is not high." And early in 1894 these uncertainties were added to by rumours of Mr. Gladstone's impending retirement. " All the world is agog about the old man's resignation. He is supposed to have made his last speech as Prime Minister yesterday and to have gone down to the Queen to-day to resign."[1] He thought that this must mean an early appeal to the country ; but the situation changed from day to day, and the political prophets were at a discount. On March the 11th he wrote : " The political world here is so full of uncertainty that from week to week one cannot tell what the day will bring forth. Gladstone's retirement and Rosebery's appointment have had the curious and paradoxical effect of temporarily strengthening their party."[2] Less than a month later the pendulum had swung back again—" The Government is going badly, and things look as though they were drawing on towards a smash."[3]

Nevertheless, he continued his preparations. The mission of which Lord Lansdowne had spoken in 1891 became an accomplished fact in the autumn of 1893. But Lord Lansdowne's term of office was then drawing to a close, a Liberal Government was in power at home, and George Curzon's request to be permitted to accompany it had been refused by an unsympathetic Secretary of State. He had determined, therefore, to see what he could do by direct appeal to the Amir himself, and in April had written him a letter in which he set forth his desires. A copy of the original draft, which covered seven sheets of foolscap in his own hand-writing, was engrossed on vellum and despatched to the Amir through the hands of Sir T. S. Pyne, then in the service of the latter at Kabul. It was a masterly document. The opening paragraphs were devoted to a lengthy statement of the writer's admiration for the Amir, of his feelings of affection for Afghanistan and of the consistency—liberally fortified with judiciously selected extracts from his speeches and writings— with which he had urged his countrymen at all costs to uphold the integrity and independence of that country. The ground

[1]Letter to Miss Leiter, March 2nd, 1894.
[2]Letter to Miss Leiter, March 11th, 1894.
[3]Letter to Miss Leiter, April 8th, 1894.

having thus been suitably prepared, he came to the heart of the matter :

> " Throughout this time it has been my principal and incessant desire to be permitted to visit the dominions of Your Highness ; so that I might both offer my salaams to the powerful and liberal minded Sovereign of whom I have so often written and spoken ; and also that I might be able to stand up in the British House of Commons, when the affairs of India and Afghanistan were being discussed, to silence the mouths of the slanderers and to say to the British Government and the British people : ' I have myself been to Kabul as the guest of His Highness the Amir. I have conversed with this great Sovereign. I can speak for his sentiments. I desire to protect his interests.' Khorasan I have seen and visited ; I have been in Bokhara and Samarkand. I have ridden to Chaman, and I have sojourned at Peshawar. But the dominions of Your Highness which are situated in the middle of all these territories like unto a rich stone in the middle of a ring, I have never been permitted to enter ; and the person of Your Highness which is in your own dominions like unto the sparkle in the heart of the diamond, I have not been fortunate enough to see. Many books and writings I have studied and have talked to many men ; but I would fain converse with Your Highness, who knows more about these questions than do all other men, and who will perhaps vouchsafe to throw upon my imperfect knowledge the full ray of truth." [1]

It was not enough, however, that he should obtain the consent of the Amir. No sooner had it become known that George Curzon had decided to make the attempt to reach Kabul than opposition in official quarters hardened. " I am terribly worried, the Russian Government having made spiteful and frivolous objections to my journey. Rosebery backs me up ; but Kimberley has developed the obstinacy of mulish ignorance." [2] He had arranged to leave

[1] Part of the above extract, together with a brief account of the circumstances in which his visit to Kabul was undertaken, appeared in a chapter on the Amir of Afghanistan in " Tales of Travel," published in 1923.

[2] Letter to Miss Leiter, dated July 10th, 1894.

England on August the 4th, and as the hour of departure approached opposition gathered strength. " Everybody is worrying, worrying, worrying about my journey and trying to put spokes in my wheel. The Viceroy has sent an idiotic telegram from India. The fact is none of these Government officials wants me to do a thing that they never have been able to do themselves, and all the forces of red tape are against me." [1]

On arrival at Bombay he was met by letters and telegrams informing him that it was useless his proceeding, since the Government of India were convinced that his proposed journey was undesirable from every point of view. All this merely stimulated him to increased activity. Letters and telegrams were brushed aside ; without an hour's delay he left Bombay, spent two days and three sleepless nights in the train, and then drove sixty miles to Simla, reaching his destination on the third day after leaving Bombay. Here he pleaded his cause in person—first with General Brackenbury, whom he knew, and then with the Viceroy, begging the latter to submit his case once more to Council. " This he did, being himself all along rather in my favour. My host (General Brackenbury) backed up the proposal, and the Council, which a fortnight before had decided *nem con* against it, finally acquiesced." [2] His point once gained, there was nothing to keep him longer in Simla, and he hurried back to rail head at Kalka and thence to Rawal Pindi. From his railway carriage he wrote on August the 25th :

> " I am now trailing up through sweltering heat to Rawal Pindi whence I hope to cover the two hundred miles that separate me from my companion in Kashmir in three days, part driving, part riding. The result, however, of all these delays before and hurry now is that it will be very difficult to get the camp together, and that I have no time to get a native servant, which is quite indispensable. How far these and other remaining obstacles will still retard my journey I cannot say. But it can scarcely be that after vanquishing so much I should still have to face failure."

[1] Letter to Miss Leiter, dated July 17th, 1894.
[2] Letter to Miss Leiter, August 25th, 1894.

He was right. Before he left Kashmir he received the Amir's invitation to visit him at Kabul ; and before the end of the year he had visited the furthermost outposts of the Indian Empire in the secluded valleys of the Hindu Kush ; had crossed its outermost boundary on the frozen fringes of the Pamir ; had located the hidden sources of the Oxus river ; had pitched his tent in the heart of Afghanistan, and had returned triumphant to India, carrying in his pocket the Amir's written acceptance of the official invitation which had been extended to him six months earlier to visit England. The whole enterprise affords an excellent example of what, all through his life, he was able to accomplish by sheer determination not to accept failure. " You have certainly had a marvellous success," wrote St. John Brodrick, on December the 27th, 1894, " and, as I told you (unlike your other journeys), you have had an admiring public here watching all your movements. To-day for instance, there is a laudatory leader in the *Morning Post*, and the paragraphs are countless."

From every point of view the achievement was a remarkable one. Some part of the journey entailed no little physical hardship and demanded considerable stamina. " Melting as I now am," he wrote from the sweltering heat of the Punjab, " on this day a month hence I should probably give the half of what I possess in the world to feel even moderately warm " ; and he added whimsically—" Why travellers do these things no one knows ; least of all the travellers themselves." [1] In the course of the double journey to the Pamirs and Afghanistan he covered on foot or on horseback close upon eighteen hundred miles, much of it over some of the worst mountain track in the world. During the Pamir section of the journey he averaged over twenty-one miles a day during fifty-four marching days, and in Afghanistan his daily march average was twenty-seven miles ; a performance all the more creditable in view of the fact that he started the journey handicapped by a recently sprained ankle.

The work of exploration in the Pamirs for which he was awarded the gold medal of the Royal Geographical Society was described in three papers in the Geographical Journal for July, August and September 1896. They excited the highest admiration of the Presi-

[1] Letter to Miss Leiter, August 25th, 1894.

dent of the Society, Mr., afterwards Sir Clement, Markham, who declared that he could not recollect any paper in the whole series of the Society which displayed such exhaustive knowledge and critical power and which would be of equally permanent value to geographical students. "I wish with your concurrence," he wrote on September the 21st, 1896, "to propose to the Council that the three parts should be published as a small separate volume, for they are much too valuable to be buried in a periodical, and ought to be in a form which will be more accessible." This was done, and the volume itself was reprinted two years later.

The grandeur of the scenery provided an apt subject for the descriptive writing that appealed so strongly to him. Of the Hunza valley above Gilgit he wrote that it was undoubtedly one of the most remarkable scenes in the world. "Nature seems to exert her supreme energy, and in one chord to exhaust almost every note in her vast and majestic diapason of sound. She shows herself in the same moment tender and savage, radiant and appalling, the relentless spirit that hovers above the ice-towers and the gentle patroness of the field and orchard, the tutelary deity of the haunts of men."

But his Monograph was far more than a descriptive narrative of his journey. It comprised learned disquisitions on the origin and meaning of names such as Pamir and Oxus ; useful information about the climate and fauna of the locality ; an elaborate and closely reasoned argument in support of his contention that a stream issuing from two ice caves at the snout of a glacier two thousand feet below the Wakjh-jir pass in the Wakhan Pamir, west of the Tagdumbash, was the true source of the river ; and finally an exhaustive account of the travellers of various nationalities who from the commencement of the Christian era were known to have visited the region. It was characterised by " the ability and completeness with which," in the words of the President, " such work is always done by you." George Curzon himself claimed for it that it was an attempt " to resume, expound, and collate the references of the past in the light of modern knowledge and to show what the Pamirs really are as viewed from the double standpoint of historical mention and personal experience." And few who are familiar with the volume will deny the success of his attempt.

The Monograph provides, indeed, an excellent example of the method and industry which have more than once been stated in these pages to have been a main source of George Curzon's success in life. When presenting him with the Patron's Gold Medal at the Annual General Meeting of the Royal Geographical Society on May the 27th, 1895, the President, after explaining that the award was made for his geographical work in Persia, which had resulted in the compilation of the best existing map of that country, his investigations in French Indo-China and Korea, his exploration of the Pamirs and his determination of the true course of the Oxus river, observed,

> " I believe that the thoroughness and excellence of your work in connection with these journeys mainly influenced the decision of the Council. . . . By diligent and exhaustive research you made yourself intimately acquainted with the history of the geography of those countries which you had intended to explore. . . Speaking with knowledge, I believe that no traveller from this country since the days when Sir Henry Rawlinson was young, has approached your excellence in this respect."

Nothing could have been truer. Oh his way out to India he had written to Miss Leiter—" I am reading hard books connected with my journey. The secret of successful inquiry is by reading to have sifted out the superfluous and well-known in advance."[1] And in thanking the Society for the honour which it had bestowed upon him he acknowledged that long, careful and studious preparation had always seemed to him to be almost the first essential of travel.

> " If any traveller came and said to me—' What would you recommend to any one going to undertake a journey in distant parts ?' I would say to him, ' In the first place, consult all the highest and most reliable authorities you can find. In the second place, read every book, good, bad or indifferent that has been written on the country you propose to visit, so that you may know what to do. In the third place, take no super-

[1] Letter dated August 8th, 1894.

fluous baggage—it only employs extra time and men; in the fourth place, realise that travel has not only its incidents and adventures, but also its humour; and in the fifth place ' "— here came the opportunity, too good to be lost, for a hit at those who had placed obstacles in his way—" ' never expect any encouragement from the Government of your country.' "

The Afghan part of the journey was in its way as remarkable an achievement as the Pamir trek. A handful of Europeans employed by the Amir had ere now made their way to Kabul. After long discussion and negotiation an official Mission from the Indian Government had been permitted to enter the country to discuss with its ruler outstanding questions concerning the demarcation of the frontier. But no private traveller had ever hitherto succeeded in extracting from Abdur Rahman an invitation to cross the border. And George Curzon was not a little elated at his success. " Here I am all right," he wrote from Kabul, on November the 20th. " I arrived yesterday, and had a great reception. Came in with an escort of about two hundred cavalry, streets lined with troops and crowds about. Am lodged in the Palace and have a suite of four large rooms, lit with innumerable candles in lustres and chandeliers. All the furniture is very sumptuous. The sheets of my bed are cerise coloured silk, the pillow is of flowered silk and the quilts of silk and brocade with gold and silver lace trimming."[1] He spent a fortnight in the capital as the Amir's guest, and during that time he had constant interviews with his host, lasting often from three to four hours at a time. That he made a very deep impression both upon Abdur Rahman himself and upon his eldest son, Habibullah Khan, is evident from the freedom with which they talked to him on every imaginable subject. It was in reply to a question put to the Amir by George Curzon that he announced for the first time that it was his definite desire that he should be succeeded by Habibullah. This in face of the ostentatious determination of the Queen to secure the succession for her own five year old son.

He found that the Amir had very definite views of the obligations

[1] Letter to Mrs. H. White.

of Great Britain towards his country. He held that on the occurrence
of any act of aggression against his frontier on the north, Great
Britain was indubitably committed to despatch troops to his aid.
He had tried to obtain financial help from the Government of India
for the construction of an elaborate series of fortifications along his
northern border, and had been bitterly disappointed at his lack of
success. He could not understand why the Government of India
went on spending money on forts on the frontier between India and
Afghanistan instead of on their true frontier against Russia. It was
in the course of this discussion that he made use of a striking phrase
which George Curzon quoted some years later in one of his most
brilliant speeches on the frontier question in the House of Commons
—" We are members of the same house, and to that house there
should be but one wall."

The Amir's relations with the Government of India were cold.
He had for long been childishly anxious to visit England, and was
annoyed because the invitation had been so long delayed. For this
reason, when at length he received an official intimation that a
visit from him would be welcomed, he refrained from answering it,
and determined that when he did so he would ignore the Viceroy
and the Secretary of State. It was in pursuance of this decision,
doubtless, that he selected George Curzon as his messenger and
entrusted him with a letter of acceptance addressed to the Prince of
Wales. Only on the former's most earnest solicitation did he agree
to follow this up with an official acceptance addressed to the Secretary of State.

It was fortunate, perhaps, that in the end circumstances prevented
him from carrying out his proposed visit, for his ideas of the Government of Great Britain and of the manner in which he would be received by it were such as were necessarily foredoomed to disappointment. " His conception of the British Government is a very
curious one. He evidently thinks that the House of Commons is
the Government ; that it consists of six hundred wise men (Great
Heavens !); that they will all be assembled solemnly to discuss the
affairs of Afghanistan when he comes to England, and that he
will be introduced with his Munshi to make a speech and to explain
to them his grievances, whereupon the whole body will behave like

the Babylonians on the Plains of Dura, and will fall down and recognise him as the greatest of men." [1]

The Amir raised no objection to his guest visiting Kandahar and returning to India *via* New Chaman. He accordingly left Kabul on December the 3rd and reached British territory once more on December the 18th.

His stay in Kabul was destined to have an important influence on his attitude towards Afghanistan in after years when, as Viceroy of India, he was called upon to take up official relations with its ruler. He learned the causes of Abdur Rahman's dislike and distrust of the Indian Government ; he formed a most favourable opinion both of the character and ability of Habibullah, and was able to correct the false estimate generally held in England and elsewhere of the position which he occupied in Afghanistan and of his chances of succeeding to the throne. Above all, he had established cordial personal relations with the Amir and was fully informed of the view which the latter took of the obligations of Great Britain towards his country. The Amir, in his turn, was very favourably impressed with his guest, whom he thought " a very genial, hard-working, well-informed, experienced and ambitious young man." He enjoyed his witty sallies and laughed at his amusing stories, and confessed his admiration for the skill with which he extracted information from him on important topics. In his autobiography he told how George Curzon had succeeded in making him commit himself on the question of the succession.

> " In a humorous conversation in 1894 he began his remarks by a joke and ended them with a most important political question as to who would be my successor. I, having already committed myself in a joke, could not refuse to give my views on the matter more fully than I originally intended. Luckily, however, the conversation took place in a small private room where there were not more than two or three persons present to hear what I said." [2]

[1] From a memorandum drawn up by George Curzon on the position of affairs at Kabul in 1895. An account of some of the more humorous portions of his interviews with the Amir will be found in Chapter III of " Tales of Travel."

[2] " The Life of Abdur Rahman, Amir of Afghanistan," published in 1900.

CURZON, 1894

On the way home George Curzon spent a week visiting the Somali coast and six days in Cairo, reaching England at the end of January. Here, as will be explained in the next chapter, he found much to occupy him, more particularly in connection with a brief visit to the United States in the following April.

CHAPTER XIV

COURTSHIP AND MARRIAGE

1890-1895

GEORGE CURZON numbered among his personal friends many talented and beautiful women. And their companionship counted for much in a life that was never lacking in fullness. Yet he remained a bachelor till comparatively late in life, being thirty-six before his marriage took place. Perhaps the memories which he entertained of one of the companions of his younger days in whose case it had once seemed likely that the cheerful camaraderie which characterised his intercourse with the women of his circle, would blossom into a warmer and more intimate relationship, held too large a place in his heart and mind to admit of the easy entry of new affections. "Well, now," he wrote to St. John Brodrick in 1886, when he realised that hopes which he had cherished were doomed to disappointment, "I suppose I settle down into a more certain (at any rate for a time) celibacy."[1]

Yet his innate love of beauty and warm-hearted sociability warred against a life of solitude, and in the end he sought and found the intimate intellectual and emotional companionship which marriage alone of all human relationships is capable of giving. He once said of a man's wedding day that it was "the commencement of extreme happiness, discreditable indifference or superlative misery."[2] There was never any doubt under which of these categories his own nuptial day had fallen. From first to last his relations with Mary Victoria, daughter of Mr. and Mrs. Leiter of Washington and Chicago, were characterised by the tender beauty of an evergreen romance.

[1] Letter dated December 24th, 1886.
[2] Letter to Mr., now Sir Ian, Malcolm, K.C.M.G. July 1st, 1902.

CURZON, 1891

A chance meeting in a London ballroom in the summer of 1890 had quickly led to something much more than mere acquaintance-ship. Each recognised in the other tastes and interests which provided the basis of a natural and easy intercourse ; and when on the eve of bidding each other farewell at the close of the London season he gave her, as a memento of the parties and pursuits which they had enjoyed together, an amulet, she returned the compliment by taking a pearl from her chain—" almost the only thing that is my very own "—and having it set as a stud and tiepin for him " as emblematic of the tear I shed on leaving London." [1]

They had already found too much in common to contemplate losing touch with equanimity, and a regular correspondence soon took the place of the frequent meetings of the London season. From the Tyrol she wrote telling him of the mountain pinnacles " like cathedral spires, reaching so far up to Heaven that I think sometimes that they must reach there," and the Alpine villages " leaning against the proud old mountain that seemed to wind its strong arms around them." [2] On her way through London to catch the steamer home they enjoyed a brief re-union, and then she wrote to him from mid ocean—" We have had a merciless voyage from Queenstown. We sailed into a furious storm, and for four days floated on a turbulent sea of misery. Almost everyone has succumbed, some fear we will sink, others hope so, but I far from it, for hope and life are sweet." Later, on hearing news of his work in his constituency, she wrote to congratulate him on his progress with the electors—" The Southport speech is splendid ; how I wish I were there to hear and help." [3]

Before long she had matters of political interest on her side of the Atlantic to write about. Life in Washington appealed to her ; it had so many interests besides gaiety which were lacking in New York. " It has been particularly interesting lately, and Lord Salis-bury has given Blaine a great surprise in bringing the Behring Sea question before the Supreme Court. . . I have seen both Blaine and the Speaker since. Blaine at heart is glad to have had the ques-tion taken out of his hands." [4]

[1] Letter dated August 1st, 1890.
[2] Ibid., August 17th, 1890.
[3] Ibid., November 4th, 1890.
[4] Ibid., January 19th, 1891.

COURTSHIP AND MARRIAGE

Early in the New Year George Curzon learned with alarm of the total destruction of Mrs. Leiter's house in Washington by fire. Miss Leiter happened to be away when the catastrophe occurred ; but she wrote him graphic accounts of the aftermath—the charred ruins from which she sought to retrieve some of her possessions and the nervous shock which some at least of its inmates had sustained. This elicited from him some typical comments on the effect of crises upon the human organism. " How is it that people ever lose their heads ? I am sure alarm, excitement, danger would steady. One might be afraid—deadly afraid—that is according to one's nature, but I do not understand loss of presence of mind or mental distraction."[1] This from St. Moritz, where he was staying for his health and was working at his book on Persia, of whose progress he wrote with obvious satisfaction. Her interest in it was certainly not simulated—" I am too delighted that Volume I is completed ; it can only be splendid since you wrote it—and all since October—wonderful !"[2]

During the summer of 1891, which the Leiters spent in London, Persia became a bond of companionship between them. " And now good-bye," she wrote, on leaving England in September ; " every blessing to you and good luck to your beloved Persia."[3] In due course she received the promised presentation copy of the book which they had discussed so frequently together, and wrote in June 1892—" ' Persia ' has come .... I am more than delighted to have it, as I feel I knew it in its infancy when, instead of being bound and printed, it covered miles of MS. and filled the old brown bag on our various journeys. I shall prove my devotion to it by reading it all as we travel through the West this summer." She next spoke of a plan to come to Europe in the autumn. " Your movements depend entirely on the elections. Even if the Liberals win, they will not stay in long, so you cannot go very far away on that ' one last wander,' as you will be too much needed at the helm of your party."[4] Nevertheless, as we have seen, no sooner was Lord

[1]Letter dated February 3rd, 1891.
[2]*Ibid.*, February 20th, 1891.
[3]*Ibid.*, September 6th, 1891.
[4]*Ibid.*, June 18th, 1892.

Salisbury's Government defeated in the House of Commons than George Curzon packed up the old brown bag and started on his second journey round the world.

In November Miss Leiter wrote to him in China, telling him of her plans for the winter—" We cross for two months sailing on the Teutonic on the 30th of November, and we go to a southern clime —Egypt or the South of France and return here in the spring to get into the new house. . . . Do take care of yourself in those destitute-of -comfort countries and don't get ill on this ' one last wander ! ' "[1]

On his return from Asia he ran across Mrs. Leiter and her daughter in Paris where they, too, were breaking their journey home, and dined with them at their hotel, the Vendôme, before crossing to England the next day to resume his Parliamentary duties.

The journey that he had just completed was not after all to be " the one last wander " ; there was still another incursion into the heart of Asia upon which he had set his heart. " The whole thing is mapped out for me by the Indian Government directly I can go." But the journey to the Pamirs and possibly Afghanistan, could only be done in the summer and he could scarcely absent himself from the House of Commons and his constituency so soon after his recent tour, and he would have to exercise patience. He could afford to wait, for his projected book on the countries of the Far East had yet to be written and the trip to the Pamirs " would exhaust my Central Asia programme and leave me a contented and sedentary slave."[2]

They saw little of one another this summer for Miss Leiter spent only a few days in London before sailing for the United States in May ; but they kept up a regular correspondence, he keeping her informed of his activities and she commenting on the political situation in England as it appeared through American glasses. " What a dreadful time you have been having in the House— Biblical epithets recklessly applied and G.O.M. as Herod, and Chamberlain as Judas."[3] A little later she gave him the American view of the attitude of Great Britain towards the Siamese question

[1]Letter dated November 7th, 1892.
[2]Ibid., March 26th, 1893.
[3]Ibid., August 3rd, 1893.

in which he was so keenly interested. There was little praise, apparently, for the figure cut by the Liberal Government in the matter, opinion at Washington being that a Conservative Government would have acted with greater credit.[1]

In August his hopes of bringing off his journey to Afghanistan were suddenly raised. An Indian mission was being despatched to Kabul, and he asked Lord Kimberley, then Secretary of State for India, for permission to accompany it—" It is one of the dreams of my life," he told Miss Leiter. But he was very far from being *persona grata* with the Liberal party, more particularly on account of what were regarded as his jingo views on Indian frontier questions. He had recently been assailed in the Gladstonian press as an alarmist and a Russophobe, and Lord Kimberley proved obdurate. In his disappointment he derived consolation from the support which he received from across the Atlantic, for Miss Leiter not only sympathised with him in his attitude towards Russia, but was able to give him information which tended to confirm his suspicions of Russian intentions on the Pamirs. A Russian gentleman of high station had been talking grandiloquently—and indiscreetly—of the intentions of the Russian forward party in that part of the world ; and in September he wrote to thank her for what she had been able to tell him. " What you told me about the G. . . D. . . A. . . . . was also *extremely valuable*, because it confirms from high quarters the suspicions which I have had for some time." [2]

But despite Lord Kimberley's refusal, he could not keep his mind away from the Pamirs, and he wrote constantly of his plans for getting there. " If the present Government stay in, as looks likely, through the impending session, then I shall try to work the Pamirs next summer—the last wild cry of freedom ! " [3] In January, 1894, he wrote hopefully—" Pamir plan is taking shape " ; and a fortnight later he told her that he hoped to have got his book on the Far East into the printers' hands " before I start for Pamirs." With spring came the political uncertainties consequent on Mr. Gladstone's resignation, and he tried to form an estimate of the extent

[1]Letter dated August 10th, 1893.
[2]*Ibid.*, August 23rd, 1893.
[3]*Ibid.*, November 12th, 1893.

to which his prospects of reaching the Pamirs were affected—" If there is no immediate probability of a dissolution, I shall make the Pamir trip ; if, owing to the fear of an election which does not, after all, take place, I lose my chance of going to the Pamirs, I shall then go to India and I believe I can get a special invitation from the Amir of Afghanistan to go up as his guest to Kabul, the first Englishman (if I succeed) who has ever been so favoured." [1]

In the meantime the Leiters were touring in America and Miss Leiter wrote him vivid descriptions of the country through which they passed—lands of a burning sun and of monotonous stretches of endless cotton fields—which must have recalled a flying visit which he had paid to the home of Amelie Rives on his way across America eighteen months earlier. As he had travelled across Virginia he had been struck by his own familiarity with the scenery gained from the description of it in that writer's books, for he found it, as he had pictured it, " wild, unkempt, sparsely and irregularly cultivated with sweeping pine-clad hills and virgin woods, everything up and down and without system or order, the soil præternaturally and sanguineously red." [2]

In June, Miss Leiter spent a day or two in London on her way to the continent, when the possibilities of the Pamir trip were exhaustively discussed and a definite decision taken to make a supreme effort to carry it through. Plans were matured, and on July the 15th he wrote—" The mail by which I go will leave England on Friday the 3rd." Nothing happened to upset this arrangement, and at last, on August the 4th, he found himself *en route* for India and wrote in high spirits from the train as he sped across Europe—" I spent the first few hours in writing my second letter about Korea to *The Times* and posted it at Aix les Bains. . . . Read my book when it reaches you and tell me what you think of it."

She did not wait for the book ; she read his articles and letters to the papers with avidity. His letters on the problems of the Far East delighted her, " they put the situation so very clearly," and, as she was careful to inform him, " not to the taste of the French papers." She found French feeling against England and the Im-

[1] Letter dated March 11th, 1894.
[2] Notes from a diary of a journey round the world in 1892.

PLATE VII. THE HON. MRS. G. N. CURZON
(afterwards Lady Curzon of Kedleston)

perialist policy with which George Curzon was identified very bitter, and from Baden Baden she wrote giving him, as was her custom, such political news as she could gather. Hatred of England was rampant, not only in the French press, but among French people generally. A French lady of her acquaintance had said to her— " La France sera toujours prêt a céder sa main à La Russie pour menacer L'Angleterre dans l'Orient." [1] And a little later she sent him an article from a French paper in which he and Sir C. Dilke were pilloried as menacing France upon every possible occasion in the House of Commons, and was able to tell him definitely of the skill with which Germany was playing upon the feelings of the French people. " The German Emperor liberating the French spies and calling upon the Empress Eugenie when in England, and now the suggested discontinuation of the annual celebration of Sedan has moved hysterical France to tears. . . . England must remain the hated reminder of Aboukir, the Nile, Trafalgar, Waterloo and St. Helena, until she prostrates herself theatrically before Napoleon's tomb with a ' pardonnez moi.' It is all amusing, isn't it ? " [2]

The reception accorded to his book delighted her. " This morning a *Times* came with an article on the book which I posted to you at once, along with a splendid Frenchy article in the *Temps*. . . . I believe you have luck with you, for your book on Korea coming out just as everyone's attention is fixed there, is a bit of capital good fortune." [3] He was able to confirm her belief, for later on he wrote from Aden on his way home from Afghanistan, that he had heard from his publishers that the book had already reached a third edition and that his share of the profits up to the end of November amounted to over £300.

During his journey he wrote as opportunity offered, telling of his doings and finally of his safe return to England. But the relief which she felt at the satisfactory completion of his journey was quickly followed by anxiety on the score of his health. He always felt the English climate after the sunshine of Asia, and he had not been home more than a few days when he wrote complaining of the cold—

[1] Letter dated August 12th, 1894.
[2] *Ibid.*, August 29th, 1894.
[3] *Ibid.*, August 23rd, 1894.

" weather too damnable and would freeze the Styx." By the end of February he was in bed suffering grievously with pain in his back. " I broke down with all the work I have had to do since coming back, with nobody to help me. The change of life, climate and exercise is very trying and nearly always on my return from a big journey I have a collapse." [1]

On March the 2nd the world learned that George Curzon was engaged to Mary Leiter. If his friends were for the most part taken by surprise, they were quick to express their approval, and on the very day of the announcement he cabled a brief message to Miss Leiter in Washington—" Universal delight." The general feeling among his friends was well expressed by Lord Pembroke in a letter of congratulation—" It was clever of you and extremely characteristic to get engaged to Miss Leiter at Washington from the top of the Pamirs ; you must tell me how it was done." [2]

Not even his most intimate friends were aware of the romantic story of his engagement ; the secret had been preserved with extraordinary fidelity. On March the 1st he had written to her—" To-morrow is the day of the great deliverance ; we are delivered of our great secret." During his lifetime George Curzon was strangely adverse to making known the story. But before his death he wrote a note, from which it is clear that he was anxious that some day the facts should be disclosed. And since his courtship and marriage played a determining part in his public as in his private life it is appropriate that the story should now be told.

For two years they had been engaged without the knowledge of a soul except Miss Leiter's parents, to whom the secret had been confided more than a year after the engagement had been entered into. In the little sitting room in the hotel Vendôme, on March the 3rd, 1893—the day that he had spent in Paris on his way home from his second journey round the world—these two had spoken to each other words which they alone in all the world might hear. What was said was wholly unpremeditated. When George Curzon had entered the hotel for dinner, it was without the slightest anticipation of what was to be the evening's issue. It was just that the hearts of these two

[1] Letter dated March 1st, 1895.
[2] Ibid., March 3rd, 1895.

people were no longer capable of containing the song which their souls were singing. From the beginning, he told her, he had felt that they were destined for each other ; but for three years he had not dared to speak, because there was certain work in his scheme of Asiatic travel and study which he had resolved to carry through and which, he thought, no married man would be justified in undertaking. The greater part of it was now accomplished, but some of it—the contemplated journey to the Pamirs and Afghanistan—was still to do. And until that journey was either completed or definitely abandoned, he did not regard himself as free to enter into matrimony.

To all of this she bowed a willing assent. To-morrow and for all time to come it would be the same with her as it was to-day and as it had been yesterday. A few more months or, if need be, years she offered up in willing sacrifice upon the altar of her devotion. The doubts and anxieties of the past three years, exaggerated by the necessity of warding off the all too frequent advances of other suitors, vanished in the joy of the present certainty. Before he left for England the mutual pledge of secrecy and fidelity had been gladly given. It was faithfully kept.

The next two years were a time of difficulty the anxieties of which were only heightened by contrast with hopes for the future in which both constantly indulged. But they laid firm the foundations of a great and abiding happiness, built up on a mutual recognition of all that each could give the other. For all the self-sufficiency which he showed the world, he was ever ready to welcome the help which she could give him. " I want you to teach me French well (I am merely passable). . . . If ever I am Foreign Minister I must be more supple and fluent at French than I am."[1] And when the strain which the uncertainties of his Afghan journey imposed upon her was over, and she wrote to catch him in Paris on his way home, she paid a generous tribute to the value of the test to which each had been subjected. " Think of your being in Paris ! It will be almost two years since our memorable meeting at the hotel Vendôme— and the two years of waiting will be nearly up. . . . The waiting years have been fruitful ones to you, and they've not been lost to

[1] Letter dated April 22nd, 1894.

me, for love and devotion and trust count for a great deal and my feminine philosophy believes in tests and patience greatly improving and developing a woman. I believe we shall be eternally happy." [1]

How severe was the test and how great the patience demanded, is abundantly clear from the voluminous correspondence between them during these two years. As the date of his departure on " the one last wander " drew near, her anxiety became acute. She spoke wistfully of what might be—if only all went well. They must take a place in Scotland " with some good shooting for you." The prospect was marvellously fair—if only all went well. " You must think if you run risks on this journey that after all Pamir is *not* worth sacrificing all we have in store for us ; for it may be the roof of the world, but rather than perish on that roof you must think of all the delights we shall have under a more modest roof in England." [2]

On his way across Europe to catch his boat for India he broke his journey for a few hours, to see her. " It was very sweet catching that little glimpse of you," he wrote from the train. " A year hence there will be no more need of patience, no more letters and telegrams and no more goodbyes." [3] But his next letter only added to her fears, already sufficiently great—" I have been writing my will and am sending it home from Port Said. In it I tell about you ; so that if the worst came to the worst my Father would understand." [4] She tried to distract her thoughts with reading and music. " I have read Max Müller's ' India and what it can teach us,' and Sir Alfred Lyall's ' India,' which is concise and good ; but it does not go very far—and yesterday I picked up a life of Lord Lawrence, by Sir Richard Temple." But all that she read brought Asia and its present dangers to all her happiness more vividly before her. " I wonder what you will decide to do on landing ? I hope not face all kinds of dangers and think, like the Latin motto, ' Dulce et decorum est pro patria mori.' Perhaps I haven't got it straight, for I have

[1] Letter dated December 15th, 1894.
[2] *Ibid.*, July 30th, 1894.
[3] *Ibid.*, August 4th, 1894.
[4] *Ibid.*, August 8th, 1894.

forgotten my Latin ; but I do remember one sentence which is a much better one than the first, ' Dum vivimus vivamus.' "[1]

Music, like literature, seemed doomed only to emphasise her disquiet. At Bayreuth, " Lohengrin, with that lovely bridal music, was beautiful and Nordica made an enchanting Elsa." But she knew not which was the most sorrowful fiancé, Elsa or herself, the former's Lohengrin " with his allegiance divided between her and knightly traditions, or mine with his adventurous propensities."[2] And a little later, when she heard rumours of the illness of the Amir of Afghanistan, she was assailed by premonitions of tragedy. " I implore you not to go to Kabul. If the Amir dies, the danger will be terrible ; it will be quite inhuman of you to go and run such a risk."[3]

Korea, like Persia, was a happy link between them ; and he wrote delightedly of the success of his book. " The book seems to have gone like wildfire in England, which is consoling. What a part you will play in the preparation of the next. Poor child, think of your lot—amanuensis to a professional scribbler, drudge to a political pamphleteer."[4] And he spoke of the gift to which he dedicated the proceeds—a gift which " I shall now feel has been fairly won by the sweat of my own brow," one which is not merely the conventional marriage present, " but a part of my veritable heart and brain."[5] By an odd mischance the presentation copy went astray.

> " The book on Korea must have gone to Dupont for it has not turned up yet. B . . . H . . . . . . spoke of it yesterday and I with difficulty repressed a desire to beg, borrow or steal her copy ; but feared to re-arouse her suspicions, which I successfully allayed summer before last at Newport—so that now she says quite seriously, ' it is a great pity that you and George Curzon didn't hit it off ' ; at which I look blandly unconscious and feel inclined to laugh."[6]

[1]Letter dated August 12th, 1894.
[2]*Ibid.*, August 22nd, 1894.
[3]*Ibid.*, October 6th, 1894.
[4]*Ibid.*, October 12th, 1894.
[5]*Ibid.*, January 2nd, 1895.
[6]*Ibid.*, October 6th, 1894.

14

She derived mild amusement from the various suggestions made to her on the subject of matrimony. " You will laugh to hear P . . . B . . . . . urges me to marry Prince B . . . . . ., saying, ' qui donc au monde y-a t'il de mieux ?' I tell him, ' quel qu'un bien sur.' " [1]

Letters came at uncertain intervals to raise her spirits. From the railway carriage on his way to Rawal Pindi he wrote : " Outside the carriage window, staring in at me, are bearded forms in huge turbans of every colour, purple and scarlet and crimson and orange and blue and white. Some day I will bring you to see them." [2] On reaching Gilgit, on his return from the Pamir, he cabled her the agreed message, " safe." The first half of the journey was accomplished, and her gratitude knew no bounds. " Bless you . . . . your cable met me here and I can't speak for thankfulness. . . . I believe I never had a moment of such transcendently blessed thankfulness in all my life. . . . Thank God, Pamir is behind." [3]

From Kabul he wrote on November the 30th that all had gone well and that he ought to be safely out of the country by December the 21st or 22nd, when his second cable, " safe," would be sent. At last it came—" The cable was a great blessing, for I've been anxious ever since you set foot in that benighted country." [4]

Her joy at hearing of his arrival in England was tempered by news of his collapse—" I have been dismally anxious about you between Pamirs and Kabul and your being ill, and to keep up my spirits through it all has been pretty hard. . . . But after we are married and landed in England a quiet week would be Paradise Regained." [5]

The wedding took place at Washington on April the 22nd, and Mr. and Mrs. Curzon crossed to England a few days later. No more charming benediction upon the consummation of their long-drawn romance, nor one more discerning in its prophetic insight, could have been penned than that of a friend who had known Mrs. Curzon from her earliest years. " I rejoice in your prospect of

[1]Letter dated August 22nd, 1894.
[2]Ibid., August 25th, 1894.
[3]Ibid., October 6th, 1894.
[4]Ibid., January 1st, 1895.
[5]Ibid., March 24th, 1895.

happiness. . . . I think over my friendship with you and with him and collect my memories and put them side by side. They all seem to fall naturally into place together, as if the two lives were made to be lived together, and as if each had found the twin soul which halved their own. I am sure it is so—sure that for you and for him life is henceforward to be a complete and beautiful thing."[1] And so it was.

[1]Letter from Mr. G. W. Smalley to Mrs. Curzon dated March 11th, 1895.

227

CHAPTER XV

1895

GEORGE CURZON'S pre-occupation with the peoples and politics
of the East had not dissipated the hopes which he had long entertained of seeing some change effected in the composition of the
House of Lords. And in 1895 an event took place which provided
him and those who were associated with him in the matter with an
opportunity of testing the validity of what they regarded as the
penalty attaching to the eldest son of a peer, namely, that of having
to relinquish his seat in the House of Commons on the death of his
father. " The world supposes him," he had written in an article on
the subject, " to be the fortunate heir of what is called the accident
of birth ; he is in reality the hapless victim of the accident of
death."

The question was a comparatively narrow one ; but, apart from
the personal interest which it naturally possessed for George Curzon
and his friends, it was hoped that the action which they contemplated, even if unsuccessful, would direct attention once more to
the broader question of the reform of the Upper Chamber, which
had always been their main objective.

Prominent among his associates was Lord Wolmer. And by
the death of Lord Selborne in the spring of 1895 Lord Wolmer
found himself faced with the immediate prospect of paying this
unwelcome penalty. He had committed himself to very definite
views on the subject twelve months earlier, when he had joined
George Curzon and St. John Brodrick in introducing a Bill " to
remove the legal disability of peers on succeeding to their titles,
in respect of sitting in the House of Commons." And when lack of

success in the ballot for private members' time in the House of Commons had deprived them of the chance of drawing attention to the matter in this way, he had added his signature to theirs at the foot of an article in the April number of the *Nineteenth Century*, in which were set forth with a wealth of argument and illustration the objections to the existing law and practice. The article had attracted a great deal of attention. George Curzon as its author had received an honorarium of fifty pounds for it, the largest sum he had ever been paid for a magazine article, and he had written to Miss Leiter in high delight—" My article in the *Nineteenth Century* has had a great success, having had leading articles written on it in nearly every newspaper." [1]

With Lord Selborne's death an opportunity presented itself of approaching the matter from a somewhat different point of view. The Bill for which they had made themselves responsible had been designed to alter what was believed to be the existing law. But was it so certain, after all, that there was any legal compulsion upon a member of the House of Commons to vacate his seat on succeeding to a peerage? Some years before, an agreement had been come to between George Curzon, St. John Brodrick and Lord Wolmer that this question should be definitely put to the test in the House of Commons by whichever of them was first called by a callous fate to the Upper Chamber, and preparations for giving effect to this agreement were at once taken in hand. " It is very essential that I should see you as early as possible to discuss Woljohn's (Lord Wolmer's) action, Askwith's opinion (in which so far as my present knowledge of the Statute goes I do not concur), and the circulation of my memo to the Committee." [2]

There was the possibility to be considered of the penalties to which a man might render himself liable by sitting and voting in the House of Commons when no longer entitled to do so, and this aspect of the case presented itself not unnaturally with special force to Lord Wolmer. George Curzon was inclined to regard it as a side issue of no great importance—"I have no copy of the Statutes with me and cannot be certain to which Statute of Anne W. refers.

[1] Letter dated April 8th, 1894.
[2] Letter from George Curzon to St. John Brodrick, undated.

I never remember the committee unearthing any Statute by which the £500 penalty could possibly apply to a peer continuing to sit."[1] However, he added that he would gladly join in a hundred pounds guarantee. On all other points he was well prepared. " Fortunately, while at sea I prepared long reasoned statement of our House of Lords case for the Committee, so I have the powder ready for Woljohn straight away."[2]

While these preparations were going forward there was a further casualty in the ranks of the peerage. The then Lord Pembroke died, his brother and heir being at the time a Whip in the House of Commons. George Curzon, alert to all possibilities, saw in him a potential recruit of obvious value. " Tell Sidney that he must not apply for Chilterns, but continue to sit. It is very important for our case."[3]

Two main lines of argument were employed by George Curzon and his friends. First, it was argued, a peer did not become a Lord of Parliament until he had received a writ of summons to the House of Lords. Such writs were issued only on the application of the peer himself, and in the event of no such application being made, it followed that the peer retained his status as a commoner, just as an Irish peer did who was not elected by his fellow peers to a seat in the House of Lords. The contention was supported by ingenious analogies. Two peers, the late Lord Tenterden and the then Lord Iddesleigh, had, in fact, refrained from applying for their writs, in order to continue in the enjoyment of posts in the Civil Service believed to be incompatible with a seat in the House of Lords. Why, it was asked, should not a peer act similarly in order to continue in the enjoyment of another disqualifying service, namely, that of the House of Commons? Failing the success of this plea, there was a second line of defence. Before the House of Commons could issue a new writ for the filling of a vacancy, it had, admittedly, to satisfy itself that a vacancy had in fact occurred. In the case of one of its members succeeding to a peerage, the proof invariably accepted by it of his having done so, was the issue to him of a writ of summons to the House of Lords. Supposing, once again, that

[1]Letter to St. John Brodrick, dated May, 1895.
[2]Letter to St. John Brodrick dated May 6th, 1895.
Ibid.

the new peer refrained from applying for such a writ, the House of Commons would be without the proof which it had always demanded before being satisfied that a vacancy had occurred. And so long as the House of Commons was without proof that a vacancy had in fact occurred, it would scarcely be justified in requiring the member concerned to withdraw.

This latter line of argument derived support from an incident which had taken place in June of the previous year. The Hon. Bernard Coleridge, then a member of the House of Commons, had become Lord Coleridge, and in due course the Chief Ministerial Whip had moved for a new writ for the Attercliffe Division, not in the room of the Hon. B. Coleridge, " called up to the House of Lords "—the usual formula employed on such occasions—but in room of the Hon. B. Coleridge, " who since his election for the said division has accepted the office of Steward of Her Majesty's Chiltern Hundreds "—the formula always employed on the retirement of a member of the House of Commons for reasons other than succession to a peerage. It was generally understood that the reason for this departure from the ordinary practice was a simple one—that it was, in fact, merely for the purpose of permitting the by-election to be held without the delay which might occur in the receipt by the new peer of his writ of summons to the House of Lords. There were persons, however, who were by no means disposed to let the innovation pass, simply because the reason for it might be plain. Mr. Chamberlain had at once detected the irregularity, and two days later had raised the matter as a question of privilege in the House of Commons. His argument was a simple one. If a week or more after the death of Lord Coleridge the Government considered it necessary for Mr. Bernard Coleridge to apply for the Chiltern Hundreds before they could move for the issue of a new writ to fill the vacancy, they must hold the view that he was still a member of the House of Commons. Both Mr. Chamberlain and Mr. Balfour had accepted this as the logical deduction from the Chief Whip's action and had attacked the Government for thus providing a precedent for the creation of a special class of persons, neither peers nor commoners, who could claim to sit in either House according to their pleasure.

Needless to say, George Curzon and Lord Wolmer, while gleefully agreeing with their leaders on the interpretation to be placed on the Government's action, had parted company with them altogether when they had made it a ground of attack. In their view, indeed, the action of the Chief Whip was a matter for congratulation rather than for censure, for here was the precedent for which they had long sought presented to them gratuitously by the Government of the day. No " Peers' Disability Removal Bill " would now be necessary ; and George Curzon had thanked Sir William Harcourt effusively for making it incontrovertibly clear that more than a week after Lord Coleridge's death Mr. Bernard Coleridge had remained a member of the House of Commons. Sir William Harcourt at first gratified and then suspicious of blandishments so pronounced from so unexpected a quarter, had agreed hurriedly to Mr. Chamberlain's suggestion for the appointment of a Committee, to which should be delegated the task of enquiring into the circumstances in which the writ had been issued and into the larger question of the law and practice of the House of Commons relating to vacancies caused by succession to the Peerage.

The incident had excited interest out of all proportion to its intrinsic importance. Mr. Chamberlain had declared with emphasis that the effect of the Government's action might be to bring about " enormous constitutional changes " ; and *The Times* had stated in a leading article that it was essential that the public should know what the law on the matter was, and that it should be laid down without the possibility of mistake, if it was in a man's own power to decide, whether he should succeed to a peerage. And now twelve months later, when Lord Selborne died, the Committee was still pondering the matter.

The evidence so far laid before the Committee seemed to have established at least two facts favourable to George Curzon's contention ; first, that a Peer of the Realm is not a Lord of Parliament until he is called by writ of summons to the House of Lords, and secondly, that he is not disqualified by Statute from sitting in the House of Commons. The circumstances seemed to be favourable, therefore, for putting the matter to the test ; and in a letter to *The Times* of May the 13th, over the signatures of George Curzon and

WHEN IS A PEER NOT A PEER?

St. John Brodrick, it was announced that Lord Selborne proposed to raise the question whether a Peer of the Realm could continue to sit in, or be elected to, the House of Commons. " He will take this step deliberately and after due forethought, not with a view to his own position or to an individual case alone, but in order to raise in a constitutional manner a grave constitutional issue upon which a Committee of the House of Commons, after sitting for eleven months and after receiving the most conflicting evidence, has as yet arrived at no decision."

On the same day when the House met, Mr. Labouchere rose to call the attention of the Speaker to the presence in the House of a nobleman who since taking his seat as a duly elected member was alleged to have become a Peer of the Realm, and to ask whether in these circumstances the Noble Lord had a right to be within the bar of the House. The Speaker in reply disclaimed any right to decide whether Lord Selborne was entitled to sit and vote, such right being vested in the House itself. But he thought it proper to point out to the House that although many cases had occurred of members finding themselves in the position in which Lord Selborne then stood, he had been unable to discover any instance on record of such a claim being put forward as that now made by the Noble Lord, to sit and vote in the Lower House. In these circumstances he asked Lord Selborne to withdraw below the bar until the question of his right had been decided by the House.

As a result of discussion on two consecutive days, the House decided on the Motion of Sir William Harcourt to appoint a Select Committee to inquire and report whether the Hon. William Waldegrave Palmer, commonly called Viscount Wolmer, had, since his election to the House of Commons, succeeded to the Earldom of Selborne in the peerage of the United Kingdom, the larger question of principle being left to the Committee which had been appointed the year before. The finding of the Select Committee was, of course, a foregone conclusion, and on receipt of its report the House straightway agreed to a Motion for the issue of a new writ for the election of a member for the West Edinburgh Division, and Lord Selborne was thereby debarred from continuing to sit in the House of Commons. Thus the attempt of the eldest sons to divest them-

233

selves of the privileges and penalties of their rank ended in failure. It attracted little support amongst members of the House of Commons, who, for the most part, displayed a mortifying indifference to their departure from their midst. Nor did it fare much better at the hands of the leader of the Conservative party in the House of Lords, who dismissed the episode with a characteristic gibe. Replying to the toast of the House of Lords at the Academy banquet, Lord Salisbury said :

> "From time immemorial it has been the custom of fathers to reform their sons. We have recently experienced the attempts of sons to reform their fathers, and from this novel and interesting ordeal the House of Lords is emerging as well as can be expected."

Interest in the matter was destined to be submerged not many days later by happenings of more immediate import. On June the 21st St. John Brodrick accused the Government of a dereliction of duty in connection with the supply of cordite for the army, and, to the surprise of most people, the Ministry was found, in the division that followed, to be in a minority of seven. It was with still greater surprise that the public learned on June the 24th that the Cabinet had resigned and that Lord Salisbury was back in office.

Amongst George Curzon's friends and admirers expectations naturally ran high. In the press, among his personal friends and by his supporters in his constituency, he had been regarded as certain to receive promotion ; and it was with somewhat mixed feelings, therefore, that he read Lord Salisbury's letter to him on June the 27th, inviting him in flattering terms to serve once more as Under Secretary.

> "I have accepted the Foreign Office somewhat against my will," Lord Salisbury wrote. "I had much rather that Devonshire had taken it. But he would not do so. And now having to undertake it at a time when much difficulty seems to impend, I am naturally trying to secure the best assistance that I can. Therefore I venture to turn to you. You are more familiar

with Eastern questions than any man on our side and your ability and position in the House of Commons will enable you to fight a good battle for us if our policy is attacked in the House. I hope, therefore, you will not refuse to accept the Under Secretaryship of Foreign Affairs."

There were two subjects to which George Curzon had for a long time past devoted his time and thought, and Foreign policy was one of them. He did not hesitate, therefore, to accept the Prime Minister's offer. But there would be no harm, he thought, in apprising Lord Salisbury of the expectations which had been entertained—rashly, no doubt, but none the less confidently—in his constituency in case something might be done to make it clear to the public that his continued employment in a subordinate position was not to be regarded as in any sense a slur upon him. Cases were not unknown, for example, of the honour of a Privy Councillorship being conferred upon particularly meritorious Under Secretaries. Any anxiety which he may have felt on this score was, as it turned out, superfluous, for Lord Salisbury's letter of June the 27th was followed by a second communication on June the 28th, in which he conveyed to him the Queen's desire that he should attend at Windsor the following day to be sworn of the Privy Council. "It may be a satisfaction to you," he added, "to remember that (so far as I know) there has been no instance of any one holding a political office of your age having received the honour within living memory."

At the election which took place in July George Curzon was returned for his old constituency by a majority of 764 over the Liberal candidate, Sir H. Naylor-Leyland, and Lord Salisbury's Government was confirmed in office by the sweeping majority of 152.

CHAPTER XVI

UNDER SECRETARY FOR FOREIGN AFFAIRS

1895-1898

IT is interesting to compare a speech made by George Curzon at Derby soon after the General Election of 1895 with his speeches and writings nine years earlier, when his enthusiasm for Democratic Toryism was at its height, for such a comparison shows how completely his own interest in politics had moved away from domestic controversies and in the direction of foreign and Imperial affairs. It was no longer a headlong dive into the " inexhaustible work of reform "[1] that he advocated ; on the contrary, he was of opinion that the Radical Party had been defeated in the recent election because of " their plethora of plans and plots and programmes," and he was convinced that the country was anxious for the respite which would now be offered it. The Conservative Party had no desire " to crowd the Statute book with ill-discussed measures ; they contemplated no gigantic revolution." This did not mean that strenuous work did not lie ahead of them. Though the people need no longer fear any " great social or domestic upheaval at home,' there were nevertheless matters of grave import that were compelling the attention of all thoughtful men abroad. " After a considerable lull, foreign affairs have once more raised their heads above the horizon. The world is unquiet. Uneasy symptoms are abroad. We hear the moaning of sick nations on their couches, and we listen to and witness the struggles of dying men." There was growing competition for the empty places of the earth for colonisation and for trade. The rivalries of the nations were becoming fiercer. The pre-eminence of the British as a colonising and govern-

[1] See back, Chapter VI.

ing race no longer remained unchallenged. If they would guard against the perils of the future they must lift their eyes across their island seas to the greater world beyond. [1]

His forecast was an accurate one. The closing years of the century saw a great outburst of activity on the part of the European Powers in all parts of the world. The rapid accumulation of wealth which had been brought about by the industrial revolution which marked its opening years had resulted in a phenomenal increase in population. Trade and population alike spilled over the brim of the European cup, and new markets and new lands for the overflow had become imperative necessities. In Great Britain this development was reflected in the popular mind. Imperialism became the accepted creed of the nation ; and George Curzon was before all else an Imperialist. His extended travels had taught him at an earlier age than some of his contemporaries to think Imperially and had imbued him with a burning faith in the Imperial destiny of Great Britain— a faith which burned all the more brightly because it was founded not merely on a recognition of the necessity of developing new lands for a surplus population or of acquiring new markets for an expanding trade, but upon an unbounded belief and pride in the moral qualities of the British race. Some years before, Rennell Rodd, who had learned to appreciate this trait in his character, at Oxford, asked George Curzon if he might dedicate to him a volume of poems entitled " Songs of England," which he was about to publish, " because they deal with the spirit which you and I admire and believe in, and will do our damndest to maintain and further. That is all." And he must be accounted fortunate in that the circumstances of the time provided him with the field best suited to the play of the particular cast of idealism in his nature.

His horror of the Little Englander was absolutely sincere, and he was perfectly willing to make Imperialism, or the lack of it, the test by which the claims of the two historic parties to represent the nation should be judged. The gravamen of his charge against the late Government was that, whatever the individual ability of its members, it was as a whole lacking in political character, had not a single dispassionate aim, and lived from day to day " by a sort of

[1] Speech at Derby on November 6th, 1895.

juggler's ability in manipulating parties and conciliating fads."
The consequence was that foreign Governments could not rely on
it, because they knew that it could not rely upon itself. But since
July it could no longer be said that the voice of the British Government was " either the murmur of a faction or the whisper of a party.
It was what it had not been for the last three years—the voice of
the British people." It was his experience that throughout the
Empire the return of a Conservative Government was always hailed
with relief, " the result of long experience and profound conviction
. . . . that the interests of this country are safer in the hands of those
who regard the British Empire as a majestic responsibility, rather
than in the hands of those who look upon it as an irksome burden."
In the case of Great Britain expansion was not the offspring of a lust
of territorial aggrandisement, but of Imperial necessity. Year by
year the number of those who failed to understand this became
smaller. Those who shirked the responsibilities of Empire found
themselves the adherents of a discredited creed. " They may cry
upon the housetops of Northampton—but the twitterings of spar-
rows have never yet interfered with the stability of an Empire."
Expansion for Great Britain meant existence ; contraction would
signify decay. " These," he declared, " are the principles by which
the foreign policy of the present Government will be guided."[1]

Indications of the increasing share of public attention which
foreign affairs were about to demand were forthcoming during the
opening weeks of the new Parliament. The Session was scarcely a
month old when George Curzon was called on to deal with a number
of matters affecting the interests of Great Britain abroad. The business community were demanding greater commercial activity on
the part of the diplomatic and consular representatives of the
country, and George Curzon took his place at the head of the Commercial Department of the Foreign Office. Then there was the
question of the completion of the Uganda railway. The late Government having decided to assume the protectorate of Uganda and the
basin of the Victoria Nyanza Lake, a railway from the coast had
been generally accepted as a necessary corollary. This obligation,
declared the Under Secretary, " tardily accepted by the late

[1] Speech at Kingston, October, 1895.

Government is assumed with readiness by the present Government." A Departmental Committee which had been considering the matter had left unanswered one important question, namely, whether the railway should stop short at Kikuyu, three hundred miles from the coast, or should be carried on as far as the Lake, a distance of six hundred and fifty miles in all? Lord Salisbury's Government had decided on the latter alternative—a decision which followed naturally on a proper understanding of the principal object of the railway, which was to bring down to the coast the products of all the lands abutting on the Victoria Nyanza. It was abundantly clear from George Curzon's speech—the first he was called upon to make as Under Secretary for Foreign Affairs—that the project was one which appealed strongly to him as being calculated to advance within its sphere the moral and material interests of Great Britain. It would strike at the slave trade, which was a reproach to the civilisation of the age, and it would bring to an end the melancholy but unhappily chronic state of petty internecine warfare which was devastating the regions to be traversed. " This railway will carry with it not merely civilisation and commerce but peace." [1]

The Uganda Railway was only one of the many questions touched upon during the discussion of the Foreign Office Vote and later of the Appropriation Bill; but his speech on the railway provided the key to his general outlook. It was at once made clear that so far as the Under Secretary was concerned British policy in pursuance of British interests, in whatever part of the world they were found to exist, would be no hesitating one. In so far as he was permitted to express his views, the world at large would be informed in clear and unequivocal tones what British interests were, and what Great Britain was prepared to do to uphold them. There can be little doubt that had he been in control of the Foreign Policy of the country, Great Britain would have been found a good deal less accommodating in her relations with other Powers during the next few years than actually proved to be the case.

This was particularly so in the case of France. He had been very unfavourably impressed by what he had seen of French Administra-

[1] Speech in the House of Commons on August 30th, 1895.

tion abroad. In French Indo-China he thought the French Services particularly badly officered. They appeared to him to have been recruited from a far lower stratum of society than similar Services—such as the Indian Civil Service—in the case of Great Britain. "Shuffling little stubble-bearded Frenchmen of the most unattractive sort," he had dubbed them in a moment of irritation; "How tired I get of the type. All civil on the lip and smirk in address, but no real bonhomie or frankness, and a desperate jealousy and hatred of the English at the bottom." He thought them cynical and superficial, and was certain that they were indolent. "They worked a little in the morning, slept all the day from 11.30 to 3.30, and drove out and dined in the evening."[1] They were deficient, in fact, in all the qualities that George Curzon chiefly valued; and judging the French nation by such representatives, he became a little contemptuous of the pretensions of the French Government to play a leading part in world affairs.

It is important to realise the strength of the opinion which from the first he held of France, because of the tenacity, to which attention has been called in the opening chapters of this volume, with which he was wont to hold throughout his life opinions formed in very early years. At the time of which I am now writing his attitude towards France brought him more than once into respectful but quite definite disagreement with his Chief. Lord Salisbury's negotiation of a Commercial Treaty with France, to take the place of the Trade Agreement which we had with Tunis prior to its becoming a French Protectorate was a case in point.

> "If I do not see you tomorrow before your talk with de Courcel," he wrote on June the 1st, 1897, "may I most respectfully implore you to secure for us our last draft or to break off negotiations? I should really be as unhappy if I had to defend anything less as I have hitherto been happy in the tasks that you have entrusted to me. I really do not think that we are grasping or contumacious. In any case, we are making a big surrender for somewhat problematical ends. But beyond a certain point it would seem to be unjustifiable that we should be asked to go."

[1] Diary of his second journey round the World.

And in reply to certain considerations put forward by Lord Salisbury as a result of this appeal he wrote again on June 2nd.

> " I can well see the advantages of a bargain, and I have surmised that such was the object of a conciliatory attitude towards France. But they seem a little reluctant to reciprocate generosity. It is all take and very little give with them. Siam, Madagascar, the Niger, the Sergeant Malmanie, Lieut. Mizon, Uganda missionaries, Tunis—they have received or are on the verge of receiving very substantial benefits or concessions all round."

Other cases of divergence of view will appear later on—divergences illustrating the difference of temperament of the two men. But before touching on these it is necessary to point out that, however outspoken George Curzon may have been in his confidential intercourse with Lord Salisbury, his liberty of speech in public was subject to obvious limitations. As Under Secretary he might aspire to influence policy, but could not hope to exercise any sort of control over it. The policy to be pursued was very definitely Lord Salisbury's policy. Some years later, when St. John Brodrick, then Under Secretary for War, was invited by Lord Salisbury to succeed George Curzon on his appointment to the Indian Viceroyalty, the former turned to Arthur Balfour for advice. He was told—" You will simply be the mouthpiece of the Chief, often defending policy you do not agree with, instead of having a very considerable share in forming the military policy of the country."[1] George Curzon had not been in office very long before he discovered the limitations of an Under Secretaryship and the extent to which such limitations handicapped him in equipping himself even for the task of expounding other peoples' views. And there was nothing that George Curzon disliked more than to find himself imperfectly equipped for any enterprise that he took in hand. It must be clear from what has been written earlier in this volume that an outstanding feature of everything that he did in life, whether it was furnishing a house or ordering a dinner, making a speech or writing a book, running a committee or exploring the earth, was

[1]Letter from St. John Brodrick to George Curzon, dated October 3rd, 1898.

the thoroughness of his preparation and the constant personal attention which he paid to minute detail. He had quite unusual powers of
switching his mind from one subject to another and closing its
doors for the time being to all else. And his habit of attending to
the minutiæ of daily life was not in the least degree affected by the
immense addition to his work and responsibilities entailed by his
acceptance of office. In the middle of a flying visit to his constituency
in September, 1895, he found time between his speeches to devote
himself to a number of matters of domestic economy on which he
proceeded to address Mrs. Curzon. " I engaged a groom yesterday.
He arrives Saturday. I also saw an excellent coachman in London,
a thorough gentleman's servant; he will come down for you to
inspect. I am communicating with butler." Later in the same year
he wrote from Windsor Castle, whither he had been summoned
by the Queen, to inform Mrs. Curzon of the progress made with
the redecoration of the house which they had taken in Carlton House
Terrace. " The house (No. 4) looked charming to-day, the drawing-
room pretty, the staircase (now quite finished) a little dark, but
decidedly handsome, the other rooms nice. I am going to have
colour of outer hall slightly altered. All carpets and curtains to be
in by Xmas."

The time and thought which he always devoted to such details
was a constant source of amazement to his friends. He gave to the
engaging of a servant the same exhaustive study that he brought to
bear upon a problem of international diplomacy. The Concert of
Europe might be riven asunder and fall in splinters to an ignomin-
ious doom, but George Curzon would still be found nonchalantly
directing the daily working of his household. When about to proceed to India as Viceroy he undertook to find a suitable nurse for
his children, and described his interview with one of the candidates
in a letter to Mrs. Curzon consisting of nine closely written sheets.

" She is not the least like her photographs . . . . is ladylike,
yet not quite a lady ; neatly dressed, shows acres of gum and
files of artificial teeth ; has a rather curious way of rolling her
lips when she speaks and an utterance very clear and precise
and sometimes almost mincing in its accuracy. She is not in the

PLATE VIII. A HOLIDAY IN SCOTLAND

The Hon. G. N. Curzon.   The Hon. W. Cochrane-Baillie

least like a nurse, but exactly like an indigent lady placed in charge of children with a scientific and practical knowledge in which indigent persons are usually deficient."

Then followed some doubts—only to be dismissed as unimportant—whether she was intimate with the life, clothing or education of young children—" all these are rudiments, however, which the meanest intelligence should acquire." The catechism to which the astonished and probably terrified applicant was subjected was exacting ; but she was to have her turn.

" Having put her through half an hour's questioning, I then asked her if she wanted to ask anything of me. She replied by the following rather extraordinary questions : (1) might she take out a bicycle with her ? I said I would enquire, but thought that if the roads permitted it, there would be no objection to her taking her exercise in that way " . . . . .

and so on for three or four more pages.

No one who was familiar with this passion of the new Under Secretary for minute detail imagined that he was ever likely to be caught napping in the House of Commons. And his critics very soon discovered for themselves that it was never safe to assume that he would not be found armed *cap-à-pié*. In whatever other respect the foreign policy of the Government might prove vulnerable, it was not likely to be in respect of any joints in the armour of the Under Secretary—in so far, at any rate, as that armour consisted in a comprehensive and detailed knowledge of the subject under discussion. " Mr. Curzon, unlike some of his predecessors," wrote one of his critics after eighteen months' experience of his defence of the Government in the House of Commons, " has taken care to inform himself of the matters which he has to explain or, perhaps, defend. No one has been able to charge him with not knowing what he talked about. He is unquestionably painstaking."[1]

The ideal which George Curzon set before himself was not attained, however, without a struggle. At a very early date he

[1] A writer in *Echo* of February 18th, 1897.

complained to Lord Salisbury of a lack of information regarding events in China. " I may be questioned or pressed any day in the House, and at present I have next to nothing to add to my reply to Gedge's question to-day." The complaint was efficacious. A telegram was despatched to the British Minister at Pekin the same evening, requesting immediate and regular reports by cable. Later on he addressed to the Prime Minister a more comprehensive request. Writing from the House of Commons on March the 24th, 1896, he asked if he might see the private telegrams and despatches issued from and received at the Foreign Office.

> " I have to be the mouthpiece of the office here, and it would, I think, be an easier task if I knew always what was going on. . . . I might also perhaps mention the records of your interviews with the Ambassadors. I think I have only seen since last July the notes of what passed on two or three occasions with the French Ambassador about Siam and with the Turkish Ambassador about Armenia. . . . I hope I am not making a very improper request. It is certainly not actuated by curiosity, and if you tell me that it is undesirable that I should see or know more I will be content. But I do feel the difficulty of having to speak here as if I knew all, whereas I only know part ; and I am sure you will exonerate me for mentioning it."

In June of the same year he found it necessary to make one more request.

> " I do not quite know how it is, and no one in the office seems able to explain, but I have never once since I have been in the office heard of any intended deputation to you till after it has been and gone. I should very much like, for instance, to have been present at the deputation about Indo-Chinese rail-ways, a subject which I have long studied and in which I take a great interest. But the first I heard or saw of it was your speech in *The Times* next morning."

UNDER SECRETARY FOR FOREIGN AFFAIRS

So by degrees and by dint of perseverance George Curzon gained access to all the sources of information which he deemed necessary to the due discharge of his onerous task.

He held the post of Under Secretary at the Foreign Office for three strenuous and pregnant years—years that are heavily burdened with material for the historian ; years over which the Future brooded darkly, nursing into a sinister existence ambitions, passions and rivalries which grew and multiplied, wrapping themselves with an embrace that became a stranglehold about the nations of the earth, until in the highly charged atmosphere of the approaching century they broke into an exuberant and poisonous efflorescence. Over all the globe, wherever one chanced to cast one's gaze during these years, man seemed to be engaged in writing his history with a pen dipped, not in ink, but in gall.

When Lord Salisbury took office, Eastern Europe had already become the scene of fierce uprisings of the Turks against their Christian neighbours, and massacres of the Armenians were being enacted on a hideous and appalling scale. Against this outrage upon civilisation the Powers of Europe were disabled from taking effective action by the suspicions and jealousies with which they were themselves consumed. Fed in some cases by a mere craving for power, in others by the urge of economic necessity, the growing rivalries of the European Powers gave birth in their turn to fierce competition, not merely for markets, but for spheres of influence accompanied by seizures of territory in Asia. The real nature of the relations which existed between the leading countries of Europe—relations which by a sort of conventional fiction were officially described as " friendly "—was given uncomfortable notoriety when the German Emperor telegraphed his congratulations to President Kruger on his success in defeating Dr. Jameson's raid across the Transvaal border. The raid itself was a sufficiently unwelcome indication of the unhealthy state of affairs prevailing in that part of the world, and was, as it turned out, the herald of worse things to come. Nor was the spirit of unrest which stalked abroad less active in the northern than in the southern half of the African Continent, and before the close of their first year of office Lord Salisbury's Government found themselves faced with the necessity of organising an expedition against insurgent hordes of Dervishes which were threatening Egypt from the Sudan.

While the unruly passions of men thus seethed and bubbled in Eastern Europe and in Northern and Southern Africa the attention of the British people was suddenly diverted to a fresh cataclysm on the Indian frontier. It was as though a spark had inadvertently been dropped in the neighbourhood of a powder magazine. At any rate, almost before the public realised what was happening the whole frontier was in a blaze and the resources of the Government of India were strained almost to breaking point before they succeeded in extinguishing the conflagration. Even America thrust itself unexpectedly and unpleasantly upon the notice of Europe when, in December 1895, President Cleveland suddenly announced, in what seemed at the time an unnecessarily peremptory tone, that the dispute between Great Britain and Venezuela over the boundary dividing British Guiana from that republic, which had been a subject of sporadic discussion between the two disputants for many years, must not merely be settled, but settled in accordance with American wishes forthwith. And no sooner had Venezuela ceased to be a potential cause of conflict between the old world and the new than its place was taken by the island of Cuba, over which, before long, war broke out between Spain and the United States.

From the point of view of this volume the interest of these tremendous and disturbing happenings lies not so much in the contribution which they make to history as in the influence which they exercised upon the subject of this biography. And my purpose in recalling them has been to indicate the nature and extent of the burden which was thereby imposed upon the British Foreign Office, and not least upon its representative in the House of Commons. No more searching test of a man's character and ability could well have been devised than to constitute him during such times the exponent in the House of Commons of the policy of a Foreign Minister in the House of Lords. And if, in the case of George Curzon, the test was one which was calculated to encourage certain tendencies—defects of manner and temperament rather than of character—it must at once be said that failure to rise at all times completely superior to them was a small thing compared with the brilliant success with which in all other respects he emerged from the ordeal.

The post of Under Secretary for Foreign Affairs, never a light one, was at this time for the reasons set forth above, unusually burdensome. Sir Edward Grey, who had preceded George Curzon in the office, told St. John Brodrick that he had been at snapping point in 1895 ; and the latter, when invited to succeed George Curzon in 1898, after obtaining from him a detailed account of the hours of work and the nature of the pressure to which he had been subjected, felt obliged to tell Lord Salisbury that there were some respects in which he thought the labour of the post might and ought to be lightened. Lord Salisbury concurred ; admitted that constant attendance at the House of Commons for the purpose of taking part in divisions—" which would drive me mad "—added unnecessarily to the burden of the office ; thought that an attempt ought to be made to prohibit supplementary questions on Foreign Affairs, and expressed the opinion that the Parliamentary Under Secretary might very well be relieved of the Commercial Department of the Foreign Office and confine himself to questions of policy and diplomacy.

George Curzon had always been a prodigious worker. His restless brain refused to contemplate repose. And those who knew him most intimately were fully alive to the danger to which, with his highly strung nervous system, he was always exposed. " The appetite for work when one is overstrained," he was once warned by St. John Brodrick, " becomes a disease." Hitherto he had countered the strain of constant work by change of scene and occupation. During his frequent journeys abroad he worked as hard and as ceaselessly as he did at home. But both brain and body responded readily to the stimulus of change where they might have succumbed to the deadening effect of work which was not merely severe and unceasing but also monotonous. In the task upon which he had now embarked the relief to which he had thus become accustomed was scarcely possible ; for even during such brief absences from London as he found practicable, he was still accompanied by his daily task.

Early in 1897 he told Lord Salisbury that he would like to spend the short Easter holiday in Germany when he hoped he might have an opportunity of paying his respects to the German Emperor. Lord Salisbury had approved. " I am glad you are going to see the Emperor William," he wrote in reply. " I hope you will be able to discover why he has been seized with such an implacable suspicion of us and what he imagines we are scheming to do."[1] This hope was doomed to disappointment ; for to George Curzon's unutterable surprise the Emperor curtly declined to see him—a snub which he imagined could scarcely be personal to himself, and must therefore, have been directed against the British Government " with whom everyone in Berlin concurred in telling me that the Emperor is just now bitterly incensed."[2] He had several conversations, however, with Baron Marschall, " a tall man of somewhat academic but most distinguished appearance, free from any Teutonic brusquerie," who traversed the whole field of foreign politics— " Crete, Greece, Constantinople, South Africa, Delagoa bay, the Emperor's telegram, Colonial policy at large, the usurper Khalid in particular, and so on." He thought British Colonial policy everywhere deliberately exasperating to Germany, and roundly abused Cecil Rhodes. " Why," he asked, " should not the German Emperor have congratulated President Kruger on the repulse of a filibustering raid ? " " Why," I answered, " should he ? If the British Government had not from the start disavowed the raid and undertaken to punish the raiders, there might have been some excuse for sympathetic protest from outside quarters. But in this case no such plea could be advanced." He wanted to know what British policy in South Africa was. " I said, the maintenance of the *status quo*, which meant the observance on both sides of Treaty rights. What was Germany's policy ? " Baron Marschall admitted that Germany's interest was only twofold, that arising from her Commercial Treaty with the Transvaal and that arising from her financial stake in the Transvaal railway and other enterprises. The safeguarding of these interests was all that concerned her. George Curzon was very favourably impressed with Baron Marschall's personality.

[1] Letter from Lord Salisbury, April 9th, 1897.
[2] Letter from George Curzon to Lord Salisbury, dated April 29th, 1897.

" I greatly enjoyed meeting so dignified and courteous an antagonist." [1]

Such brief holidays did nothing to take his mind off his work ; and in this respect his excursions to Scotland when Parliament rose were scarcely more successful. During the summer of 1895 he took Inverlochy Castle and experienced once again something of the delight which he had always taken in handling a gun. But it is doubtful if he derived much real rest from these few weeks of retreat. He walked too far and too hard, shooting over dogs all day, fishing during what remained of daylight after his return from the moor and embarking on an exacting correspondence at an hour of the night when his guests were glad enough to retire to rest. At 7.30 a.m. the head keeper was summoned to his room to go over the programme for the day ; and he has told me how he invariably found George Curzon in bed with Foreign Office papers strewn around him. At 9 o'clock a start would be made and throughout the day George Curzon would walk without a pause, except for lunch. Sometimes, when sending his guests home in a carriage at the end of a day on the distant beats, he would himself walk back with the keepers, asking innumerable questions about the lives and habits of the people and imparting in return information that he had gathered during his tours abroad. [2]

The following summer he again took a place in Scotland— Beldorney Castle—but spent some part of the time paying visits and fishing on the Tay. Finding himself on one occasion within driving distance of Butterstone, where Mr. and Mrs. Gladstone were staying, he went over to see them, and wrote Mrs. Curzon a vivid account of this his last interview with the great statesman, with whom he had come into contact in so many different connections since, as captain of the Oppidans, he had first invited him to visit Eton. He found him " immensely old and a good deal bent," his hearing and eyesight both failing him. " He talked, however, with perfectly clear and resonant voice ; descanted upon the size of

---

[1] The above quotations are from a letter from George Curzon to Lord Salisbury, dated April 29th, 1897.

[2] I am indebted to Mr. D. Robertson of Corrour, who served Lord Curzon as keeper at Inverlochy Castle, for an account of his tenancy.

Aberdeenshire men's heads, upon the inability of Jew or Greek to compete in business with the canny Scotsman, upon the national characteristics of Bulgarians and Armenians, upon questions in the House of Commons, upon the merits of the station hotel at Perth, upon Scotch air, upon the health of Arabi Pasha, and upon the code of honour of John Bright." After luncheon he rested and later in the afternoon took a drive. " He wished me all success in fishing ; but betrayed not the faintest interest in my public life or career." [1]

Less than a year later, on May the 28th, 1898, he walked in the funeral cortège which followed Mr. Gladstone's body through Westminster Hall to its last resting place in the Abbey. Seventeen years earlier, when an undergraduate at Oxford, he had been a curious spectator at the funeral of Lord Beaconsfield—" a somewhat jarring combination of public display and quiet modesty," which had prevented it from being " either impressive as a sight or moving as a function." [2] He had thus attended to the grave the two men of whom he had once said that when they passed from public life, the country would confess that its two greatest and only statesmen had gone. [3] The chapter of history throughout which they had been the dominant figures had been more than half written when George Curzon had made his own entrance into public life ; the ink was still wet on the pages of a new chapter in which he himself was to play so conspicuous a part, when the moving notes of Handel's Dead March in " Saul " apprised the great concourse of people which had assembled in the precincts of the Abbey that an era which had profoundly influenced the political evolution of Great Britain had passed definitely into history.

[1] Letter dated September 21st, 1897.
[2] Letter to St. John Brodrick, May 1st, 1881.
[3] See back, chapter V. p. 102.

CHAPTER XVII

THE TRIALS OF AN UNDER SECRETARY

1895-1898

WHEN Arthur Balfour told St. John Brodrick that as Under Secretary for Foreign Affairs he would frequently have to defend a policy with which he did not agree, it is probable that he had in mind the experience of his predecessor in the post. George Curzon entertained feelings of profound respect for Lord Salisbury's wisdom and ability. Writing of the three years which he spent under him at the Foreign Office, he declared that he had learned to some extent " how premature first judgments are apt to be ; what rewards there are for prudence and courtesy and consideration ; and how wonderfully perseverance is justified of her children." [1] But this did not prevent him from thinking that he sometimes acted with a caution greater than was called for in the case of a country occupying the position and commanding the resources of Great Britain. He was always more ready than Lord Salisbury to adopt a policy which depended for its success upon a willingness to appeal in the last resort to arms. This difference between the Foreign Minister and his Under Secretary was the outcome to a great extent of temperament. George Curzon's gaze was fixed on the goal which he wished to reach rather than on the ground that intervened. He was impatient of obstacles standing in the way and a little inclined, therefore, unduly to discount them. On the other hand, Lord Salisbury brought a coldly critical mind and a dispassionate judgment to bear upon the difficulties to be encountered before any particular object could be attained. And if as a result he was satisfied that the obstacles were insurmountable except at a disproportionate cost, he shrugged his shoulders and accepted the inevitable.

[1]Letter to Lord Salisbury, dated June 20th, 1898.

251

The different standpoints from which they approached the problems with which they had to deal, may be seen from perusal of a brief correspondence which passed between them on the subject of an appointment soon after George Curzon began his duties. Sir Nicholas O'Connor was shortly vacating the post of Minister at Pekin, and George Curzon, impressed by the importance of developments in the Far East, addressed Lord Salisbury on the subject. The next ten years, he urged, would have a far-reaching effect upon the position of Great Britain in the Far East, and it was essential, therefore, that our representative should be a man " of first-rate abilities, of resolute character and with Eastern experience." [1] Lord Salisbury agreed as to the importance of the appointment, but wondered if George Curzon was prepared to produce the man having the qualifications which he deemed essential. For his own part he had " looked in vain down the Foreign Office list to find the man ' of first rate abilities, resolute character and Eastern experience,' who is likely to accept the post." And then followed the dispassionate analysis of the situation which laid bare the limits of what was practicable. " The last condition will exclude all except Wade, Alcock, B——, S——, and H——. The two first are octogenarian, and certainly would not go, and I do not think your first condition will apply to the other three." It would be possible, no doubt, to promote the senior man who knew anything of China, but Lord Salisbury could not flatter himself that he would have " a far-reaching effect on our position in the Far East." [2]

When it came to questions of policy, it was inevitable that Lord Salisbury should regard George Curzon's conclusions as having been rashly formed, while the latter looked upon Lord Salisbury's decisions as lacking in enterprise. This divergence grew more pronounced as time went on, and later, when George Curzon became responsible for the foreign policy of the Indian Government, led to differences of a fundamental character. " I am much obliged to you," he once told Lord George Hamilton, " for prodding up that very slumberous lion, the Foreign Office. If only it would now and then roar, or even show its claws ! But it is so very deferential

[1] Letter dated September 28th, 1895.
[2] Letter dated September 30th, 1895.

and polite to all the other lions and to many who are not even leopards." [1] There is every reason for supposing that there were only too frequent occasions during his tenure of the Under Secretaryship when he found the slumberous lion's politeness to the other lions more than trying. The deference shown to France always seemed to him to be excessive. Early in 1898 Lord Selborne, who was then serving under Mr. Chamberlain at the Colonial Office, wrote to him on the subject of French aggression in West Africa. " I am full of anxiety about West Africa. . . . The position is most critical. If the Cabinet decides in favour of Monson's terms, I doubt very much if Chamberlain will be prepared to be responsible for defending them in the House of Commons." George Curzon heartily agreed. " The point upon which I am most strongly with you," he replied, " is about the East Niger regions, where Monson's argument is that the proximity of the French forces over rides our Treaty rights. . . . I hope to see Mr. Chamberlain's reply to-morrow ; and if it is open to me, as I think it may be, to put in a word in favour of ' courage,' you may rely upon me to do so." [2] On this occasion he met with some success in his attempts to make the lion roar, for he wrote a few days later—" The point about which you and I felt so keenly, viz., treating a French advance to the east of the Niger as a hostile act, has, I hope, been attained. Its importance did not seem at an earlier stage to be as much recognised in our office as it perhaps was in yours ; but Lord Salisbury gave Bertie instructions this evening as to a Despatch to the French Government which should leave the matter in little doubt." [3] This did not conclude the matter, however, and the following day he wrote again full of apprehension. " Of course, it rests with the Cabinet whether the Government stand firm or not. Monson's last ' wobbles ' is being printed for Saturday's Cabinet and they must decide whether we are to stand out or once more cave in. I can't tell you how anxious and even how miserable I am. And next week I have got to be defending all this without the slightest idea what

[1] Letter dated April 11th, 1900, when he was urging upon the Home Government the desirability of a more enterprising policy in Persia.
[2] Letter dated January 26th, 1898.
[3] Letter dated February 2nd, 1898.

the Cabinet really think or by what steps they arrive at their mysterious conclusions."

Some years later he had occasion in a letter to the same correspondent to make some observations on British foreign policy which throw further light on the views which he held at this time.

> "I never spend five minutes in inquiring if we are unpopular. The answer is written in red ink on the map of the globe. Neither would I ever adopt Lord Salisbury's plan of throwing bones to keep the various dogs quiet (Madagascar, Tunis, Heligoland, Samoa, Siam). They devour your bone and then turn round and snarl for more. No; I would count everywhere on the individual hostility of all the great Powers, but would endeavour so to arrange things that they were not *united* against me. And the first condition of success in such a policy is, in my opinion, the exact inverse of your present policy; for I would be as strong in small things as in big. This may be a counsel of perfection; but I should like to see the experiment tried." [1]

It is greatly to George Curzon's credit that disagreement with him on many points made no difference to his loyalty to his Chief. Loyalty was, indeed, the keynote of his relations with him, and any hint at possible disloyalty caused him acute distress. In connection with Lord Salisbury's eventual choice of a candidate to fill the vacancy in Pekin, George Curzon was charged by a writer in a provincial newspaper with having expressed his disapproval. He wrote in a fever of irritation, begging Lord Salisbury to pay no attention to the slander—"In case this grotesque fabrication should reach your ears, I hasten to say that I have never even mentioned the subject to a single soul outside the Foreign Office. . . . Please do not trouble to answer; but if there is a suspicion calculated to wound, it is that of disloyalty." [2]

He had not been long in office before his loyalty was put definitely to the test. The settlement of the Siamese question effected by Lord

[1] Letter to Lord Selborne, dated April 9th, 1900.
[2] Letter dated June 20th, 1896.

Rosebery in 1893 was hanging fire. The project of a buffer State which was to keep Great Britain and France from coming into direct contact on the upper waters of the Mekong river, was soon seen to have been still born. Every circumstance was against its prospect of life. The French Colonial Party were determined not to have it. And even if they had been favourable instead of hostile to the project, it is difficult to see how it could have survived, for the simple reason that there was no one to take charge of such a State, even if it had come into being. George Curzon had no illusions on this point; and since it seemed to him that to attempt to set up "a rulerless Alsatia" between the French and British frontiers was absurd, he saw no advantage in persevering with the plan. Something else, then, had to be attempted, and he promised Lord Salisbury that as soon as his election was over he would draw up a Memorandum, setting forth the points of a settlement at which the Government should aim. The Agreement with the French Government eventually reached by Lord Salisbury early in 1896 fell far short of what George Curzon had urged; yet he defended it as stoutly as he had attacked the Agreement arrived at by Lord Rosebery three years before.

He himself inclined to the view that unless we could obtain substantially what we wanted, it would be better not to enter into any agreement with France at all. Lord Salisbury thought that any agreement was better than no agreement. "If no arrangement is come to, France will swallow up Siam in ten years, and I greatly doubt the English being disposed to run any risk in its defence."[1] The most serious blot on the Agreement was undoubtedly the free hand which it conceded to France in Eastern Siam; but it was upon the cession to France of a small piece of Burmese territory on the east of the Upper Mekong that the critics of the Government seized. Lord Salisbury had given away slightly less territory than Lord Rosebery had been prepared to cede; on the other hand, he had ceded the territory to France, whereas Lord Rosebery could claim that his cessions were to have been to a neutral and not to a rival State. To the average man these differences were scarcely appreciable. The two solutions of the question could not in the

[1] Letter from Lord Salisbury to George Curzon, December 3rd, 1895.

nature of things differ materially for the reason that Lord Salisbury was no more prepared to go to war with France over Siam than was his predecessor. No one, of course, knew this better than George Curzon, and for all his spirited defence of it, he can have viewed the Agreement with little enthusiasm. It was one of the bones thrown to the dogs ; and as we have seen, the policy of throwing bones to dogs was not one which commended itself to him.

Later on, when difficulties arose in China, George Curzon must have found acquiescence in such a policy still more irksome, all the more so on account of the very definite views to which he was committed by his own previous writings on the Far East. It was, indeed, made a cause of serious reproach against him by *The Times*— as will be seen hereafter—that the Far Eastern policy of the Government and his defence of it in the House of Commons, differed so markedly from that which, when in a position of greater freedom and less responsibility, he had himself so forcibly urged. Such criticism must have been hard to bear, for the policy, as has been pointed out before, was not his policy. He pressed his own views as far as he was able ; in some cases, notably in that of the acquisition of Wei-hai-wei, he did so with success. But for the rest he could do no more than loyally accept the decisions of his superiors and lend them the aid of his extremely powerful advocacy. Of the success with which he discharged his difficult task, there can be no question. Writing of his defence of Lord Salisbury's policy some years later, the Parliamentary Correspondent of one of the Opposition news-papers declared that it was " China which elevated Mr. Curzon's Parliamentary reputation to its zenith " ; and drew a flattering picture of a brilliant lieutenant gallantly fighting his Chief's not too popular cause. " He was ready for all comers, and his audacity . . . . combined with his undoubted knowledge and ability ultimately triumphed over all prejudices and dislikes. Cleverly and undauntedly he fought the fight without, however, unduly exalting Lord Salisbury (to whose condemnation he was often believed tacitly to assent), or once failing to give you the impression that there was only one man really capable of riding the Celestial whirlwind, his name being George Nathaniel Curzon."[1]

[1] *Leeds Mercury*, June 15th, 1900.

The strain which was consequently imposed on the Under Secretary was a particularly severe one. " I have been utterly dead beat to-day," he wrote to Mrs. Curzon from Southport, where he had been speaking in the Spring of 1896, " and have not done a thing beyond walk out and take the air. I spoke for sixty-seven minutes. How it will look on paper, if reported at all, I have no idea. I tried to be very careful and hope I did not anywhere put my foot in it." The anxieties and responsibilities of the office would have weighed heavily enough on the most phlegmatic—and George Curzon was by temperament the very reverse of placid. With his emotional nature, he was acutely sensitive to criticism of any kind and was apt to take censure very much to heart. In the course of a debate on slavery in Zanzibar, he thought that Sir Edward Grey had impugned his good faith. Sir Edward Grey had, needless to say, done nothing of the sort ; but George Curzon dashed off a letter of indignant protest. [1] Later in the Session he took deep offence at a remark by Sir William Harcourt in the course of a debate on the Uganda railway. The Uganda railway was beginning to get a little on the nerves of men like Mr. Labouchere. He attacked it in Parliament and he held it up to ridicule in the pages of *Truth* in the sort of doggerel for which, as has been shown in the pages of this book, George Curzon himself had a lively taste :

" What it will cost no words can express ;
What is its object no brain can suppose ;
Where it will start from no one can guess ;
Where it is going to nobody knows.

" What is the use of it no one can conjecture ;
What it will carry there's none can define ;
And in spite of George Curzon's superior lecture,
It clearly is naught but a lunatic line." [2]

On the other hand, the Uganda railway, as we have seen, appealed strongly to George Curzon's Imperialistic instincts and was a project,

[1] Letter dated July 28th, 1896.
[2] *Truth* of July 30th, 1896.

consequently, in which he took a special interest. He had warmly commended it to the House in the first speech which he made as Under Secretary ; early in July, 1896, he had again spoken strongly in favour of it, and on the 27th of the same month he had been called on to reply to an attack made on it by the member for Northampton. In bringing his speech to a close, he had observed parenthetically that if Great Britain refused to recognise her obligation to establish railway communication between the interior and the coast, Germany would undoubtedly step in and do so in her place Sir William Harcourt had immediately taken him to task for dragging in references to Germany, " which he is so constantly making and which, coming from the Foreign Office, are singularly impolitic." If George Curzon's passing reference to Germany was impolitic, it may well have seemed to the onlooker that Sir William Harcourt was equally unwise in calling further attention to the matter. But it is unlikely that any disinterested person would have assigned any importance to either reference, interpolated casually in such a debate. Yet George Curzon was so greatly affected by it, that he read into Sir William Harcourt's reference a grave charge against himself fraught with serious international possibilities, and he wrote him a letter of resentful protest. Indeed, he did more, for he did a thing which he can have done on very few occasions throughout his life—he went to the trouble of making an autograph copy of it.

> " Your words, whether read in this country or in Germany, cannot fail to convey a damaging impression, which I am now powerless to remove. I should have had no cause of complaint if this criticism had been merely part of the ordinary cut and thrust of Parliamentary warfare, still less if the rebuke had been justly earned. But I feel that it is rather different when a charge that I believe to be wholly groundless is publicly brought against me as Under Secretary by the Leader of the Opposition; and I am the more hurt that it should have come from one whose friendship I have always regarded it a privilege to claim."

Sir William Harcourt wrote in friendly terms, dismissing the suggestion that he felt any personal animus in the matter, and explaining that he took any opportunity that presented itself of trying to counter the feelings of hostility to Germany which seemed to him to be harboured by so many people and particularly on the Conservative benches, to say nothing of the Foreign Office itself, whose cherished tradition it was to gain support for its own policy by fostering jealousy of the designs of other foreign Powers.

Two more letters passed between them in the course of the same day. " Thank you for your genial and friendly reply," wrote George Curzon.

> " What vexed me was not, however, your criticism of my remark about the German railway, which may or may not have been a wise one, but your suggestion that it was only one of a series of similar affronts from my lips to that Country. If the feeling that you complain of exists in the Foreign Office or elsewhere, it certainly is not shared by me, since I may confess that I have always been an ardent advocate of the *entente cordiale* with Germany, which no one rejoices more than myself that Lord Salisbury has successfully re-established."

Of this letter he also took the almost unprecedented course of making an autograph copy.

These may seem small matters, and so in themselves no doubt they are. But they are important in that they provide illustrations of a particular trait in George Curzon's nature which was due as much, perhaps, to physiological as to psychological causes ; but which exercised as time went on an increasing influence on his career. He was undoubtedly prone to sudden accessions of hyper-sensitiveness which led to conduct which can scarcely be explained on any other grounds—notably the suddenness and completeness with which at a later period of his life he cut himself off from friendships which had been both intimate and prolonged. An intensification of the trouble with his back was the physiological sympton of the strain imposed upon his nervous system, just as hyper-sensitiveness was the psychological indication of the same thing.

Lord Salisbury's absence in the South of France in the Spring of 1898 increased the burden which devolved upon his shoulders to such an extent that he succumbed temporarily to the strain and was obliged to retire to The Priory, near Reigate, the country house which he had taken soon after his marriage, for a period of recuperation. Alarmist paragraphs appeared in the newspapers, hinting at his possible retirement from public life. These, happily, proved to be exaggerations, though from a letter which he wrote to Lord Salisbury at the time, it is clear that the rumours which spread were not wholly without foundation.

> " I promised and had meant to write to you immediately on coming down here last Wednesday. But I am sorry to say that I have been in bed almost ever since and am there now. The work of the past few months has been very heavy, and I do not think that since the beginning of the year I have ever got to bed till 1.30 or 2 a.m. The fatigue has affected my back, which is my weak spot and from which I have suffered before. I am afraid I shall pass the whole of my holiday upon it—and in bed, for I do not think I shall be able to move for some days. However, it will not matter if I get right again when I resume." [1]

He returned to his duties in the House of Commons on May the 9th ; but before the end of the session he was laid up once more and for some days at the beginning of August was wholly incapacitated for work. His friends were becoming seriously alarmed on his account, and on the eve of his departure for labours in another sphere, their fears for the future and their remonstrance with him at his recklessness were conveyed to him by St. John Brodrick—

> " I, with many others, am sorely troubled about your health. For years I have envied your marvellous nervous energy and recuperative power and it is only because I seem to see that the one has been overtaxed and the other has ceased to come to the rescue that I now write—not on my own behalf alone. You

[1] Letter dated April 14th, 1898.

have lived a fuller life for the laſt ten years than any man alive, and for the laſt nine months you have hardly known a day's real health. . . . Please remember that all of us have but one aim. You cannot carry on as you have done these laſt ten years. A man with heart complaint would not run a hundred yards if he were late, and you with overtired back and nerves have no right to work when you are tired. . . . You will not be angry with me for writing this. I have been asked over and over again lately to speak to you and have declined to worry you. But now, and for the only time I speak as I feel." [1]

To these words of kindly warning George Curzon paid little heed. He was conſtitutionally incapable of living a life of ease. In health it was from conſtant work that he derived his zeſt for life ; in suffering and sorrow it was in fierce and concentrated labour that he found the only effective anodyne. If during his life-time his devotion met with brilliant, though fitful, reward, he was deſtined at the laſt to pay the penalty of his all too-consuming passion.

CHAPTER XVIII

THE CONCERT OF EUROPE

1895-1898

THE key to Lord Salisbury's policy in Europe was the maintenance of the Concert of the European Powers. It was not a popular policy in Great Britain, because the policy of the Concert in its turn seemed, so far as it could be said to possess any positive quality at all, to be one of calculated inaction. And if there was one thing which the conscience of the British people demanded, it was that something definite should be done to purge Eastern Europe of Turkish misrule and the shocking outrages for which it was responsible.

George Curzon's brilliant defence of the Government in these unpromising circumstances added greatly to his reputation and won for him a position in the country seldom attained by a politician not holding Cabinet rank. During the autumn recess of 1896, he spoke at Glasgow with an ability and a weight of authority which made a deep impression. It was remarked at the time that he was the first Under Secretary of State who had ever had a platform speech reported in full by the morning papers ; and it was generally agreed that the speech itself was fully deserving of the respect which had been paid to it. He spoke for an hour and twenty minutes, devoting the whole of his speech to foreign affairs. Lord George Hamilton, among others, wrote to congratulate him on it in a strain of high praise. " Let me congratulate you upon your speech. It was first-rate in tone, finish of expression ; exposition of policy equally good, and a very high level was maintained from start to finish. I am now becoming such an old Parliamentary bird that I only read and note exceptional performances. Your speech is the best thing you have done."[1]

The speech was a lucid exposition of the difficulties with which Great Britain was faced, particularly in Eastern Europe, and a dispassionate defence of Lord Salisbury's policy in refusing to be driven into isolated action against Turkey, with the almost certain risk of breaking up the Concert of Europe and precipitating war. It was singularly free from party spirit. Only when referring to the success of the Egyptian expedition in recovering Dongola for Egypt, did memories of the fate of General Gordon betray him into an attack on the Liberal Party. For all the foolish denunciation of the Liberal leaders, the people of Great Britain might rest assured, he declared, that sooner or later the flag would fly again over Khartum ; for only then would we have struck at the tap root of Mahdist ferocity and misrule ; only then should we have wiped out the follies and blunders of our Egyptian policy in the past ; only then should we have avenged on the very spot on which he fell, the memory of General Gordon.

By far the greater part of the speech was devoted to the affairs of Eastern Europe. The question was one on which feeling in Great Britain ran high. A fresh outbreak of massacres in Constantinople had seared the conscience of the British people. A storm of passionate protest against what appeared to be a selfish and callous inactivity on the part of the Powers had swept over the country. The agitation was all the more formidable in that it was undoubtedly the outcome of a revolt of conscience, a spontaneous outburst of moral indignation. Demands had even been made by Mr. Gladstone himself for the withdrawal of the British Ambassador from Constantinople. It was in these circumstances that George Curzon, whose own natural inclination was always to shake the sword in the scabbard, was called upon to urge his countrymen to trust to the continued efforts of diplomacy to unravel the Turkish tangle.

"I observe it is the fashion to speak disparagingly of diplomacy. Yes, gentlemen, but I tell you the only road to successful

[1] Letter dated October 19th, 1896.

action lies through the gates of diplomacy. You may have action, if you like, without diplomacy, but that action will be war. You may lay down the pen, but you are then bound to take up the sword."

His defence of the Concert of Europe was a brilliant piece of advocacy.

Towards the close of his speech he surveyed briefly the activities of Great Britain in other parts of the world—a survey which led up to a glowing peroration. " As the scroll of history unfolds before our eyes, the page on which we are inscribing the characters of British influence grows wider and wider, until it seems to embrace almost the destinies of mankind. Truly this is a great, an august and Imperial work that lies before us. I pray God that we may be equal to the task."

Less than a month later he was himself an interested listener to a speech delivered by Lord Salisbury on the same topics—" Most of his arguments were verbatim, those which he told me to use at Glasgow," he told Mrs. Curzon in a letter written the same night. Yet he found the speech curiously disappointing. The occasion was the Lord Mayor's banquet, on November the 9th, and he wrote his impression of the speech immediately on his return home from dinner. " Lord Salisbury did not (in my opinion) make at all a good speech. He revealed nothing ; left things just as they were ; derided the Opposition criticism ; made jokes about Providence ; almost kneeled to the Concert of Europe ; and said nothing about the really admirable efforts that he has been making—not without some success—to lead that Concert into a more reasonable way. . . . I daresay it may look different in print, and the Concert of Europe will no doubt be pleased. But no one can say that it was a great speech or worthy of the occasion or the speaker."

Within the House of Commons George Curzon's reputation as a debater kept pace with his rapidly growing fame outside. The pages of Hansard during the three years that he represented the Foreign Office in the Lower Chamber bear eloquent testimony to his powers. Late one night in March, 1896, he received notice of the terms of a Motion which was to be moved the following day, expressing sympathy with the sufferings of the Christian population in Asiatic Turkey and a hope that "further endeavours" would be made to improve their lot. George Curzon sent it across to Lord Salisbury with his suggestion that the Government might safely accept the Motion. The latter returned it with his approval of the course proposed, but with a characteristic note of caution written across it in red ink—"Make it clear that in voting for the Motion we do not pledge ourselves to *armed* endeavours."

His instructions were carried out the next day in a speech which was described as "far away the best speech he has yet made in the House"; one which by "its courage, frankness and dexterity charmed the gathering audience."[1] The speech was unusually free from provocation. The jibes and jeers which so exacerbated the feelings of his opponents and in which he often took so mischievous a delight were in abeyance. Once only did the spirit of malice peep out, when, in recalling the truculent demands for action which had not so long before been a commonplace of the Radical press, and comparing them with the sober tone of the Motion before the House, he referred to "these heroics raked up from the dustbin of forgotten follies," as being foolish indeed.

Before the end of the month he was defending Lord Salisbury, not this time for inactivity, but for displaying too great enterprise. The despatch of troops up the Nile in the direction of the Sudan was the occasion of the attack. In defending Lord Salisbury's action he contrasted the highly imaginative picture of what was taking place in Egypt drawn on the Radical benches with the sober realities of the case. They had spoken of unwilling Egyptian troops being dragged on step by step into the heart of Africa and to probable disaster, followed at a respectful distance by British legions. The facts were that in order to protect Egypt against a threatened invasion of fanatical Dervish hordes from the Sudan, the Egyptian army had been ordered to make a cautiously planned and carefully guarded advance of eighty miles, with the possibility of proceeding later to Dongola. "Is there any resemblance," asked the Under Secretary, "between the lurid phantasmagoria which has been conjured up by the imagination of hon. members opposite and the

[1] Mr. (afterwards Sir) H. Lucy in *Punch* of March 4th, 1896.

sober realities which I have attempted to put before the Committee ? " There were doubtless members of the Committee who resented the somewhat contemptuous language in which their arguments were dismissed—there were comments in the press on the tone of the speech, " approaching an insolence of manner which Mr. Curzon would do well to check as much as possible " [1]—but impartial opinion agreed that the Opposition had marred their case by overstatement and that the rebuke was justified.

It was not long before Lord Salisbury was to be assailed once more for lack of initiative in dealing with a fresh difficulty in Eastern Europe ; and it was in the course of his defence of the attitude of the Government toward the Cretan question that George Curzon made a speech which, judged by the effect which it produced, must be accounted one of the most successful of the many which it fell to his lot to deliver.

Among the many storm clouds which rose above the horizon to darken the sky of Europe during these troublous years, the Cretan cloud was undoubtedly one of the most threatening. With a spirit of violent unrest abroad in Eastern Europe, it was inevitable that the little island of Crete with its age-long, hereditary, religious vendetta should sooner or later be drawn into the storm centre. And it was not surprising, therefore, that the year 1896 should be marked by one of the periodical outbursts to which the island had become accustomed. Crete was inhabited by three hundred thousand people of Greek descent. It was misgoverned by Turkey and it was coveted by Greece. No one denied the unsatisfactory character of Turkish rule ; and the whole of the population may well have groaned under the maladministration from which the island suffered. Yet not all of its three hundred thousand people were willing to transfer their allegiance from Turkey to Greece ; for while all were of Greek descent, not all were of the Christian faith, and the bond of religion proved more potent than the ties of race. When, therefore, the embers of unrest flared into open flame, as they did with monotonous periodicity, the people ranged up automatically into two opposing camps, the two hundred thousand Christians in a pro-Greek, and the hundred thousand Moslems in an anti-

[1] The *Evening News* of March 21st, 1896.

Greek camp. It would have been difficult, surely, to find in the compass of a single island the seeds of more certain trouble.

With the Armenian atrocities fresh in memory, Greek sympathy for the Christian population of the island burned dangerously hot, and in the end set light to a serious conflagration. The Greeks wanted Crete for themselves ; they believed what they wanted to believe about what was happening in the island ; and what they wished to believe was that the Cretan Moslems, with the help of the Turkish troops, were treating the Cretan Christians in the island much as the Turks on the mainland had treated the Armenians. Not only did they smuggle arms and reinforcements into Crete, but they despatched raiding expeditions across their own northern frontier into Turkish territory, thus compelling Turkey to declare war. There were many persons in Great Britain whose natural sympathies were all with the Greeks ; but the hard facts of the matter undoubtedly were that the conduct of the Cretan Christians was as much, if not more, to blame than that of the Cretan Moslems. They displayed as much readiness to murder, pillage and burn as did their opponents ; they were, in fact, the aggressors, and the naval forces of the European Powers which assembled in Cretan waters for the purpose of discharging the obligations which they had incurred under the Treaty of Berlin, found themselves obliged by force of circumstances to demonstrate against the Christian insurgents rather than against the Muhammadan peasantry or the Turkish troops.

When, therefore, George Curzon was called upon to defend the policy of the Government in the House of Commons, he was met with an undercurrent of hostility, due to an impression that as a member of the Concert of Europe, Great Britain was backing the Turk against the Christian. " I read out a long list of reports from the admirals this afternoon," he told Mrs. Curzon, on March the 31st, 1897, " amid uproarious and disgraceful cheers from the Irishmen at every step taken by the insurgents in Crete at the expense either of the Turks or the Powers. It was all I could do to keep my temper. . . . The Rads are going to raise Crete again to-night after midnight and I shall probably be kept till the early hours of the morning." Crete had, in fact, become the favourite stick with which to beat the Government, and the Under Secretary was kept busy warding off a constant stream of attack from the radical and Irish benches. " My speech was not really worth much," he wrote after one such attack, " but I was genuinely angry, as you may have inferred, Dillon having three times accused me of lying." [1]

On May the 7th an attack was made in force with a Motion to reduce the Foreign Minister's salary, and it was George Curzon's reply to a speech delivered by Sir Robert Reid, who had served as Attorney General in the previous Government, that left so deep an impression on the House. The pro-Greek sentiment which draped the speeches of his critics was mercilessly torn aside by a cold analysis of the actual sequence of events in Crete itself; the success of the Concert of Europe in localising the war precipitated by the passionate folly of the Greeks, was insisted on. " I venture to say that that success constitutes an incalculable—and will be regarded as an historic—service in the history of European politics." And before they realised it, the organisers of the attack upon the Government found themselves with the point of their weapons broken, suddenly hard pressed to resist a powerful and dramatic counterstroke. " It is very easy to denounce the Concert of Europe " ; but he would ask them to pause for a moment and consider whether in doing so they were really wise ? " If you had an alternative, I could understand it. Denounce the Concert if you have something to set up in their place." And then followed one of those biting phrases with which he was wont to raise the temperature of the debate to fever heat—" but you come here barren of any suggestion—with your mouths full of denunciation and your brains empty of suggestion."

On all sides it was admitted that the speech marked an epoch in George Curzon's career. It was strangely effective in silencing criticism. The stream of questions on the Cretan problem, which had been a feature of the Session, unaccountably dried up. Men who were habitually exasperated by his tone and manner yet admitted the undeniable ability of his performance. Mr. T. P. O'Connor, M.P., who declared that the speech was one the whole tone of which

[1] Letter to Mrs. Curzon, March 30th, 1897.

he detested, confessed, nevertheless, that it constituted " one of the very strongest and most masterful defences of a policy " to which he had ever listened. And he predicted a brilliant future for the man who made it. " His triumph will be as much of temperament as of sheer intelligence. He has a great deal of intelligence, it is true ; but he has more temperament. Self-confident, ambitious, masterful, hard—he is determined to be a master of men and he will be." [1]

George Curzon's natural aptitude for language certainly served him well in these days of stress. His style may sometimes have invited criticism at the hands of those who came into conflict with him ; for he had never quite succeeded in shaking off the manner which had won for him at Oxford the sobriquet which stuck to him for life, and men like Mr. H. Labouchere were never tired of urging him to be " a little more careful in the use of grandiose and recondite words " in his speeches and to cultivate in his mien " an air of modesty." [2] But his speeches excited genuine enthusiasm among his friends and supporters and he derived solid satisfaction from their outspoken praise. " Everybody seems very pleased with my speech," he wrote to Mrs. Curzon on April the 5th, 1897. " All our men come up and congratulate me and say it is just what was wanted and will do a lot of good. *Westminster Gazette* very flattering about it and *Pall Mall* even more so."

No amount of speechifying, however, could altogether drown the discords which were so palpably marring the harmony of the Concert, and George Curzon did not always find his task of defending it an easy or agreeable one. Towards the end of 1897, when the attitude of the leading members of the Concert towards Great Britain had become so hostile that it was frankly recognised that she was for the moment the best hated country in the world, he was billed to speak in his constituency. It was only too apparent to him that the proceedings of the Concert could not possibly be passed over in silence, and he appealed to Lord Salisbury for instructions. The latter replied that he did not think that it was necessary to praise the Concert.

[1] The *Weekly Sun* of May 9th, 1897.
[2] *Truth* of April 2nd, 1896.

" In fact, if you hinted without saying it that the extreme views of Germany have done much to mar its action, I do not see that you would be doing any harm. But we often think ill of the proceedings of Parliament ; we do not in that see any reason for abandoning Parliamentary Government. The same with respect to the Concert of Europe. In spite of constant defects and errors, it is on the whole a beneficent institution. The thing which our critics have to show and which they have not shown is that on any occasion things would have gone better if we had broken away from the Concert. On several occasions our participation has done some good, though perhaps not much. On no one occasion has our participation hindered any good or done any harm. And this is the crucial question to be decided when it is disputed whether we ought to have withdrawn from the Concert as soon as we had ascertained that it was far from being likely to achieve all the good we desired." [1]

The resulting speech, delivered in Southport on December the 10th, provides an excellent example of the skill with which George Curzon could speak to a brief. His hint at the obstruction of Germany was a delicate one, the significance of which was probably understood in Berlin even if it was not fully apparent to his immediate audience.

" You may say that the Concert of Europe is very slow in its operations. I grant you that it is very slow. Its operations have on more than one occasion been retarded by what appeared to us to be the exaggerated views that are entertained by some of its members. There are quarters where, as regards the give and take which is the essence of international diplomacy, more stress seems to have been laid upon the take than upon the give. These are the inevitable drawbacks of a combination in which each unit retains its absolute freedom, both of opinion and of action."

Having thus pointed a warning finger at the bad boys of the

[1] Letter dated December 6th, 1897.

PLATE IX. DISCUSSING THE FUTURE OF CHINA

Concert who refused to play in tune, he proceeded to a defence of the Concert as a whole, following with remarkable accuracy the wording of his brief.

" But though there are anomalies or weakness in an institution, you do not therefore necessarily condemn it. . . . The House of Commons itself is not free from imperfections. There are many people who think it is tolerably full of them. But we should not for that reason applaud the action of any modern Cromwell who advanced to the table, removed the mace, expelled the members and ordered the doorkeepers to shut the door. . . . It is very easy for our critics to denounce the Concert of Europe. What they have to show, what they have not shown yet, is that matters would have proceeded any better or more smoothly if in the first place there had been no such Concert, or if in the second place Great Britain had broken away from it. I have shown you, I think, a number of occasions on which the Concert and the influence of this country in the Concert have done positive good. I know of no occasion on which our influence there has hindered any other Power from doing good ; still less do I know of any occasion on which it has done harm. The Concert may not have done all the good we expected of it or desired ; but if we had deserted it, we should have made ourselves ridiculous and should have retarded and not advanced the solution of the European problem."[1]

The Concert itself paid its apologists in Great Britain a poor return for the fidelity with which they championed it. The assembly of the Powers which for some time past had been a Concert in name rather than in reality, rapidly lost all cohesion. Sentiment in Russia was altogether hostile to Turkey ; in Germany, on the other hand, there was noticeable a marked development of pro-Turkish tendencies. When, therefore, early in 1898 Prince George of Greece was definitely put forward by Russia as a candidate for the Governorship of Crete, Germany showed her disapproval by withdrawing her naval and military forces from the island and carrying Austria

[1]Speech at Southport, on December 10th, 1897.

with her in her train. It was all very well for George Curzon to assert in the House of Commons that the withdrawal of the single German ship and her small detachment of troops had no practical effect on the position in Cretan waters. His statement was, no doubt, literally correct; but the significance attaching to Germany's action was plain enough—the Concert of Europe was no longer a Concert even in name. Nor was George Curzon under any illusions in the matter. "We are no forwarder with Crete," he told Lord Salisbury on April the 11th, 1898. "I wish Russia had proposed anyone but Prince George. We may get him into the island, but will there not straightway be a fresh war of the roses between the two sects? And how are we to get rid of those dreadful Turkish troops?" Doubts such as these, however, were never allowed to show themselves in his public utterances, which excited the admiration of the Foreign Secretary. "I have carefully followed your numerous utterances on behalf of the F.O.," wrote Lord Salisbury on April the 6th, 1896. "They have been admirable. Our critics have certainly left you no rest."

But speech-making was neither the most arduous nor the most difficult part of the Under Secretary's task in the House of Commons. With complicated problems arising almost daily, first in one part of the world and then in another, it was inevitable that the representative of the Foreign Office should have to meet and parry a constant stream of questions on a multitude of matters requiring the most delicate handling; and it was the dexterity which he displayed in dealing with his catechists, even more than his ability in debate, that excited the passions of the House and established his Parliamentary reputation. The question hour became the feature of the sitting, and George Curzon became the feature of the question hour. He was written about almost daily by the newspaper paragraphists and he became the central figure in innumerable cartoons. His adroitness never left him. Pestered with supplementary questions by Mr. Gibson Bowles, he replied on one occasion—" The hon. member asked me the same question last year and he can refer to my answer." He was pictured next day in the *Westminster Gazette* as the haughty youth in "Alice through the Looking Glass" into whose ear Humpty Dumpty Bowles was shouting:

THE CONCERT OF EUROPE

" I said it very loud and clear,
I went and shouted in his ear ;
But he was very stiff and proud ;
He said, ' You need not shout so loud.' "

He coined at least one phrase which has passed into the English language. Irritated by an attempt made to draw him with a question containing an insinuation that the press was in advance of the Foreign Office in obtaining news of happenings abroad, he referred in a vein of sarcasm to " the intelligent anticipation of facts before they occur," as a legitimate art in the case of a newspaper correspondent, but as altogether improper in the case of a Government official. *The Times*, at whose correspondent in China this was a deliberate thrust, did not easily forget it, as will be seen later on.

There were many questions to which it was expedient to give replies while withholding information, and at this art practice soon made George Curzon an adept. His dexterity excited the ire of all those whose curiosity he baffled. " Your friends," wrote an anonymous correspondent, " may legitimately congratulate you on the high stage of perfection to which you have attained in the art of keeping a still tongue. Speechlessness is a beautiful accomplishment which you share in common with the mummy and the cabhorse. Of course, it is a matter of no moment that as a consequence of your policy—and the Government's want of one—the markets are overborne by a keen sense of anxiety ; speculation is at an end and confidence exhausted. Nor will it even fractionally disturb the wonderful balance of your intellect when you learn that most business men have long since written you down a congenital idiot. With every expression of my unalterable esteem, allow me to subscribe myself—A Fervent Admirer." [1]

Mr. Labouchere and Sir Charles Dilke on the Radical benches and Sir Ellis Ashmead Bartlett and Mr. Gibson Bowles on the Conservative side of the House, vied with the Irish members in the ingenuity and persistency of their attempts to throw the Under Secretary off his guard. The growing violence of their indignation provided a measure of their failure, and Mr. Labouchere admitted

[1] Letter dated March 26th, 1898.

ere long that his victim was acquiring so pretty a talent in evading a direct reply to a direct question, " that although I am sometimes the sufferer, his ability in this line fills me—politics apart—with genuine admiration."[1] Elsewhere he was compared to Grattan, who once noted in his memoranda—" I wrote a reply to George Grenville which I thought very good, for I had taken much care. It touched every point except the question. It kept clear of that."

At the close of the session of 1897, two members of the Government were generally regarded as having added markedly to their Parliamentary reputation; one was Mr. Chamberlain and the other was George Curzon. " This year has been an especially good one for you," wrote St. John Brodrick on December the 26th, " your last two speeches have caught on, and your treatment by *The Times* is in itself a testimony."

[1] *Truth* of April 2nd, 1896.

CHAPTER XIX

CLOUDS IN THE FAR EAST

1898

IN the matter of Crete and other problems which had been occupying the public mind, George Curzon had the advantage of starting with a clean slate. Not so in the case of the troubles and difficulties which now thrust themselves with unwelcome insistence upon the attention of the British public. On Far Eastern affairs and on Russian ambitions in Asia, and not least on the methods which she habitually adopted in pursuing them, he had expressed very definite views, both in speech and writing. With reference to possible developments in the China seas, he had asserted in very outspoken language that a Russian port and fleet in the Gulf of Pechili would constitute a serious menace both to China and to British interests. The balance of power, he declared, would be gravely jeopardised by such a development, and he warned his readers that England was prohibited " alike by her Imperial obligations and her commercial needs from lending her sanction to any such issue."[1] In such circumstances his task as spokesman of the Foreign Office in the House of Commons throughout the year 1898, when the rapidly growing ambitions of Russia, France and Germany in the Far East forced China into such unenviable prominence, was very far from being an enviable one. The rapid sequence of events which so alarmed the public and embarrassed the Government in Great Britain may be briefly recalled.

When, as George Curzon had predicted, China collapsed before the victorious forces of Japan, it became evident that an important alteration had been brought about in the balance of power in the

[1] " Problems of the Far East," revised edition of 1896.

Far East. Japan's success on sea and land had left her in possession of certain portions of Chinese territory of great political and strategic value. Her occupation of the Liao-tung Peninsular in particular placed her in a position from which it seemed likely that she would be able to bring undue influence to bear upon the Chinese Government at Pekin. Her presence there was consequently viewed with serious alarm by Russia, and it soon became clear that not all the spoils to which her victories seemed to entitle her were to be left to her enjoyment. In April, 1895, she had, in fact, received a Note addressed to her by Russia, with the support of France and Germany, in which the Imperial Russian Government had told her in very plain language that her contemplated possession of the Liao-tung Peninsular would not only constitute " a menace to the capital of China," but would render the independence of Korea illusory, and so " jeopardise the permanent peace of the Far East " ; and " in a spirit of cordial friendship " had counselled her to renounce the definitive possession of this territory. Since Great Britain, from her position of voluntary isolation, had looked on at these proceedings with folded arms, Japan had been obliged to withdraw her claims to Port Arthur as gracefully as she could.

The significance of Russia's action had not been lost on George Curzon. He had explained it with disconcerting candour in the revised edition of " Problems of the Far East," issued in 1896.

> " Russia does not render this assistance (to China) from a superfluity of unselfishness or for no end. She has her price and she will receive her reward. That reward will involve the still further enfeeblement of the victim for whose inheritance she is waiting and to whose invalid gasps she prescribes with tender hand the dose that imparts a transient spasm of vitality, to be followed presently by an even more profound collapse."

But the British Government, anxious if possible to break down the traditional hostility between Great Britain and Russia, had paid little heed to this warning, and had made it known early in 1896 that, far from wishing to stand in the way of Russia's legitimate aspirations, they would welcome an arrangement which would secure for her a commercial outlet on the Pacific. This declaration was abruptly called to mind during the closing weeks of 1897, when Germany landed a force of marines at Kiao-Chau in support of certain demands which she had made as compensation for the murder of two German missionaries, and Russia followed suit by despatching a squadron to spend the winter at Port Arthur.

George Curzon, whose whole previous study of the Russian advance in Asia had familiarised him with her methods, was under no illusion as to what these steps foreboded. And on December the 29th he wrote to Lord Salisbury setting forth his views upon the situation which was rapidly developing. " Does not the point at which our interests are threatened and at which retaliation may become necessary arise," he asked, " when we know for certain that some other Power has appropriated some portion of Chinese soil ?" It was true that neither Russia nor Germany had yet done this, though the latter might be found at any moment to have done so ; and in this event

> " the pleas that she will thereby be, from a strategical point of view, more vulnerable in the future, or that a German Hong Kong must be a commercial failure, or that she will be a thorn in the side of Russia, do not, it seems to me, alter the fact that she will have violently affected the balance of power in ncrth China to our detriment and in her interest, and that we are consequently entitled to receive compensation."

Where should such compensation be found ?

> " The dangers of the German and Russian position in the north seem to consist in the command that it gives them of the Gulf of Pechili and the approaches to Pekin (for the Court dares not move to Nanking) and in the pressure which they will be able in consequence to exercise on the Chinese Government. It is here that our position, already a good deal shaken by Russian ascendency in Korea, seems most likely to suffer. Russia is always at the door of China by land ; and if her occupation of Port Arthur is made permanent, will be so also

by sea. Germany (if she makes a dockyard and a coaling Station of Kiao-Chau) will be on the other side of the door-Step ; and it will be more difficult for others to get in."

He sketched with remarkable prescience the lines on which public opinion in Great Britain would be likely to cryStallise if the tendencies already visible on the part of the continental Powers developed further.

"The point which it is a little difficult to demonStrate mathematically, but which, 1 think, affects British merchants who know the Far EaSt and all who have been there—and through them public opinion—is this. Up till the present t'me England has enjoyed an undisputed supremacy, naval and mercantile, in the China seas. She was the greateSt Power also at Pekin. No queStion affecting the future of China could be decided without consideration of her Standpoint, almoSt without her consent. The force of circumStances has changed this. Rival nations have Stepped in and claim to exercise a similar control without reference, often in open hoStility, to British intereSts in China, although they possess no Stake at all compared to our own in that part of the world."

Public opinion would undoubtedly demand in these circumStances that definite Steps should be taken to retain for Great Britain in the Far EaSt a position compatible with her paSt achievements and the importance of her present intereSts. And he foretold with accurate prevision the course which in the end she would be compelled to pursue.

"If the European Powers are grouping themselves againSt us in the Far EaSt, we shall probably be driven sooner or later to aft with Japan. Ten years hence she will be the greateSt naval Power in those seas, and the European Powers who now ignore or flout her will be then competing for her alliance."

Returning to the immediate situation, he Stated plainly his view of what our attitude ought to be. Our China squadron might with advantage be sent to Wei-hai-wei as a counter-demonstration to the action of Russia in despatching her ships to winter at Port Arthur, and as an indication that we were not prepared to view with acquiescence any act of a definitely aggressive nature on her part.

> " I argue for a watching attitude, but for a determination to pounce the moment anyone else pounces (and if possible in the same area) ; and for a decision beforehand as to the point of operation, possibly accompanied by an intimation to the Chinese Government that in certain eventualities we shall be bound to protect ourselves."

These views were not shared by the Government as a whole, most of whom seem to have been satisfied that the policy of the open door for which they stood was not seriously threatened. Mr. Balfour, indeed, admitted later on that Russia's seizure of Port Arthur had come as a " shock " to the Government ;[1] while Mr. Chamberlain, speaking his thoughts aloud as was his custom with a candour that was always so refreshing, declared bluntly at Birmingham on May the 13th, when referring to the means by which Russia had succeeded in installing herself at Port Arthur, that as to the representations which had been made and repudiated as soon as they had been made, and as to the promises which had been given and broken a fortnight afterwards, we had better say—" Who sups with the Devil must have a long spoon." No hint of what was impending was to be found in the speeches delivered by the spokesmen of the Government either in the country before Parliament met, or in either House at the beginning of the session of 1898. On the contrary they were of an entirely reassuring nature. On January the 10th Mr. Balfour speaking at Manchester immediately after a meeting of the Cabinet, declared that our interests in China were not territorial but commercial. He admitted that there were two ways in which foreign Governments might inflict injury upon them. They might bring pressure to bear upon the Chinese Government to discriminate against British enterprise, or they might dot the coast of China with stations over which they exercised control and at

[1] Speech in the House of Commons, April 5th, 1898.

which they might establish hostile customs barriers. But he did not think any such development probable and in any case the public might rest assured that the Government was alive to the importance of guarding against any infringements of our rights. A week later Sir Michael Hicks-Beach said the same thing in much more bellicose language. He declared that he did not regard China as a place for conquest or acquisition by any Power, European or other; that Great Britain could not tolerate the acquisition of privileged positions by anyone and that we were determined that the door should be kept open to the trade of all nations on a footing of complete equality, even, if necessary, at the cost of war. When Parliament met on February the 8th, China found no mention in the Queen's speech; but in reply to enquiries by the leader of the Opposition, Lord Salisbury declared that nobody had indicated the least intention to infringe our Treaty rights nor did he believe that any such intention would ever be entertained. On the contrary the Russian Government had given written assurances that any port which might be assigned to it as an outlet for Russian commerce, should be a port free to the commerce of Great Britain, while the German Government had acted in a similar spirit in regard to Kiao-Chau.

As the representative of the Foreign Office in the House of Commons George Curzon was, of course, obliged to frame his speeches in harmony with the note of optimism which dominated the outlook of his superiors; and as late as March the 1st he accepted a Motion by Sir Ellis Ashmead Bartlett laying down the importance, in the interests of British commerce, of maintaining the integrity and independence of China. In accepting the Motion he said that while he could conceive of circumstances arising in the future gravely affecting, or even imperilling our interests in China, which might compel us to modify our attitude, yet " the seizure of Chinese territory, the alienation of Chinese territory, the usurpation of Chinese sovereignty," was not primarily any part of British policy; and that which we repudiated ourselves it was not likely that we should regard with a welcoming eye if attempted by others. Neither his speech nor his action in accepting the Motion was calculated to prepare the public for the news telegraphed to *The Times* only a week later, that Russia had made important demands of

China in connection with Port Arthur and Manchuria; nor for the more definite news received before the end of the month, that the Chinese Government had signed a Convention leasing Port Arthur and Talienwan to Russia and that these two ports were to be occupied by Russian troops forthwith.

Indeed one of the chief sources of George Curzon's embarrassment was the well founded suspicion of the British public which grew steadily during February and March, that there was little enough cause for the optimism which the Government continued to display. His position was undoubtedly one of extreme difficulty. The public, particularly well served in the matter of information by the newspapers with correspondents in the Far East, saw with far keener insight than the Government the trend of events in that quarter, and developed what Mr. Balfour described later on as " an almost irritable anxiety " on the subject. George Curzon's own estimate of the situation coincided with that of the public rather than with that of the Government; yet loyalty demanded of him that he should side with the Government and against the public. The difficulty of the position was increased by the reticence of the Government and the enterprise of the Press. Information appearing daily in the columns of the latter was almost invariably confirmed sooner or later—usually later—by the Foreign Office. On March the 29th Mr. Dillon enquired in the House of Commons how it was that the Pekin correspondent of *The Times* was able to publish facts of the highest importance several days before the Foreign Office had knowledge of them ? Stung by the taunt—and still more no doubt by his realisation that it was deserved—George Curzon replied :—

" It is the business of Her Majesty's representatives abroad to report to us facts of which they have official cognisance and to obtain confirmation of them before they telegraph. I hesitate to say what the functions of the modern journalist are ; but I imagine they do not exclude *the intelligent anticipation of facts even before they occur* and in this somewhat unequal competition I think the House will see that the journalist whose main duty is speed, is likely sometimes to get the advantage over the diplomatist whose main object is accuracy." [1]

Had he paused to consider the almost certain effect of such a jibe upon so powerful an organ as *The Times*, he would probably have foregone, willingly enough, any temporary satisfaction which he derived from its utterance. He was soon to realise how ill advised he had been, for in a report of the proceedings in the House of Commons which he wrote to Lord Salisbury on April the 11th, he told him that *The Times* had thrown itself into the fray " with the passion of a ferocious partisan " ; and he added by way of comment—" It is usually faithful to its old employés ; but some mild chaff in which I indulged in a spirit of subdued compliment to its Pekin correspondent, brought it down on me with the tread of an elephant."

How strongly he disapproved of the attitude of the Government at this time is made abundantly clear by letters which he wrote at a later date. " We have never had and we have not (now) any policy towards China," he asserted in a letter to St. John Brodrick on May the 3rd, 1899. " No one knows that better than you or I who have successively had to conjure up make-believes. But of course the supreme lesson of the F.O. is that there is no pre-determined policy about anything." A year later—on June the 18th, 1900—he returned to the subject. " I forget if I said in a recent letter that I hope F.O. are keeping their eye on Wei-hai-wei. . . I have never been able to understand what seems to me the inexcusable apathy shown about turning it to some purpose. But then it is a part of the Chinese policy of H.M.G. which has always been to me—and I believe to everybody else—a riddle insoluble by man." The Boxer rising in the summer of 1900 recalled once more his own past connection with the Foreign Office in its attempts to grapple with the affairs of China. " You are very good and faithful about letting me know the goings on, particularly in your F.O. world where I follow your movements and struggles with the liveliest interest. I know what an uphill job it is with the Parl. Under Sec. so to speak outside the show and with that strange, powerful, inscrutable, brilliant, obstruc-

[1] *Hansard*, March 28th, 1898.

tive dead-weight at the top."[1] And again on August the 22nd, 1900; " How well I remember the difficulty of making speeches on China with no instructions, no policy, and not too much heart."

It may be argued that in the circumstances in which he found himself George Curzon should have resigned rather than permit himself to be associated with a policy with which he disagreed. The same dilemma arose at a much later period in his life, when, as Foreign Secretary, he seemed to acquiesce in a policy with which he was not in sympathy, and which to all appearances was imposed upon him by the masterful will of the then Prime Minister, Mr. Lloyd George. In both cases resignation would have been easy—though from a personal point of view distasteful. But would resignation have advanced the cause which George Curzon had at heart ? He was, I think, quite sincerely convinced in each case, not merely that his resignation would not help matters, but that it would be positively injurious to the interests of the country. So long as he remained he could bring influence to bear upon his colleagues, and could hope to carry them some part of the way, at least, if not the whole way with him. True, such a decision necessitated his defending in public some things that in other circumstances he would have preferred to attack. But this seemed to him to be the lesser of the two evils ; and it was in keeping with his temperament that the vehemence of his defence should have been in proportion to what he believed to be the weakness of his case. At such times the artist triumphed over the man ; the satisfaction which he experienced was derived from the skill which he was called upon to exercise in presenting his case. In the year 1898 he was more than justified by results, for in one matter of the first importance he carried the Cabinet with him.

The views which he had laid before Lord Salisbury in his letter of December the 29th had not then carried conviction. Russia was still protesting the innocence of her intentions, and the Government were content to accept the assurances " spontaneously " offered to them. But when George Curzon saw that his own doubts of Russian *bona fides* were once more being confirmed by the inexorable march of events, he returned to the charge, and on March the 13th drew up a

[1] Letter to St. John Brodrick, July 19th, 1900.

more elaborate statement of his case for submission to the Cabinet. It was certain, he urged, that whatever assurances might be given to the contrary, Port Arthur, when it passed into Russian hands, would become Russia's naval base in China. When promises were given that it should remain a commercial port, let them remember the fate of Bizerta. Nor was it of the least use delaying their protest until the assurances given had been violated, for experience showed that a *fait accompli* was almost invariably accepted. Great Britain had not gone to war either for Bizerta or for Batoum. He could not agree with those who argued that if Russia and Germany were detemined on the dismemberment of China, Great Britain should accept such an outcome of the crisis as inevitable and withdraw from northern China with a view to concentrating on the Yangtsze valley. Such a step would deprive us of all influence at Pekin, where the Chinese Government would be left at the mercy of our rivals. There were three naval ports in the north of the China sea—Kiao-Chau, Port Arthur and Wei-hai-wei. Germany had seized the first, Russia was on the point of appropriating the second, should we not be wise to occupy the third ? We could do so with complete propriety, for before the demands of Russia had been definitely formulated on March the 7th the Chinese Government had actually invited us to take this step. Acceptance of her invitation would constitute a declaration on our part that we had no intention of abandoning the field in northern China to our rivals and would give us a lien upon the continued confidence and, in due course, upon the alliance of Japan. On the other hand, to retire from northern China would be fatal to our position in the Far East. Our power, once paramount, had already been gravely compromised ; only by decisive action could we hope to retain even a greatly curtailed influence where once we had been supreme. No hesitation need be shown on the score of the reception which such action would meet with at home, for the British public would be the last to complain if the valiant declarations which had been made—a reference doubtless to the bellicose speech of the Chancellor of the Exchequer in January—were followed by corresponding deeds.

Before the end of the month it became known that at the invitation of Mr. Balfour, who, in the absence of Lord Salisbury through illness, was acting as Foreign Secretary, George Curzon was attending frequent meetings of the Cabinet. It was assumed at the time that he was called in to give the Government the benefit of his intimate knowledge of the Far East. The assumption was not far from the truth, though the actual circumstances in which he had been called in remained a secret. The Government had protested with too great emphasis against territorial acquisitions in China to make acceptance of George Curzon's plea for the occupation of Wei-hai-wei easy; and those members of the Government to whom he had first submitted it—Mr. Balfour, Mr. Chamberlain, Mr. Goschen, the Duke of Devonshire, Sir Michael Hicks-Beach and Lord Lansdowne—had begun by being unanimously opposed to it. Mr. Chamberlain urged concentration on the Yangtsze valley; Sir Michael Hicks-Beach stood resolutely against occupation, and it was only when George Curzon succeeded in gaining the support of Mr. Balfour that he got the chance of arguing his case before the Cabinet as a whole. The latter body were not easily persuaded, and it was not until its fifth sitting that George Curzon won the day. With the approval of Lord Salisbury, who was consulted in his retreat in the South of France, a decision in favour of the occupation was finally arrived at and was communicated to the House of Commons in the course of a debate on the Chinese question on April the 5th.

George Curzon felt legitimate pride at his success. " I think our China debate on the whole went off well," he wrote Lord Salisbury, on April the 11th. " Arthur's statement was judicious and well delivered ; but its effect had been somewhat discounted by the revelations of the newspapers. I think, however, everyone on our bench (including the anti-Wei-hai-wei party, such as Chamberlain, Goschen, etc.) realised that but for Wei-hai-wei we should have fared badly." To Mrs. Curzon he confessed that he did not think very much of his own speech. " But people say it was good. General reception of our case fair, not enthusiastic. Without Wei-hai-wei we should have been simply nowhere."[1] And more than two years later, when the situation in China suddenly took a new and alarming turn and the anti-foreign rising known as the Boxer Rebellion had

[1] Letter dated April 5th, 1898.

all the appearance of being the prelude to a racial cataclysm on a vast scale, he was able further to congratulate himself on his foresight. As Viceroy of India he was called upon during the summer of 1900 to despatch an expeditionary force to co-operate with the troops of the other Powers engaged upon the relief of the Legations at Pekin ; and he wrote with satisfaction to Lord George Hamilton, then Secretary of State for India, of the value of Wei-hai-wei. " I have been quite pleased to hear that Wei-hai-wei—which was in a particular sense my own child . . . has turned out such trumps. I only regret that we have not done more to utilise and develop it during the past two years." [1]

There was, however, a great deal still to be done before the situation could be regarded with anything approaching satisfaction.

> " I think our next step in China should be to get some reliable syndicates to undertake the trunk lines N. and S. from the Yangtsze—N. towards Pekin, S. towards Canton. People talk as if we could absorb, protect and administer the whole Yangtsze valley in the twinkling of an eye. I calculate that it contains over 150 million people, or two thirds of the whole population of China. Fifty years hence we shall not have done it, if we ever do. But I expect that railways are the best way of getting at the people and making your sphere of influence practical." [2]

Throughout the summer the Chinese crisis dragged on, and George Curzon continued to urge a more vigorous policy upon the Government in private, while defending what he undoubtedly looked upon as a weak and vaccilating policy in the House of Commons. In June he returned to the question of railways centering upon the Yangtsze valley. The northern section of a trunk line running from Pekin to Hankow was already being built by a syndicate with Russian money behind it ; and now, it was learned, negotiations were on foot for the construction of the further section to Hankow on the Yangtsze through the same agency. " Is not this

[1] Letter dated August 22nd, 1900.
[2] Letter to Lord Salisbury, April 11th, 1898.

railway demand more than we should allow?" he asked in a letter to Lord Salisbury on June the 2nd. "And need a protest against it necessarily involve the immediate production of a rival offer from ourselves?... I am sure we shall have trouble if once the Russians get a serious footing (even through the medium of a State bank or a mortgaged railway) on the Yangtsze. Is it not desirable that Mac-Donald should oppose any such scheme by all means in his power, and that the Chinese Government should know that we cannot admit of such an intrusion into the Yangtsze?" Lord Salisbury, with his gaze riveted on what seemed practicable rather than on what was merely desirable, replied two days later in a tone which George Curzon always found so hard to bear. "I understand you to propose that we should resist and prevent the construction of any Chinese railway to whose expenses any Russian bank has subscribed. Is this practical? Yet if you do not accept this general principle, I do not see how the particular offence of financing the Hankow railway can be detected and punished. I do not see my way, if Russian Capitalists will throw their money about, to preventing the Chinese from picking it up. We must find some equally patriotic Capitalists on our side; otherwise we must say sorrowfully of the Russian coin—'Roublet.'" And two months later he said the same thing in slightly different language in the House of Lords—"If our Capitalists are able and willing to make railways in the Yangtsze valley or anywhere else, we will give them the utmost possible support, but if they cannot we will not try to deprive the Chinese people of the benefits of railway construction."

In the House of Commons criticism came from all quarters. On the Conservative benches the flag of revolt was raised by a little band of stalwarts which, under the leadership of Mr. Yerburgh, came to be known as the Pigtail Committee. If George Curzon had been a private member he would assuredly have been found leading the Pigtail Committee. As it was he had to bear the brunt of its attack; and it must be admitted that in his frequent bouts with Mr. Yerburgh and his friends he was sometimes betrayed into making statements which accorded ill with views which could be—and, of course, were—quoted against him from his own previous writings. His airy dismissal of Russia's action in converting Port Arthur into a closed naval base as being of little importance, on the ground that with Talienwan close by there was no commercial need for a second Treaty port in the neighbourhood, lacked conviction, in face of the very definite views on the subject which were on record in the pages of " Problems of the Far East."   And in the last speech on the affairs of China which it fell to his lot to deliver in the House of Commons he had the misfortune to fall foul of *The Times* once more. It was all very well for the Government to cling to their belief in the policy of the open door, declared that journal ; but with our rivals establishing preferential rights over great areas, what became of the open door ? Mr. Curzon had based his defence on the fact that the rights claimed by Germany in Shantung were preferential but not *exclusive*, as some of his opponents had described them. " Accuracy of statement is an excellent thing, but it is possible to sacrifice substantial accuracy to verbal precision and to irritate without either convincing or confuting." And its summing up of the performance was characterised by a note of extreme acidity. " A Government cannot be said to be particularly fortunate when it has to depend for the presentation of its policy to the House of Commons upon such speeches as that made by Mr. Curzon."[1]

Yet, in spite of a certain measure of odium which he incurred as a result of his zealous championship of the Far Eastern policy of the Government, the ability which he displayed in doing so set the seal upon his Parliamentary reputation. And a realisation of the difficulty of his position won for him a large measure of sympathy. " All of a sudden," wrote an onlooker when the Chinese crisis was at its height, " Mr. Curzon has made a great stride in advance, and the last few speeches he has delivered in the House have marked enormous improvement in temper, in language and in thought. He has abandoned almost completely the aggressiveness which made him so many enemies and so many difficulties."[2] Even more significant of the growing appreciation of the House of Commons was the genuine concern which it displayed on learning, in April 1898, that he had been obliged by ill health to withdraw temporarily from active participation in its work. " I see it stated in the papers," wrote his

[1] The quotation is from a leading article in *The Times* of August 3rd, 1898.
[2] A writer in The *Weekly Sun* of March 3rd, 1898.

old enemy H. Labouchere, on April the 27th, " that you are so bad that you will have to withdraw for sometime from H. of C. Then I see it contradicted. I sincerely hope that the contradiction is the right version, for you have made yourself such a splendid position in Parliament that it would be too bad if your health were to break down for any length of time." And when he returned to the House after an absence of two to three weeks, he received a welcome from both sides which took him completely by surprise. " George Curzon back to-night after long bout of sickness," wrote Toby, M.P., in his diary of May the 9th. " Pleasant to see the hearty welcome that cheered his return. Both sides vied with each other in genuine heartiness of congratulation. The House always prompt with kindliness of this nature. But there are degrees of warmth, and the warmest was showered on the young Under Secretary. This all the more gratifying because it is a position won against certain disadvantages." Moreover, the events of these strenuous days brought prominently to the surface the indomitable courage of the man. The grim fight with ill health could not be altogether hidden from sight. It was more apparent, perhaps, to those who viewed the daily struggle from the comparative detachment of the press gallery than it was to those engaged in the constant thrust and parry on the floor of the House itself. " It was curious, and sometimes almost pathetic," wrote one witness, " to observe the palpable struggle which was going on between the remnants of recent illness and the determination to state his case. At times, indeed, it seemed as if the strain would be too much and as if tired nature would have to give in."[1] George Curzon was himself acutely conscious of the extent to which his aspirations and ambitions were threatened by the spectre of ill health, and he had special reasons for wishing to satisfy Lord Salisbury on the matter. It was with very real relief, consequently, that, as the result of a consultation with an eminent physician in June, he was able to give his chief a definitely reassuring report.

On August the 5th, a few days before Parliament was prorogued, George Curzon made what was to prove to be his last speech in the House of Commons. He was attacked, as he had been on many occa-

[1] A writer in the *Daily Telegraph*, June 11th, 1898.

sions, in connection with the attitude of the Government towards the vexed question of slavery in East Africa. It was not the subject which he would himself have chosen for his farewell speech, for earlier in the Session he had gravely offended the House by a certain flippancy with which he had treated the misgivings which it entertained as to the intentions of the Government in dealing with the matter. But no one who heard him on August the 5th had any reason to suppose that he was listening to him for the last time ; nor, indeed, did George Curzon himself imagine—though he was then aware that his career in the House of Commons was about to be interrupted—that the break was to be anything more than temporary. A few days later the House learned that changes were impending in the Ministry and that thenceforth the battle of the Foreign Office was to be fought by someone else. But George Curzon was not present to witness the display of genuine emotion which the news evoked, for he was a prisoner once more upon a bed of sickness.

CHAPTER XX

1898

LORD ELGIN had assumed charge of the office of Viceroy and Governor General of India in January 1894. He was due to retire in January 1899, and throughout the summer of 1898 rumour had been busy with the names of those upon whom it was thought that the mantle might fall. The importance of the appointment was widely recognised, for events in India had been attracting considerable attention in Great Britain.

The peace which brooded over the sub-continent when Lord Elgin took over from his predecessor, Lord Lansdowne, had been rudely disturbed. A poor rainfall in 1895 had been followed by a disastrous drought in 1896, and the machinery of Government had been strained to the utmost in fighting the grim spectre of want that stalked naked through the land. Echoes of the tragedy being enacted on the sun scorched plains of its remote Dominion had reached the public of Great Britain when an appeal to its generosity had been made on behalf of the suffering survivors of this calamity. But this had not been all, for to famine had been added pestilence in the form of bubonic plague, which, making its sinister appearance in the crowded slums of Bombay in the autumn of 1896, had spread with alarming rapidity, and had presented the Administration with a new and baffling problem, demanding urgent and drastic treatment. Sedition, not yet clearly dissociated from the ferment caused by these inflictions and the measures taken to combat them, had given unwelcome proof of its existence. In the summer of 1897, amid its celebration of the Diamond Jubilee of Queen Victoria, the public had been startled and momentarily shocked by the news flashed

across the wires from Poona of the murder of two British officials ;
and a little later considerable stir had been created by the trial and
sentence of a prominent Indian publicist, Mr. Bal Gangadhar Tilak,
for inciting to disaffection in the columns of his newspaper, the
Kesari.

But grave as these symptoms of trouble in the internal situation
were, it was the perennial problem of the North West Frontier
that was most seriously exercising the public mind at home.   The
picture presented by an Englishman beleaguered with a handful of
companions in a hostile land, hard pressed, but keeping the flag
flying with cheerful optimism against heavy odds, common though
it has been in the long history of her Imperial growth, is one which
never fails to capture the imagination and quicken the pulses of the
British nation.   It illustrates the courage and tenacity which it
complacently regards as the special prerogative of its race.   And in
1895, amid the rugged mountains on the borders of Afghanistan, a
British officer, charged with duties in connection with the demarcation of the frontier, had been beleagured in the isolated fort of
Chitral.   The siege and subsequent relief of this remote outpost
had proved to be but a prelude to still graver happenings over a
greatly extended field.   In June of the year 1897 the latent fanaticism
of the border tribes had burst into flame, and from the Tochi valley,
tucked away in the ample folds of the mountains of Waziristan, the
fire had spread with alarming rapidity, enveloping the whole
frontier in fierce conflagration.   The most peace-loving of Viceroys
had found himself confronted with a rising, officially described as
" unprecedented alike in the suddenness with which it broke out
at each point, in the large extent of country affected and in the simul-
taneous action of distinct tribes," and compelled to concentrate all
his thought and energy upon the prosecution of a military episode
on a grand scale, which came to be known as the Tirah Campaign ;
while the British Cabinet had been faced with the necessity of
coming to grave decisions as to its future attitude towards these
powerful and truculent neighbours.

In such circumstances there was no room for doubt as to the
importance attaching to the selection which Lord Salisbury had to
make, and the qualities required for the successful mastery of the

problems peculiar to the Indian continent were canvassed in the press and became the subject of desultory discussion round the dinner tables at which society met and gossipped. Five years earlier Mr. Gladstone's choice had fallen on " a cautious, silent young Scotch peer," and there were many who thought that search might be made for a man with characteristics similar to those which had served Lord Elgin so well during his five strenuous years. Little difficulty was experienced in hitting on such a man. In Lord Balfour of Burleigh, then Secretary for Scotland, the prophets discovered an ideal example of the type. Able, cautious, essentially sound, here was the man to tread warily amid the pitfalls with which British Government in India was beset. Fears of a perilous policy of adventure across the North West Frontier which were agitating the minds of many eminent persons would be laid to rest by such an appointment ; the difficult and delicate problems arising out of plague and famine would be capably and safely handled ; financial questions—notably that of currency—would be under the supervision of one whose familiarity with business would be an undoubted asset. So confidently was his appointment predicted that in India itself, and particularly among the Services whose members had naturally a personal interest in the matter, it came to be regarded as a foregone conclusion.

It would have been strange, however, if rumour had concerned itself only with one name. There was another nobleman of Scotch descent whose thoughts were turning towards what he himself had once described as " the way of ambition."[1] And if Lord Minto's personal friends looked to Canada rather than to India to provide him with the means of satisfying his aspirations, it was nevertheless no secret to them than if offered the Viceroyalty of the latter he would not refuse it. There were others again who thought that qualities of a very different kind marked out Mr. Curzon as a man unusually well fitted for the post. Brilliant imagination, specialised knowledge, outstanding personality, self-confidence and assiduous industry combined with great gifts of speech and writing—these were attributes, surely, which went to create a figure worthy of so spacious and brilliantly illumined a stage. And when in due course his

---

[1] " Lord Minto—A Memoir," by John Buchan.

appointment to this great office was announced, previous predictions were forgotten in face of the obvious appropriateness of the choice which had been made.

The appointment, the official announcement of which appeared in the papers on the morning of August the 11th, had been made known the previous evening in the House of Commons. Mr. Curzon himself was kept away from the House by illness, and Mr. Balfour, to whom fell the task of replying to an attack upon the foreign policy of the Government in his absence, expressed his regret that the Under Secretary should have been prevented from attending the House on the last occasion on which it would have been in his power to address it on a subject in which he had made "so great and so deserved a reputation." At the moment the significance of this casual interjection was lost upon those present; but when its import was realised, it elicited a chorus of warm approval. The first words of congratulation came from Mr. Dillon who, in the past, had broken many a lance with the man he now rose to praise, and met with such universal endorsement that the Parliamentary correspondent of one of the leading organs of the Opposition, was fain to admit that "the tributes from the House . . . show that Mr. Curzon has more than half out-lived his early unpopularity."[1] They did more; they showed that with its unerring judgment in the matter of men, it had detected behind the manner of which at first it had been so resentful, not only the brilliant intellectual attainments of the scholar and statesman, but a strong sense of courtesy and a sincere kindness of heart.

On the whole, Mr. Curzon had little cause to complain of the manner in which his appointment was received by the press. It would have been too much to expect that his political opponents should altogether resist the temptations of a thrust at one who had himself not always been over tender towards those with whom he differed; and here and there an acid note could be detected in the comments of the party press. Not Mr. Curzon's most indulgent friends could deny that what had been described somewhere as his "little tricks of condescension, the almost Johnsonian pomposity of his rhetoric and other perceptible angularities" had, during his

[1] The *Daily Chronicle* of August 11th, 1898.

early Parliamentary days, created an impression of superciliousness of character, than which, as Mr. T. P. O'Connor observed at the time, " there is no quality in a man which the House of Commons more seriously resents." But if there were those amongst his critics who lamented that the Viceroy-designate had still " many of the defects of the youthful temperament " ; that he was " flippant, omniscient and not unfrequently hard and cynical as only blasé youth can be,"[1] or who predicted that his " restlessness and conceit " would not improbably " bring us into trouble in India ";[2] the great majority agreed with those who regarded the appointment as " a personal triumph almost unique in Parliamentary history,"[3] and found in it reason for believing that " the Government of India and the people of India would very greatly profit by it."[4] Nor was approval confined to the press of his own party. Leading organs of the Opposition paid generous tribute to his ability and to the conscientious manner in which he had prepared himself for the great office to which he had been raised ;[5] and the conclusion of the *Pall Mall Gazette* that " when those whose duty it is to pick holes in Ministerial appointments have recited all possible objections to Mr. Curzon, they are constrained to admit that this appointment is a good one," was in the main well founded.

Not all the criticism, however, could be discounted as being due to personal antipathy or party prejudice. Beneath the general chorus of approval there existed a thin but perceptible undercurrent of uneasiness, which tended to crystallise into fear of a policy of adventure beyond the Indian frontier, fed by the reputation which Mr. Curzon enjoyed of being an ardent supporter of the forward school. In the Russian press it was regarded as a foregone conclusion that he was being sent to India to give effect to a policy which challenged Russian aspirations in Central Asia and the Middle East. In a prominent article in the *Novoe Vremya* he was depicted as a member of " the most extreme Russophobe party, who close their

[1] The *Liverpool Mercury*.
[2] The *Saturday Review*.
[3] The *Morning Post*
[4] The *Daily Graphic*.
[5] The *Daily News*.

eyes to everything that does not seem to confirm their hardly intelligible hatred towards Russia " ; and the writer urged his countrymen " to follow with a keen eye the acts of Mr. Curzon," and warned them that as Viceroy of India he would proceed to give effect to the theories which he had hitherto developed in his books and in the columns of the press. [1] These apprehensions found an echo in London in the columns of the *Spectator* and the *Westminster Gazette*. The former feared that the new Viceroy was a man who by temperament was " inclined to ambition and delighted by personal victories," whereas the most essential requisite in a Viceroy of the great Eastern Dependency was, in its opinion, a capacity for self-effacement ; while the ideal Viceroy in the view of the latter was, generally speaking, " a sober middle-aged gentleman with a cool head and such insight into men and character as experience alone brings," and, in particular, " a man of weight and authority who could stand up to all encroaching military gentlemen and refuse to be pushed into a forward policy by an exaggerated alarm about remote dangers."

The events leading up to the Tirah campaign had brought the frontier to the forefront of Indian questions, and had opened the door to a reconsideration of the existing policy. Decisions of grave import had to be taken, and fears as to the direction which such decisions might take under the influence of an ambitious Viceroy were seriously exercising the minds of persons who counted in the public life of the nation. They were formulated half jestingly by Sir William Harcourt at the end of a letter of good wishes to Mr. Curzon himself—" P.S. The most important thing is always put in a postscript. Let me beg as a personal favour that you will not make war on Russia in my life-time " ; and Mr. H. Labouchere, in a letter of warm congratulation, while careful to dissociate himself from such anxieties, made pointed reference to them—" Campbell Bannerman, who is here, spent this morning conclusively proving to me that you will drag us into a war with Russia." Nor was the expectation that the new Viceroy would pursue a vigorous frontier policy confined to those who viewed the prospect with feelings of anxiety and dislike. General Sir Bindon Blood, who had been in

[1] The *Novoe Vremya* of 3/15 September, 1898.

command of the Malakand Field Force during the previous year, wrote—" it will amuse you to hear that I am being told by the Acute-Forward-Policy people, of whom I know several well, that now I shall have as many wars as I want !" He added, however, speaking for himself, that in a way this was doubtless correct, for he wanted no wars, and " I am sure you are the man to prevent them, unless they are absolutely necessary." Another eminent soldier, Sir W. Lockhart, who had directed operations in Tirah and who, as Commander-in-Chief in India, was destined to be associated with the future Viceroy in working out the military aspect of frontier policy, wrote to him in an enthusiastic strain—" The next five years will be stirring ones for India. Your own personal influence with the Amir will be of untold value—as the world will see ; but the Amir may not last long, and I think we should have a plan beforehand of what is to be done when his death takes place." Perhaps he had in mind something which Mr. Curzon had himself written some years before—" so long as Abdur Rahman lives a buffer Afghanistan may continue to figure in the lists of independent States " ; but upon his death " it is to be feared that a time of trouble will again recur more critical than any of its predecessors, inasmuch as Russia notoriously looks to such an emergency as providing an excuse for her next advance." [1]

It cannot be said that these apprehensions were altogether without justification. Mr. Curzon's study of Russian policy in Central Asia and his personal observation of her methods, had aroused in his mind serious misgivings regarding her intentions. These he had proclaimed with no uncertain voice in speech and writing ; and if he ridiculed the idea of a Russian conquest of India, he was profoundly impressed by the danger of a Russian invasion of her frontiers, not in the expectation, or, indeed, with the intention, of wresting the sceptre from Great Britain ; but with the purpose of disabling the British Government from checking further her own ambitions in Europe. Russia's object was not Calcutta, but Constantinople ; not the Ganges, but the Golden Horn. " She believes that the keys of the Bosphorus are more likely to be won on the banks of the Helmund than on the heights of Plevna. To keep England

[1] " Russia in Central Asia," page 357.

quiet in Europe by keeping her employed in Asia, that, briefly put, is the sum and substance of Russian policy."[1] All this was so plain to him that he could not understand how any one could deny the existence of " an Anglo-Russian question of incalculable seriousness and vast proportions " : and he refused to believe that any such could still be found. " The school of politicians who described anxiety at Russia's advance as ' old women's fears,' have closed the doors of their discredited academy."[2] The actual steps necessary for combating this menace he was prepared to leave to the soldiers ; but he had made it clear that he would certainly not dissent from measures involving a forward frontier policy. There was at least the possibility of Russia deciding in favour of the Balkh-Kabul line of advance, and we must, therefore, keep a very watchful eye on the Afghan capital, which, " twice within the last half century, has been made the cockpit of British disaster," but which may yet " come to be regarded as a citadel of British salvation." The construction of a railway up the Khyber and the establishment of an advanced British position at the head of the Kurum valley were proposals which seemed to meet with his approval. Of the former he had written—

> " to those who detect in such a proposal the glimmer of Jingo war paint I make the unhesitating and unequivocal reply . . . that there is no such means of pacifying an Oriental country as a railway, even a military railway ; and that if for bullets and bayonets we substitute roads and railroads as the motto of our future policy towards Afghanistan, we shall find ourselves standing on the threshold of a new and brighter era of relations with that country."[3]

It was not only in connection with Afghanistan that he had spoken with impatience of a policy of " masterly inactivity " towards the lands beyond the Indian frontier. Our relations with Afghanistan had been successively those of " blundering interference and un-masterly (I have always supposed it to be a *lapsus calami* to write *masterly*) inactivity " ; but Persia " stands a good second to Afghanistan in the category of British diplomatic failure in the East, the

[1]" Russia in Central Asia," page 321. [2]*Ibid*. page 333. [3]*Ibid*. page 372.

result in this instance less of positive error than of deplorable neglect."[1] Why had we looked on while from the north Russia had been driving her influence further and further into the heart of Persia? Were not her intentions writ large over her doings, so that he who ran might read? Was it not clear that with Khorasan in her grasp, the Khojak defences and Quetta might be disregarded and the newly fortified British frontier in Pishin might find itself in danger of being turned from the west? As also that with her penetration of southern Persia we might wake up one morning to find a Russian naval station on the Persian gulf? " Are we content to see a naval station within a few days sail of Karachi and to contemplate a hostile squadron battering Bombay?"[2] These grim possibilities could only be averted if Great Britain herself was willing to adopt a vigorous Persian policy. British political and commercial interests in southern Persia must be actively upheld. Britain herself must build the railways that Russia desired to lay; in short, Russian ascendancy in the north must be countered by British supremacy in the south. Among possible railway schemes a line from the British system in the neighbourhood of Quetta across Baluchistan to Sistan in eastern Persia—to be extended at some future time across the whole of southern Persia—was in the first rank of importance. " Of all the possible suggestions for counteracting the Russian menace to India by pacific and honourable means, the construction of such a railway is at once the least aggressive, the cheapest and the most profitable."[3]

These views had been recalled only a short time before by a speech in the House of Commons in reply to an amendment to the Address moved by Mr. J. Walton Lawson on behalf of the Liberal party, disapproving a frontier policy which involved such forward steps as the permanent military occupation of Chitral. In the course of a spirited reply, Mr. Curzon had pointed out that however anxious we might be to leave the tribes on our frontier alone, they would not let us alone. Moreover, we were under certain obligations not only to the tribes themselves, but to the ruler of Afghanistan. This was a legacy which had been bequeathed to us by no Conservative jingo, but by Mr. Gladstone. The Lawrence policy of 1868,

[1] " Russia in Central Asia," page 374.   [2] *Ibid.* page 380.   [3] *Ibid.* page 378.

which had been so fervently acclaimed in some quarters of the House, had been rendered obsolete by Mr. Gladstone's Government when it sanctioned the occupation of Quetta, established political influence over the Afridis in the neighbourhood of the Khyber pass, and contracted to defend Afghanistan against unprovoked aggression. It had been designed to protect India from a danger which was, when it was formulated, separated from it by many thousands of miles. " It is not equally suited to a position where the Cossacks are at your gates." Indeed, it was clear that unless we were to repudiate our obligations, we might have, at some time or other, " to advance to the external frontier of which I have been speaking, or, at any rate, to take a forward, although less forward, position on the line of Kabul, Ghazni and Kandahar." We were bound, therefore, to select the lines of communication which should be kept open in the interests of the Empire; to enter into confidential relations with the tribes, and to concentrate our forces in necessary spots instead of diffusing them over a scattered area.

The means by which these objects were to be attained were reasonable enough. While we must enter into relations with the tribes, our relations with them " should involve the very minimum of interference with the lands and independence of the tribesmen." Military occupation on a large scale was not necessary. Our position could be assured by a handful of frontier officers, provided they were selected with sufficient care

> " I believe that all along the frontier we are capable of finding scores of men . . . capable of winning, or who had already won, the confidence and affection of the tribes, men who know their language and are in sympathy with their customs. . . . I put my whole faith in the work of such men, and I believe that our security rests, not upon the number of battalions we place there, but upon the individual character of the men whom we choose."

And he rounded off his profession of faith with an admirable apophthegm—" It is a question not of rifles and of cannon, but of character and of all that character can do amid a community of free men." The significance of this declaration became apparent at a later date, for it formed the basis of the successful frontier policy which in later years was to be associated with his name. At the time, however, the essential soundness and moderation of the views which he expressed were overshadowed, for those who feared a forward policy, by the stress which he laid upon the binding nature of the obligations which we had incurred. To those who shrank from commitments beyond the border there was an ominous ring about a question which, Mr. Curzon declared, had been insistently put to him by the Amir of Afghanistan himself in the course of his interviews with him. " England and Afghanistan are one house," asserted the Amir. " One house should have one wall. Are your soldiers going to join mine in defence of that wall ?" [1]

The fact that Mr. Curzon interested himself actively in the question of frontier policy from the moment that he received Lord Salisbury's offer of the Viceroyalty, if natural enough in the circumstances, did not tend to allay anxiety where it existed. The Secretary of State was engaged in drawing up a reply to a letter from the Government of India containing proposals for the future control of the Khyber pass and for its retention under the jurisdiction of the Punjab Government. Mr. Curzon was critical of the reply which had been drafted by the India Office, and he wrote to the Secretary of State and to Lord Salisbury and Lord Lansdowne on the subject. On July the 26th, in a letter to Mrs. Curzon, he mentioned a long Cabinet discussion on the question, and added that as a result of his intervention the reply was to be rewritten " and put in a much more tentative way." An intimation conveyed in one of his earliest letters to Lord Elgin, that one of his first steps after reaching India would be to visit the frontier, drew a mild protest from the Viceroy. The Budget would certainly keep the Head of the Administration in Calcutta until the very end of March, after which the heat on the frontier would be very great. " But, if I may say so, there is not so much to be learnt on the spot as might appear at first sight. The problem is how best to arrange the wheels of the administrative machine and to arrive at a conclusion you will have to study, not so much the physical surroundings of Peshawar, or even the men there, as the Foreign Department and its capabilities,

[1] Speech in the House of Commons, February 15th, 1898.

the Punjab Government and its methods, the military authorities and their aspirations. A good deal of this you will be able to do in Calcutta." [1]

In the meantime Mr. Curzon was able to add to what he had written to Mrs. Curzon on the subject of the India Office Despatch : " I saw Lord S. this afternoon. He is backing me up very loyally over the G. H. [2] business, but says Beach is frightened to death at my appointment, because he thinks I am such a jingo. I must try to smooth him down." [3]

But if Mr. Curzon could afford to ignore criticism based on personal antipathies and was willing enough to profit by the genuine anxieties which his appointment had aroused in more serious quarters, there was one direction from which he felt that he had hardly met with the treatment which he deserved. The leader-writer in *The Times*—to whose columns he had contributed so frequently in the past—while paying tribute to his attainments, was not prepared to regard the success of the appointment as a foregone conclusion. The whole tone of the article was non-committal ; its approval was cautious rather than convinced ; its expectations hopeful rather than confident. " We sincerely hope, for Mr. Curzon's sake and that of the Empire, that Lord Salisbury's very interesting experiment will succeed." [4]

It must be remembered that for some time past foreign affairs had ousted domestic controversies from the pride of place which they normally occupy in the House of Commons ; that Lord Salisbury's foreign policy had evoked widespread criticism, which had found vigorous expression in the columns of *The Times*, and that Mr. Curzon, as the official exponent of it in the Lower House, had necessarily incurred a large share of the odium which the policy itself had called forth. So much was this the case, that one of his fellow members and relative, Sir W. Lawson, in writing to congratulate him was moved to record the state of affairs in his customary manner, in verse :—

[1] Letter from Lord Elgin to Mr. Curzon, dated October 12th, 1898.
[2] Lord George Hamilton, Secretary of State for India.
[3] Letter to Mrs. Curzon, July 27th, 1898.
[4] *The Times*, 11th August, 1898.

APPOINTED VICEROY OF INDIA

Armenia and Crete will no longer depress you ;
No more will the cracking of China distress you.
Poisoned arrows from Bartlett and Bowles may fly on,
But vain is their flight, for the victim is gone.
In the realms of romance in those regions afar
He sits on the throne of the mighty Akbar.
St. Stephens regrets you and Southport feels low,
But life is all coming and going we know.
Then away to the Indies, fresh laurels to earn,
In peace sally forth and in honour return.

Nor did the writer in *The Times* deny that herein lay the main cause of its attitude. " It is not our only ground of quarrel with him that this brilliant ex-correspondent of *The Times* has lately seemed to entertain a less favourable opinion of correspondents of *The Times* than he used to have. The policy of which he has been the mouthpiece has disappointed us, as have sometimes Mr. Curzon's tactics in the exposition of it." [1] It is still clearer from the letters which passed between Mr. Curzon and Mr. George Buckle, who at that time filled the editorial chair. The former had made it plain that he attributed the criticisms of *The Times* to personal animus against him on the part of the editorial staff. The latter repudiated the suggestion with some warmth, and went on to dot the " i's " and cross the " t's " of the references in the article in question. " You must bear in mind that we of *The Times* base our Chinese policy largely on your writings, to the teaching of which we think most of your speeches in the House run counter ; and that you have lost no opportunity of endeavouring to create the impression that our Peking correspondent, who has been substantially right and far ahead of other sources of information throughout, is not to be trusted." [2] Mr. Moberley Bell, at that time manager of *The Times*, said the same thing in rather milder language—" *The Times* has criticised you sometimes favourably, sometimes the reverse—no doubt it will do so still, but I am sure you will recognise in such

[1] *The Times*, August 11th, 1898.
[2] Letter from Mr. Buckle to Mr. Curzon dated August 11th, 1898.

criticism nothing but fair difference of opinion—in fact, something akin to hating the sin, but loving the sinner !" [1]

Any wounds inflicted by this or any other criticism must, however, have been salved by the warmth of the congratulations which poured in with every post from a wide circle of friends and acquaintances. Nothing could have born more striking testimony to the place which Mr. Curzon had already won for himself in public estimation than the wide range of those who hastened to express satisfaction at Lord Salisbury's choice. Political supporters and political foes ; authorities on the problems of the East both British and foreign ; the army and navy ; letters and art ; diplomacy and the church— all found numerous representatives anxious to convey to the Viceroy-designate their congratulations and good wishes. Within little more than a month from the announcement of his appointment he wrote with obvious pride to Mrs. Curzon that the telegrams and letters of congratulation which he had received already numbered seven hundred and fifty. The tone of the letters from persons promi-nent in the ranks of his political opponents was in marked and pleasant contrast with the captious comments of a section of the party press, and must have been particularly gratifying to him. Sir Henry Fowler (afterwards Lord Wolverhampton) wrote— " . . . although I may not always have agreed with some aspects of your policy, none wishes you success more heartily than I do " ; and he expressed regret that the House of Commons was losing " one of its most brilliant ornaments," and that Her Majesty's Opposition would no longer be confronted with one of its " ablest, fairest and most courteous antagonists." [2] Other leading members of the Opposition in the House of Commons wrote in a similar strain. Mr. Asquith (afterwards Lord Oxford), while he could not help regretting that Mr. Curzon's career in the House of Commons was to be interrupted, declared that it was splendid to think he had beaten the record—and beaten it, " not by the aid of anything adventitious, but by brilliant natural gifts developed and applied with the most strenuous labour." [3] Mr. (afterwards Lord) Haldane, M.P., thought that " no more brilliant appointment could have

[1]Letter from Mr. Moberley Bell to Mr. Curzon, dated August 23rd, 1898.
[2]Letter dated August 11th, 1898.   [3]*Ibid.*

been made."[1]   Mr. John (afterwards Viscount) Morley, M.P., wrote that his good wishes were tinged with a pang of regret that "so much free courage and brilliant capacity" were being withdrawn from the House of Commons "which so much needs these high qualities."[2]   Sir Edward Grey, speaking for Her Majesty's Opposition, asserted that since Mr. Curzon had represented the Foreign Office in the House of Commons there had been no member of the Government whose work in the House "has been more respected and admired by us";[3] Sir William Harcourt, M.P., declared that, in spite of the din of battle, "I shall always cherish the recollection of your courteous kindness to myself and of our mutual friendship, which no differences of opinion have disturbed";[4] and, finally, Mr. (afterwards Sir) Courtney Warner, M.P., averred that "even we Radicals, who wish to find fault with everything Lord Salisbury does, will be unanimous in thinking he has made a very good appointment this time."[5]

Not less gratifying must have been the testimony of those who had been brought into official contact with him at the Foreign Office. "Having worked with you now for some time," wrote Sir H. Bergne, "I know well your qualifications for your new high office, and am well assured that it could fall into no worthier hands." But this was not all—". . . before you go I must thank you very heartily for your many kindnesses and courteous consideration which have made the last few years very pleasant for me in my office work."[6]   In the letters from his more intimate friends we get glimpses of the lighter and more human side of Mr. Curzon's character, of which the public saw so little.   "And here is the top place of the Empire for you, my dear," wrote the Hon. A. Lyttelton, M.P.   "I knew you would get to it, as I wrote once when first you got your foot on to the ladder, and some Dryasdust ventured to question.   So here's to you, old boy, with every blessing for the future and every memory of the past."[7]   Another of the companions

[1] Letter dated August 10th, 1898.
[2] *Ibid.*, August 11th, 1898.
[3] *Ibid.*, August 12th, 1898.
[4] *Ibid.*, August 13th, 1898.
[5] *Ibid.*, August 11th, 1898.
[6] *Ibid.*, August 13th, 1898.   [7] Letter undated.

19

of his leisure hours lamented that the body social should have to go under for the general welfare, but added hopefully—"Calcutta will now be a holiday resort—at any rate, I trust it will be for me—as your companionship, whether in its most outrageous or most subdued moments, cannot be dispensed with for five years, or anything like it."[1] From Mr. Wilfred Blunt he received a letter in which, with a characteristically light and satirical touch, the writer succeeded in congratulating Mr. Curzon without in any way retracting his own well-known views as to the folly of Empire—that form of Empire, at any rate, involving the dominion of one people over another. "I write to condole with you on the appointment which I grieve to think severs your long and meritorious connection with the Crabbet club." In another sense, however, the Crabbet club was to be congratulated—"As in H's case I notice that you have no single qualification but that of Crabbet club membership fitting you for the high post you are called on to fill, and the appointment is a new tribute, and the most conspicuous the club has yet obtained, of its inestimable merits as a nursery of irresponsible statesmen." The pith of the letter lay in the tail of its benediction. "I trust . . . that you may prove the best, the most frivolous (even remembering Lytton), and the *last* of our Viceroys."[2]

[1]Letter from the Hon. Evan Charteris, dated August 11th, 1898.
[2]Letter dated August 11th, 1898.

CHAPTER XXI

PREPARATIONS FOR DEPARTURE

JULY-DECEMBER 1898

IT was arranged that the Viceroy-designate should sail before the end of the year, and the next four or five months were full to overflowing. Mr. Curzon had before him five years of absorbing interest in the discharge of a task for which he had prepared himself with remarkable foresight and assiduous care. Surprise had been expressed in some quarters at his willingness to interrupt an assured career in the House of Commons, even for so dazzling a post as the Viceroyalty of India. It had been voiced among others by Sir Alfred (afterwards Lord) Milner, who was himself busily engaged in building up a reputation as a great Pro-Consul in South Africa. "My only doubt was whether you would care to leave the House of Commons. I think the choice must have been difficult, still, I feel quite sure that in the national interest your decision was the right one." [1] Such surprise was, surely, not warranted. It is hard to believe that the Viceroyalty of India had not always been the Mecca of his political pilgrimage ; and looking back over a life full of the most varied interests, all enthusiastically pursued, at a date, it is true, which is perhaps too near to permit of its being viewed in strict historical perspective, it is nevertheless difficult not to see in the period of his Viceroyalty the central goal of his ambition and the culminating point of his career.

Whether it was the resemblance of the stately building erected by Lord Wellesley in Calcutta to the family seat of the Curzons at Kedleston in Derbyshire, or the spirited address of Sir James

[1] Letter dated August the 15th, 1898.

Stephen to the Eton Literary Society, telling of an Empire on the Continent of Asia " more populous, more amazing and more beneficent than that of Rome," that first fired Mr. Curzon's imagination and directed his gaze eastward, we have it on his own authority that from these early days onwards the fascination, nay, the sacredness, of India grew upon him until he had come to think that "it is the highest honour that can be placed on any subject of the Queen, that in any capacity, high or low, he should devote such energies as he may possess to its service." [1] That this was no mere oratorical flourish called forth by the emotional stress of the moment there is ample evidence to show. The extent to which Asia gripped his imagination and absorbed his energies was early apparent from the journeys which he projected and carried out, and from the writings for which they provided the material. It would have been still clearer had he ever completed the amazing programme which he deliberately set before himself for accomplishment. This was no less than a series of volumes covering in its different aspects—geographical, historical, ethnological and political—the whole continent of Asia. And, wide as was the field covered by the books actually issued before his appointment to the Viceroyalty—Persia in the Near East, the Russian possessions in Central Asia, Japan, Korea, and China in the Far East—it was but a part of that which it had been his intention to traverse. Among the works of this comprehensive series, begun but never completed, was a volume on the Indian Frontier, which was to be a compendium of frontier history, geography and ethnology, as well as a reasoned analysis of the principles underlying the frontier policy of the Government of India ; another on the political problems and future of Indo-China ; and finally, an elaborate work in two volumes on Afghanistan.

Both in private conversation and in his public speeches and writings the place which he assigned to Asia had been plainly stated. To him the most wonderful piece of natural and human mechanism which the nineteenth century provided was the political evolution of the Asian continent which he perceived in progress ; and the part played by the different nations of the East in the process—" how far they individually retarded its progress or contributed to the

[1] Speech at dinner given by Old Etonians, October 28th, 1898.

PLATE X. KEDLESTON HALL, DERBYSHIRE.

collective thunder of its wheels "—the most absorbing of problems. And as he had probed deeper and deeper into his subject the paramount position of India in the scheme had been steadily brought home to him. " As I proceed . . . the true fulcrum of Asiatic dominion seems to me increasingly to lie in Hindustan. The secret of the mastery of the world is, if they only knew it, in the possession of the British people " ;[1] and a little further on in the same volume

> " within her borders may be studied every one of the problems with which the rest of Asia challenges our concern. But her central and commanding position is nowhere better seen than in the political influence which she exercises over the destinies of her neighbours far and near ; and the extent to which their fortunes revolve upon an Indian axis. The independence of Afghanistan, the continued national existence of Persia, the maintenance of Turkish rule at Baghdad are one and all dependent upon Calcutta. Nay, the radiating circle of her influence overlaps the adjoining continents and affects alike the fate of the Bosphorus and the destinies of Egypt. Nor is the effect less remarkable if examined on the eastern side. . . Such and so supreme is the position enjoyed in the Asian continent by the Empire of the Kaiser-i-hind."[2]

No declaration could have been clearer ; and no one with any knowledge of the writer could doubt, on reading it, where the height of his ambition lay.

Nor had he ever been at any pains to hide it from his friends. " How well I remember just eight years ago in the House of Commons a tiny dinner," wrote Lady Granby—afterwards Duchess of Rutland—on hearing of his appointment. " And the talk was of ambition—G. W. proudly asserting that he had none ! And you as proudly stating that you had a deal—and that India was your greatest !"[3] A similar admission was recalled by another correspondent, Sir Edgar Vincent—" Do you remember telling me at dinner at

[1] " Problems of the Far East."
[2] " Problems of the Far East," pages 10 and 11.
[3] Letter dated August 21st, 1898.

least four years ago that the Viceroyalty was in your view the finest object of ambition and the one most worthy to be sought after? I thought then that you would surely achieve this ambition; but I did not venture to hope that you would reach the pinnacle before turning the corner of forty." [1]

Letters have, indeed, been preserved which not only dispose of all possible doubt on the point, but show how passionately his heart was set on obtaining the Viceroyalty. As far back as April 1897, when Lord Elgin's term of office had still all but two years to run, he had confided his ambition and his hopes to Lord Salisbury. " A report, very likely unauthorised, in an English newspaper the other day has tempted me to write to you about something that has long been in my mind, and with regard to which, if I am premature in disclosing it to you, I at any rate have not committed a similar indiscretion with anybody else." It might be regarded as presumptuous, he continued, that he should himself aspire to the Indian Viceroyalty; but he could at least claim that he had done what lay within his power to qualify himself for the post, and he was profoundly convinced that a very great work could be done in India by an English Viceroy who was young and active and intensely absorbed in his work and who would take to India what very few men did take there—" a great love of the country and pride in the Imperial aspect of its possession." He did not deny that he was influenced to some extent by the fact that as the eldest son of a peer he could not in any case look forward to a very prolonged career in the House of Commons; but at the end of a letter of sixteen pages he returned to his original plea—" my strongest impulse is, I can most honestly say, not a personal one at all; it is the desire, while one is still in the hey day of life, to do some strenuous work in a position of responsibility and in a cause for which previous study and training may have rendered one in some measure less unfit for the effort." [2] Lord Salisbury had replied that he quite understood and sympathised with Mr. Curzon's feelings in the matter, but whether it would be in his power to make the appointment was another question, to which he could not even suggest an answer. " A year and a half is

[1] Letter dated August 11th, 1898.
[2] Letter to Lord Salisbury, April 18th, 1897.

a long way off—where shall we all be then ?" [1] This was reassuring, in that it seemed to indicate that Lord Salisbury was, at any rate, not committed to any one else ; and a year later he returned to the charge. " It is just a year ago since I was writing to you about India ; and the contingency that you discussed in your reply, viz. of having to make the appointment yourself, seems likely to arise. Perhaps, unless you have already made other and wiser arrangements, you may let me have a word or two with you about it when you return." [2] Lord Salisbury replied that the matter had much occupied his thoughts, but that he was not yet in a position to speak definitely on the subject. When, therefore, on June the 24th Mr. Curzon received a letter from the Prime Minister, telling him that he was about to submit his name to the Queen, his satisfaction knew no bounds.

> " Your letter, so characteristically generous in its terms, is one that it has been a great pride to me to receive and one that I shall always treasure as one of my most valued possessions. . . I have read with great interest the remarkable words of the Queen in her letter to you ; and I shall not fail to bear in mind her wise injunctions. . . That I should at my years receive from her hand this high post of trust which you are recommending her to confer upon me will lend a distinction to the honour that the winning of no other prize in life could give." [3]

Those who knew him best always realised, I think, that in Asia and its problems was centered the consuming passion of his life, and understood the readiness with which he turned his back on the lure of a brilliant Parliamentary career at home. Some few of his most intimate friends guessed, perhaps, how the consummation of the other great passion of his life—his love for Mary Leiter—had been postponed, in order that his preparation for a future career in India might not be cut short or even interrupted ; and they made no mistake in their estimate of his real ambition. " You will have many

[1] Letter from Lord Salisbury, April 26th, 1897.
[2] Letter dated April 11th, 1898.
[3] Letter to Lord Salisbury June 25th, 1898.

years of life in which your thoughts will be directed backwards and in which you will feel that what is (no matter what you become) cannot quite compare with what has been "; [1]—words which were to prove prophetic, for, looking back over his life a quarter of a century later, he came to the conclusion that, if he were to tell the naked truth, he had derived far more pleasure in life from tastes and pursuits which were not connected with politics than from political life itself, with all its glamour and bright and fitful rewards, save only in so far as India was concerned. For before he died he expressed a hope that sooner or later an authoritative account of his Indian Administration, to which, he always declared, he had given all that was worth having of his spirit and his strength, might be written. It was by his work in India in particular that he desired to be judged, and it was here that he cherished the hope—should history pause to notice him—that he would be held not to have laboured in vain. There is a great pathos, surely in these words from the lips of a dying man, tinged as they are with the regrets of a strong and ambitious personality gazing back down the vista of time, to days which have slid imperceptibly but inexorably into the irrevocable limbo of the past.

But at the date of which I am now writing these days were still in the womb of time. They were of the future, and the future was calling with beckoning finger to one who thrilled at her voice. The picture which we look on as the year 1898 draws towards its close is that of a man absorbed by the prospect of that which lies before him, throwing himself heart and soul into the many matters demanding attention during the rapidly flitting weeks before departure—from the preparation of those resonant phrases which gave to his farewell speeches so great a distinction to the arrangement of his private affairs, and from the selection of his personal staff to the packing of the family plate. " I have had a very hard day ; Elkington's man in. Place clogged and blocked with plate. F. wandering about like a forlorn viking ; Appleton executing internal rumbles and displaying mingled anxiety and stupidity." [2]

[1]Letter from the Hon. E. Beckett, M.P.—afterwards Lord Grimthorpe—dated August 19th, 1898.
[2]Letter to Mrs. Curzon, July 27th, 1898.

PREPARATIONS FOR DEPARTURE

In the interests of his health, which had been a source of considerable anxiety to his friends, he went in September to Strathpeffer, and later to Cromer, where Mrs. Curzon and their second daughter, who had been born in August, were able to join him. On his way north he went to Balmoral, whither he had been bidden on a visit to the Queen. In the comparative seclusion of Strathpeffer he was able to proceed with his preparations for departure, undisturbed by the constant interruptions inseparable from residence in London. He devoted much time and thought to the question of his personal staff. Lord Dufferin had once said of his private secretary that he relieved him of half his labours, enjoyed everybody's confidence, completely effaced himself and worked eighteen hours a day. Lord Elgin, whom Mr. Curzon consulted, admitted that there were such men, but added that they were not always to be found. Mr. Curzon was determined to find one, and the energy and resolution with which he prosecuted his search met with their meet reward. The person whom he sought appeared on the scene unexpectedly, but with the happiest results. His engagement was the subject of considerable correspondence before the difficulties which stood in the way were finally overcome ; but the successful outcome of the search was imparted to Mrs. Curzon in a brief and characteristic message—" I wrote to Walter Lawrence "—at that time agent to the Duke of Bedford—" asking him to recommend priv. secretary like himself, whereupon he offered me the latter commodity." This laconic message did not tell the whole story. Walter Lawrence in the first instance recommended someone else, and it was only when Mr. Curzon returned to the charge, rallying him on his obtuseness and reminding him of a promise made half in jest when they had met in India some years before, that he approached the Duke on the subject and ended by offering his services.

The more serious matters which engaged his attention were not permitted to dim the whimsical sense of humour with which he viewed the little comedies which he was always detecting on the surface of life's waters. From Balmoral he wrote to Mrs. Curzon describing his conversations with Queen Victoria, " who talked incessantly and with great animation about Elgin, Lockhart, Warburton, Indian Civil Service, etc., etc., " and about the Sudan and

Kitchener, news of whose victory over the Dervishes arrived by telegram in the middle of this discussion ; and then, with obvious delight—" I have had an advertisement sent me of the ' Curzon ' collar ! copied from mine and described as all the rage in London now !"[1] A few days later, in a letter from Strathpeffer, he is describing with a puckish pen his entertainment at a neighbouring mansion. " I lunched to-day with the H . . . s at Castle . . . . Nice old M.P. Elderly wife, whom I had to arm into lunch, where she sat next her husband. At least three or four grown-up, yellow-haired girls. Butler three feet high. Footman whom we would not have taken as usher. An appalling meal, atrociously cooked ; Yorkshire pudding like slabs of bread poultice."[2]

Among the personal matters which engaged his anxious thought were the question of the peerage which Her Majesty desired to bestow upon him, and that of a permanant home to which Mrs. Curzon could turn when visiting England during the period of their exile. There were some doubts in Mr. Curzon's mind whether objections might not be entertained to the title which he wished to bear by the family of which the Earl of Howe, whose second title was Viscount Curzon, was the head. If any such existed they were not pressed, and in due course Mr. Curzon, who was anxious that the door of the House of Commons should not be closed against him, became a member of the Irish peerage with the title of Baron Curzon of Kedleston. Lady Curzon was much entertained at first by her new rank—" Oh ! the ladyships, I feel like a ship in full sail on the high seas of dignity !" The question of a residence was likewise brought to a successful issue, for in October after negotiations to which he devoted much personal attention, he acquired the stately mansion in Carlton House Terrace which was thenceforth to be his London home.

The arrangement of these domestic matters was followed by a succession of public engagements, and on October the 28th, came the first of the series of farewell functions with which his last weeks in England were punctuated. The gathering was a distinguished one of Old Etonians, assembled at dinner at the Café Monaco under

<hr>

[1]Letter dated September 4th, 1898.
[2]Letter dated September 18th, 1898.

314

the chairmanship of Lord Rosebery, in honour of three famous sons of the old school—Lord Curzon of Kedleston, Viceroy-designate of India, the Earl of Minto, Governor-General-designate of Canada, and the Rev. J. E. C. Welldon, Bishop-designate of Calcutta. In his reply to the toast of his health, proposed with all the grace and wit which placed Lord Rosebery upon so high a plane as an after dinner speaker, and in his speeches on subsequent occasions of a similar nature, he made clear the place which India held in his estimation, and the part which he had always resolved she should play in his own life. He had seen during the past few weeks his acceptance of the Viceroyalty attributed to a variety of causes—to personal ambition, to the disappointment of Parliamentary hopes, to failing health. " Is it permissible, therefore, for me to say in this company of old school-fellows and personal friends that ... I gladly accept it because I love India, its people, its history, its Government, the absorbing mysteries of its civilisation and its life ?" Ten days later at a dinner given to him at the Royal Societies' club he returned to the subject. " I have said on a previous occasion that I am glad to go to India ; and my main reason for being so is the fact that India has always appeared to me to be the pivot and centre—I do not say the geographical but the political and Imperial centre—of the British Empire." Possessions had been acquired and Colonies had been founded by other nations. But for the experiment upon which we were engaged in India no analogies could be quoted, no precedents invoked. " It is there that we are doing a work which no other people has ever attempted to do before, and by the doing of which we shall be judged by history. There lies the true fulcrum of dominion, the real touchstone of our Imperial greatness or failure." [1]

It was, indeed, when speaking of India that his oratory soared on its loftiest flights. The splendour and mystery in which her past lay buried, the baffling complexity of her present problems, the resplendent future to which, under the guidance of Great Britain, she was destined to attain—these were the topics which called forth his most resonant phrases, his richest and most vigorous prose. It was then that from the brightly illumined chambers of his mind, there poured forth glowing periods burnished by the enthusiasm

[1]Speech at dinner at Royal Societies' club, November 7th, 1898.

that burned within, and that the flicker of the flame of inspiration as it rose and fell was reflected in the swift and subtle changes that played across his countenance. He approached the tremendous responsibilities of the trust which had been laid upon him with a humility akin to reverence, which purged his speech of the self-satisfied assurance of which his critics had been so ready to complain.

"For after all—and I speak to those if there are any here present, who have travelled in the East and have caught the fascination of its mysterious surroundings—the East is a University in which the scholar never takes his degree. It is a temple where the suppliant adores but never catches sight of the object of his devotion. It is a journey the goal of which is always in sight but is never attained. There we are always learners, always worshippers, always pilgrims, I rejoice to be allowed to take my place in the happy band of students and of wayfarers who have trodden that path for a hundred years. I know that I have everything to learn. I have, perhaps, many things to unlearn. But if the test of the pupil be application, and if the test of the worshipper be faith, I hope that I may pass through the ordeal unscathed." [1]

The round of farewell functions bore witness to the prominent position which Lord Curzon occupied in academic, political and social life. There were dinners at Oxford, a rousing reception and the presentation of a piece of plate by his former constituents of the Southport division, and an elaborate dinner planned by a large number of his personal friends. At this intimate gathering in the gilded hall of the Hotel Cecil, a happy reference was made in a poem written and recited by George Wyndham, to a gathering eight years before at which George Curzon himself had been the host—the dinner party at the Bachelors' Club at which the sobriquet of " the Souls " had first been accorded to the little coterie of brilliant society men and women, whose frequent meeting in town and country had given rise to stories of a mysterious society with esoteric rites :—

[1] Speech at Eton dinner, October 28th, 1898.

PREPARATIONS FOR DEPARTURE

Eight years ago we sat at your table
We were the guests and you were the host
You were young, said the world, but we knew you were able
To justify more than your friends dared boast.
We knew you would win all wreaths in the end
And we knew you would still be the same dear friend
And that's what we cared for most.

You wrote us some rhymes wherein friendship and laughter
Played in a blaze of affection and jest,
Round the name of each one for whom no years thereafter,
Could blunt the sharp edge of that festival's zest.

So, go in and win ! what's five years but a lustre
To shine round a name that already shines bright ?
Then come back, and we'll greet you and go such a ' buster,'
As never was seen ; no, not even to-night !

Come back in five years with your sheaves of new fame :
You'll find your old friends ; and you'll find them the same
As now when you gladden their sight."

But, perhaps, one of the most notable of all the farewell functions was the presentation by the people of Derbyshire, in whose midst his family had been resident for the past eight hundred years, of an Address of congratulation and good wishes. He found time to write a hurried note describing it to Lady Curzon—" Function a great success — two thousand people. I spoke for twenty minutes very hoarse, voice nearly gone from cold. Old Louis XV fan for you, very pretty. Address for me. Great enthusiasm." [1] This put the seal on what Lord Scarsdale had written to him earlier—" I begin to realise what a splendid position you have deservedly won. Congrats pour in from every quarter and the county generally are as proud of you as I, your Father, am, and more I cannot say." [2]

These various gatherings attracted a great deal of attention and

[1] Letter dated November 25th, 1898.
[2] Letter dated August 12th, 1898.

Lord Curzon's speeches created a deep impression. By an ironic decree of Fate, in view of what the future held in store, he and Lord Kitchener stood prominently together in the limelight. The victor of Omdurman and the Viceroy-designate of India were singled out as " the most remarkable and conspicuous figures in public life "[1] at the time ; and the admirable strain in which Lord Curzon had been speaking of his coming duties was commented upon most favourably in the press. " No one can doubt that Lord Curzon of Kedleston goes out to rule our great Eastern Dependency fully impressed with the gravity of his task and better equipped by previous knowledge to grapple with it than many of his predecessors " ;[2] and a month later when, on December the 15th, he bade farewell to the large and distinguished gathering which had assembled on the station platform to see him off, the voice of criticism was finally hushed beneath the spontaneous expression of goodwill with which the nation speeded its distinguished representative on his way. With a gesture as graceful as it was appropriate, *The Times* emphasised Lord Curzon's special qualifications for dealing with the problems with which he would be faced and, notably, that of the frontier which dominated the situation.

> " Lord Curzon will approach it with a very different training and from a widely diverse point of view from that in which it is usually regarded either by the strategic experts or their critics." He would be vigilant but not aggressive. " It is no longer the brilliant young writer who wanted to hear someone cry ' Halt !' to the Cossack that now becomes Viceroy of India ; it is the mature statesman who has been for the House of Commons and the nation the mouthpiece of the foreign policy of England during the greatest crisis in Asia since 1857."[3]

END OF VOLUME I

[1] *The Times* of November 15th, 1898.   [2] *Ibid.*
[3] *The Times*, December 15th, 1898.

CPSIA information can be obtained at www.ICGtesting.com
Printed in the USA
BVOW02s1017250116

434140BV00025B/311/P